Word For Windows® 95 For Dummies®

P9-DES-395

Cheat Sheet

The Formatting Toolbar

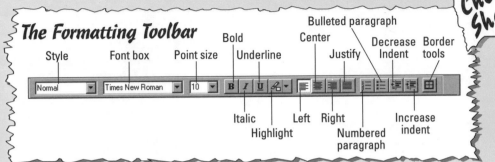

Labels: Style, Font box, Point size, Bold, Underline, Center, Bulleted paragraph, Justify, Decrease Indent, Border tools, Italic, Highlight, Left, Right, Numbered paragraph, Increase indent

Fields shown: Normal | Times New Roman | 10

The Standard Toolbar

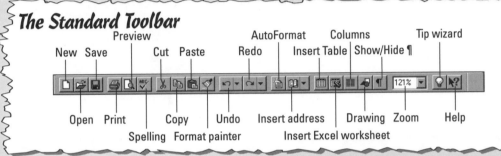

Labels: New, Save, Preview, Cut, Paste, Redo, AutoFormat, Insert Table, Columns, Show/Hide ¶, Tip wizard, Open, Print, Spelling, Copy, Format painter, Undo, Insert address, Insert Excel worksheet, Drawing, Zoom, Help

Field shown: 121%

Helpful Tips

- Let the computer do the work! Let Word format your pages, insert page numbers, headers and footers. Don't ever do that stuff "manually" on-screen.
- Always save your documents to disk!
- If a document has already been saved to disk, press Ctrl+S to update the document on disk.

Useful Tools

- To check your spelling, press the F7 key or Alt,T,S.
- To use the thesaurus, press Shift+F7 or Alt,T,T.
- To print envelopes, press Alt,T,E.

Document Filenames

A document must be saved to disk using a Win 95 filename. Here are the rules:

- Be brief and descriptive with your filenames.
- The filename can be from 1 to 255 characters long.
- The filename can contain letters and numbers in any combination.
- The filename cannot contain these symbols: \ < > * ? " | ; : /

Getting Around in a Document

↑	Moves toothpick cursor up one line of text
↓	Moves toothpick cursor down one line of text
→	Moves toothpick cursor right to the next character
←	Moves toothpick cursor left to the next character
Ctrl+↑	Moves toothpick cursor up one paragraph
Ctrl+↓	Moves toothpick cursor down one paragraph
Ctrl+→	Moves toothpick cursor right one word
Ctrl+←	Moves toothpick cursor left one word
Ctrl+PgUp	Moves toothpick cursor to top of the screen
Ctrl+PgDn	Moves toothpick cursor to bottom of the screen
PgUp	Moves toothpick cursor up one screen
PgDn	Moves toothpick cursor down one screen
End	Moves toothpick cursor to end of current line
Home	Moves toothpick cursor to start of current line
Ctrl+Home	Moves toothpick cursor to top of document
Ctrl+End	Moves toothpick cursor to bottom of document

...For Dummies: #1 Computer Book Series for Beginners

Word For Windows® 95 For Dummies®

Word for Windows 95 Screen
Common WinWord

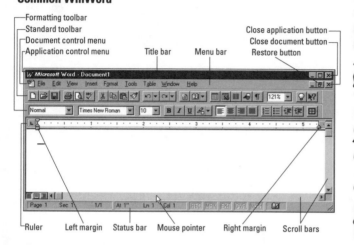

- Formatting toolbar
- Standard toolbar
- Document control menu
- Application control menu
- Title bar
- Menu bar
- Close application button
- Close document button
- Restore button

- Ruler
- Left margin
- Status bar
- Mouse pointer
- Right margin
- Scroll bars

IDG BOOKS WORLDWIDE™

Copyright © 1995 IDG Books Worldwide, Inc. All rights reserved.

Cheat Sheet
$2.95 value.   Item 932-X

For more information about IDG Books, call 1-800-762-2974.

The Kindergarten Keys

Copy	Ctrl+C
Cut	Ctrl+X
Paste	Ctrl+V
Undo	Ctrl+Z

General Information

To start Word, first start Windows by clicking the Start button, then Programs, then Microsoft Word.

- Use the Insert key to switch between insert and overtype modes.
- Use the Backspace key to backup and erase.
- Use the Delete key to delete a character.
- Press the Enter key to start a new paragraph.
- Press the Tab key to indent or align text.
- F1 is the Help key.
- Press the Escape key to cancel things and make dialog boxes go away.

Ctrl+S means to hold down the Ctrl (control) key and press the S key. Release both keys. Alt,F,N means to press the Alt key, release it, press the F key, release it, press the N key, and release it.

Select the Exit command from the File menu when you're ready to quit Word. Follow the instructions on-screen; save your document to disk.

Always quit Word, and then quit Windows when you're done working for the day. Don't turn off your computer until you see the message telling you it's "safe" to do so.

Common WinWord Formatting Key Commands

Bold	Ctrl+B
Italic	Ctrl+I
Underline	Ctrl+U
Center text	Ctrl+E
Left align	Ctrl+L
Right align	Ctrl+R
Justify	Ctrl+J

Common WinWord Key Commands

Cancel	Escape
Go back	Shift+F5
Help	F1
Mark Block	F8
New document	Ctrl+N
Open	Ctrl+O
Print	Ctrl+P
Quick save	Ctrl+S
Repeat Command	F4
Repeat Find	Shift-F4

...For Dummies: #1 Computer Book Series for Beginners

®

References for the Rest of Us! ®

COMPUTER BOOK SERIES FROM IDG

Are you intimidated and confused by computers? Do you find that traditional manuals are overloaded with technical details you'll never use? Do your friends and family always call you to fix simple problems on their PCs? Then the *...For Dummies*® computer book series from IDG Books Worldwide is for you.

...For Dummies books are written for those frustrated computer users who know they aren't really dumb but find that PC hardware, software, and indeed the unique vocabulary of computing make them feel helpless. *...For Dummies* books use a lighthearted approach, a down-to-earth style, and even cartoons and humorous icons to diffuse computer novices' fears and build their confidence. Lighthearted but not lightweight, these books are a perfect survival guide for anyone forced to use a computer.

> *"I like my copy so much I told friends; now they bought copies."*
> **Irene C., Orwell, Ohio**

> *"Quick, concise, nontechnical, and humorous."*
> **Jay A., Elburn, Illinois**

> *"Thanks, I needed this book. Now I can sleep at night."*
> **Robin F., British Columbia, Canada**

Already, hundreds of thousands of satisfied readers agree. They have made *...For Dummies* books the #1 introductory level computer book series and have written asking for more. So, if you're looking for the most fun and easy way to learn about computers, look to *...For Dummies* books to give you a helping hand.

TM

IDG BOOKS
WORLDWIDE

WORD FOR WINDOWS® 95 FOR DUMMIES®

WORD FOR WINDOWS® 95 FOR DUMMIES®

by Dan Gookin

IDG Books Worldwide, Inc.
An International Data Group Company

Foster City, CA ♦ Chicago, IL ♦ Indianapolis, IN ♦ Southlake, TX

Word For Windows® 95 For Dummies®

Published by
IDG Books Worldwide, Inc.
An International Data Group Company
919 E. Hillsdale Blvd.
Suite 400
Foster City, CA 94404
http://www.idgbooks.com (IDG Books Worldwide Web site)
http://www.dummies.com (Dummies Press Web site)

Library of Congress Catalog Card No.: 95-80445

ISBN: 1-56884-932-X

Printed in the United States of America

10 9 8 7

Distributed in the United States by IDG Books Worldwide, Inc.

Distributed by Macmillan Canada for Canada; by Transworld Publishers Limited in the United Kingdom and Europe; by WoodsLane Pty. Ltd. for Australia; by WoodsLane Enterprises Ltd. for New Zealand; by Longman Singapore Publishers Ltd. for Singapore, Malaysia, Thailand, and Indonesia; by Simron Pty. Ltd. for South Africa; by Toppan Company Ltd. for Japan; by Distribuidora Cuspide for Argentina; by Livraria Cultura for Brazil; by Ediciencia S.A. for Ecuador; by Addison-Wesley Publishing Company for Korea; by Ediciones ZETA S.C.R. Ltda. for Peru; by WS Computer Publishing Company, Inc., for the Philippines; by Unalis Corporation for Taiwan; by Contemporanea de Ediciones for Venezuela. Authorized Sales Agent: Anthony Rudkin Associates for the Middle East and North Africa.

For general information on IDG Books Worldwide's books in the U.S., please call our Consumer Customer Service department at 800-762-2974. For reseller information, including discounts and premium sales, please call our Reseller Customer Service department at 800-434-3422.

For information on where to purchase IDG Books Worldwide's books outside the U.S., please contact our International Sales department at 415-655-3172 or fax 415-655-3295.

For information on foreign language translations, please contact our Foreign & Subsidiary Rights department at 415-655-3021 or fax 415-655-3281.

For sales inquiries and special prices for bulk quantities, please contact our Sales department at 415-655-3200 or write to the address above.

For information on using IDG Books Worldwide's books in the classroom or for ordering examination opies, please contact our Educational Sales department at 800-434-2086 or fax 817-251-8174.

For press review copies, author interviews, or other publicity information, please contact our Public Relations department at 415-655-3000 or fax 415-655-3299.

For authorization to photocopy items for corporate, personal, or educational use, please contact Copyright Clearance Center, 222 Rosewood Drive, Danvers, MA 01923, or fax 508-750-4470.

is a trademark under exclusive license to IDG Books Worldwide, Inc., from International Data Group, Inc.

About the Author

Dan Gookin got started with computers back in the post slide rule age of computing: 1982. His first intention was to buy a computer to replace his aged and constantly breaking typewriter. Working as slave labor in a restaurant, however, Gookin was unable to afford the full "word processor" setup and settled on a computer that had a monitor, keyboard, and little else. Soon his writing career was under way with several submissions to (and lots of rejections from) fiction magazines.

The big break came in 1984 when he began writing about computers. Applying his flair for fiction with a self-taught knowledge of computers, Gookin was able to demystify the subject and explain technology in a relaxed and understandable voice. He even dared to add humor, which eventually won him a column in a local computer magazine.

Eventually Gookin's talents came to roost as he became a ghostwriter at a computer book publishing house. That was followed by an editing position at a San Diego computer magazine, at which time he also regularly participated in a radio talk show about computers. In addition, Gookin kept writing books about computers, some of which became minor best-sellers.

In 1990, Gookin came to IDG Books with a book proposal. From that initial meeting unfolded an idea for an outrageous book: a long overdue and original idea for the computer book for the rest of us. What became *DOS For Dummies* blossomed into an international bestseller with hundreds and thousands of copies in print and many foreign translations.

Today, Gookin still considers himself a writer and computer "guru" whose job it is to remind everyone that computers are not to be taken too seriously. His approach to computers is light and humorous yet very informative. He knows that the complex beasts are important and can help people become productive and successful. Yet Gookin mixes his knowledge of computers with a unique, dry sense of humor that keeps everyone informed — and awake. His favorite quote is, "Computers are a notoriously dull subject, but that doesn't mean I have to write about them that way."

Gookin's titles for IDG Books include: *DOS For Dummies, More DOS For Dummies, PCs For Dummies, Word For Windows For Dummies, Illustrated Computer Dictionary For Dummies, C For Dummies (Volume 1),* and *Real Life Windows 95.* Gookin holds a degree in Communications from the University of California, San Diego, and lives with his wife and boys in the as-yet-untamed state of Idaho.

ABOUT IDG BOOKS WORLDWIDE

Welcome to the world of IDG Books Worldwide.

IDG Books Worldwide, Inc., is a subsidiary of International Data Group, the world's largest publisher of computer-related information and the leading global provider of information services on information technology. IDG was founded more than 25 years ago and now employs more than 8,500 people worldwide. IDG publishes more than 275 computer publications in over 75 countries (see listing below). More than 60 million people read one or more IDG publications each month.

Launched in 1990, IDG Books Worldwide is today the #1 publisher of best-selling computer books in the United States. We are proud to have received eight awards from the Computer Press Association in recognition of editorial excellence and three from *Computer Currents'* First Annual Readers' Choice Awards. Our best-selling *...For Dummies*® series has more than 30 million copies in print with translations in 30 languages. IDG Books Worldwide, through a joint venture with IDG's Hi-Tech Beijing, became the first U.S. publisher to publish a computer book in the People's Republic of China. In record time, IDG Books Worldwide has become the first choice for millions of readers around the world who want to learn how to better manage their businesses.

Our mission is simple: Every one of our books is designed to bring extra value and skill-building instructions to the reader. Our books are written by experts who understand and care about our readers. The knowledge base of our editorial staff comes from years of experience in publishing, education, and journalism — experience we use to produce books for the '90s. In short, we care about books, so we attract the best people. We devote special attention to details such as audience, interior design, use of icons, and illustrations. And because we use an efficient process of authoring, editing, and desktop publishing our books electronically, we can spend more time ensuring superior content and spend less time on the technicalities of making books.

You can count on our commitment to deliver high-quality books at competitive prices on topics you want to read about. At IDG Books Worldwide, we continue in the IDG tradition of delivering quality for more than 25 years. You'll find no better book on a subject than one from IDG Books Worldwide.

John J. Kilcullen

John Kilcullen
CEO
IDG Books Worldwide, Inc.

*Eighth Annual
Computer Press
Awards ≥1992*

*Ninth Annual
Computer Press
Awards ≥1993*

*Tenth Annual
Computer Press
Awards ≥1994*

*Eleventh Annual
Computer Press
Awards ≥1995*

IDG Books Worldwide, Inc., is a subsidiary of International Data Group, the world's largest publisher of computer-related information and the leading global provider of information services on information technology. International Data Group publishes over 275 computer publications in over 75 countries. Sixty million people read one or more International Data Group publications each month. International Data Group's publications include: **ARGENTINA:** Buyer's Guide, Computerworld Argentina, PC World Argentina; **AUSTRALIA:** Australian Macworld, Australian PC World, Australian Reseller News, Computerworld, IT Casebook, Network World, Publish, Webmaster; **AUSTRIA:** Computerwelt Österreich, Networks Austria, PC Tip Austria; **BANGLADESH:** PC World Bangladesh; **BELARUS:** PC World Belarus; **BELGIUM:** Data News; **BRAZIL:** Annuário de Informática, Computerworld, Connections, Macworld, PC Player, PC World, Publish, Reseller News, Supergamepower; **BULGARIA:** Computerworld Bulgaria, Network World Bulgaria, PC & MacWorld Bulgaria; **CANADA:** CIO Canada, Client/Server World, ComputerWorld Canada, InfoWorld Canada, NetworkWorld Canada, WebWorld; **CHILE:** Computerworld Chile, PC World Chile; **COLOMBIA:** Computerworld Colombia, PC World Colombia; **COSTA RICA:** PC World Centro America; **THE CZECH AND SLOVAK REPUBLICS:** Computerworld Czechoslovakia, Macworld Czech Republic, PC World Czechoslovakia; **DENMARK:** Communications World Danmark, Computerworld Danmark, Macworld Danmark, PC World Danmark, Techworld Denmark; **DOMINICAN REPUBLIC:** PC World Republica Dominicana; **ECUADOR:** PC World Ecuador; **EGYPT:** Computerworld Middle East, PC World Middle East; **EL SALVADOR:** PC World Centro America; **FINLAND:** MikroPC, Tietoverkko, Tietoviikko; **FRANCE:** Distributique, Hebdo, Info PC, Le Monde Informatique, Macworld, Reseaux & Telecoms, WebMaster France; **GERMANY:** Computer Partner, Computerwoche, Computerwoche Extra, Computerwoche FOCUS, Global Online, Macwelt, PC Welt; **GREECE:** Amiga Computing, GamePro Greece, Multimedia World; **GUATEMALA:** PC World Centro America; **HONDURAS:** PC World Centro America; **HONG KONG:** Computerworld Hong Kong, PC World Hong Kong, Publish in Asia; **HUNGARY:** ABCD CD-ROM, Computerworld Szamitastechnika, Internetto online Magazine, PC World Hungary, PC-X Magazin Hungary; **ICELAND:** Tolvuheimur PC World Island; **INDIA:** Information Communications World, Information Systems Computerworld, PC World India, Publish in Asia; **INDONESIA:** InfoKomputer PC World, Komputek Computerworld, Publish in Asia; **IRELAND:** ComputerScope, PC Live!; **ISRAEL:** Macworld Israel, People & Computers/Computerworld; **ITALY:** Computerworld Italia, Macworld Italia, Networking Italia, PC World Italia; **JAPAN:** DTP World, Macworld Japan, Nikkei Personal Computing, OS/2 World Japan, SunWorld Japan, Windows NT World, Windows World Japan; **KENYA:** PC World East African; **KOREA:** Hi-Tech Information, Macworld Korea, PC World Korea; **MACEDONIA:** PC World Macedonia; **MALAYSIA:** Computerworld Malaysia, PC World Malaysia, Publish in Asia; **MALTA:** PC World Malta; **MEXICO:** Computerworld Mexico, PC World Mexico; **MYANMAR:** PC World Myanmar; **NETHERLANDS:** Computer! Totaal, LAN Internetworking Magazine, LAN World Buyers Guide, Macworld Netherlands, Net, WebWereld; **NEW ZEALAND:** Absolute Beginners Guide and Plain & Simple Series, Computer Buyer, Computer Industry Directory, Computerworld New Zealand, MTB, Network World, PC World New Zealand; **NICARAGUA:** PC World Centro America; **NORWAY:** Computerworld Norge, CW Rapport, Datamagasinet, Financial Rapport, Kursguide Norge, Macworld Norge, Multimediaworld Norge, PC World Ekspress Norge, PC World Nettverk, PC World Norge, PC World ProduktGuide Norge; **PAKISTAN:** Computerworld Pakistan; **PANAMA:** PC World Panama; **PEOPLE'S REPUBLIC OF CHINA:** China Computer Users, China Computerworld, China InfoWorld, China Telecom World Weekly, Computer & Communication, Electronic Design China, Electronics Today, Electronics Weekly, Game Software, PC World China, Popular Computer Week, Software Weekly, Software World, Telecom World; **PERU:** Computerworld Peru, PC World Profesional Peru, PC World SoHo Peru; **PHILIPPINES:** Click!, Computerworld Philippines, PC World Philippines, Publish in Asia; **POLAND:** Computerworld Poland, Computerworld Special Report Poland, Cyber, Macworld Poland, Networld Poland, PC World Komputer; **PORTUGAL:** Cerebro/PC World, Computerworld/Correio Informático, Dealer World Portugal, Mac*In/PC*In Portugal, Multimedia World; **PUERTO RICO:** PC World Puerto Rico; **ROMANIA:** Computerworld Romania, PC World Romania, Telecom Romania; **RUSSIA:** Computerworld Russia, Mir PK, Publish, Seti; **SINGAPORE:** Computerworld Singapore, PC World Singapore, Publish in Asia; **SLOVENIA:** Monitor; **SOUTH AFRICA:** Computing SA, Network World SA, Software World SA; **SPAIN:** Communicaciones World España, Computerworld España, Dealer World España, Macworld España, PC World España, PC World; **SRI LANKA:** Infolink PC World; **SWEDEN:** CAP&Design, Computer Sweden, Corporate Computing Sweden, Internetworld Sweden, it.branschen, Macworld Sweden, MaxiData Sweden, MikroDatorn, Nätverk & Kommunikation, PC World Sweden, PCaktiv, Windows World Sweden; **SWITZERLAND:** Computerworld Schweiz, Macworld Schweiz, PCtip; **TAIWAN:** Computerworld Taiwan, Macworld Taiwan, NEW ViSiON/Publish, PC World Taiwan, Windows World Taiwan; **THAILAND:** Publish in Asia, Thai Computerworld; **TURKEY:** Computerworld Turkiye, Macworld Turkiye, Network World Turkiye, PC World Turkiye; **UKRAINE:** Computerworld Kiev, Multimedia World Ukraine, PC World Ukraine; **UNITED KINGDOM:** Acorn User UK, Amiga Action UK, Amiga Computing UK, Apple Talk UK, Computing, Macworld, Parents and Computers UK, PC Advisor, PC Home, PSX Pro, The WEB; **UNITED STATES:** Cable in the Classroom, CIO Magazine, Computerworld, DOS World, Federal Computer Week, GamePro Magazine, InfoWorld, I-Way, Macworld, Network World, PC Games, PC World, Publish, Video Event, THE WEB Magazine, and WebMaster; online webzines: JavaWorld, NetscapeWorld, and SunWorld Online; **URUGUAY:** InfoWorld Uruguay; **VENEZUELA:** Computerworld Venezuela, PC World Venezuela; and **VIETNAM:** PC World Vietnam.
1/24/97

Acknowledgments

I'd like to formally apologize to all Canadians for the joke in Chapter 17, which didn't have to use "Canadians," but the Editorial Staff at IDG Books won't have it any other way. So it's not my fault and I promise never to do it again. Really, I love hockey. I do, I do.

I'd also like to acknowledge the contributions made by Ray Werner, who assisted with the original *Word For Windows For Dummies*.

Publisher's Acknowledgments

We're proud of this book; please send us your comments about it by using the Reader Response Card at the back of the book or by e-mailing us at `feedback/dummies@idgbooks.com`. Some of the people who helped bring this book to market include the following:

Acquisitions, Development, and Editorial

Project Editor: Bill Helling

Product Development Manager: Mary Bednarek

Permissions Editor: Joyce Pepple

Copy Editors: Tamara S. Castleman, Suzanne R. Packer

Technical Editor: Jim McCarter

Editorial Manager: Mary Corder

Editorial Assistants: Constance Carlisle, Chris H. Collins

Production

Project Coordinator: Sherry Gomoll

Layout and Graphics: Shawn Aylsworth, Elizabeth Cardenas-Nelson, Dominique DeFelice, Lee Hubbard, Angela F. Hunckler, Shelley Lea, Mark C. Owens, Carla Radzikinas, Theresa Sánchez-Baker, Gina Scott

Proofreaders: Henry Lazarek, Melissa D. Buddendeck, Dwight Ramsey, Robert Springer

Indexer: Sherry Massey

General and Administrative

IDG Books Worldwide, Inc.: John Kilcullen, CEO; Steven Berkowitz, President and Publisher

IDG Books Technology Publishing: Brenda McLaughlin, Senior Vice President and Group Publisher

Dummies Technology Press and Dummies Editorial: Diane Graves Steele, Vice President and Associate Publisher; Judith A. Taylor, Brand Manager; Kristin A. Cocks, Editorial Director

Dummies Trade Press: Kathleen A. Welton, Vice President and Publisher; Stacy S. Collins, Brand Manager

IDG Books Production for Dummies Press: Beth Jenkins, Production Director; Cindy L. Phipps, Supervisor of Project Coordination, Production Proofreading, and Indexing; Kathie S. Schutte, Supervisor of Page Layout; Shelley Lea, Supervisor of Graphics and Design; Debbie J. Gates, Production Systems Specialist; Tony Augsburger, Supervisor of Reprints and Bluelines; Leslie Popplewell, Media Archive Coordinator

Dummies Packaging and Book Design: Patti Sandez, Packaging Specialist; Kavish+Kavish, Cover Design

♦

The publisher would like to give special thanks to Patrick J. McGovern, without whom this book would not have been possible.

♦

Contents at a Glance

Cartoons at a Glance

By Rich Tennant • Fax: 508-546-7747 • E-mail: the5wave@tiac.net

page 7

page 277

page 207

page 319

page 96

page 341

page 109

page 233

Table of Contents

Part II: Formatting — or Making Your Prose Look Less Ugly 109

Part VII: The Part of Tens 341

Chapter 30: The Ten Commandments of Word 343

Chapter 31: Ten Cool Tricks 347

Chapter 32: Ten Weird Things You Probably Don't Know About 353

Introduction

*W*elcome to *Word For Windows 95 For Dummies*, a book that should have been called Word 102 for Dummies, eliminating the need for numbers altogether. But I digress.

The book you hold in your hands is not afraid to say, "You don't need to know everything about Microsoft Word to use it." Heck, you probably don't *want* to know everything about Microsoft Word. You don't want to know all the command options, all the typographical mumbo-jumbo, or even all those special features that you know are in there but terrify you. No, all you want to know is the single answer to a tiny question. Then you can happily close the book and be on your way. If that's you, then you've found your book.

This book informs and entertains. And it has a serious attitude problem. After all, we don't want to teach you to love Microsoft Word. That's sick. Instead, be prepared to encounter some informative, down-to-earth explanations — in English — of how to get the job done by using Microsoft Word. After all, you take your work seriously, but you definitely don't need to take Microsoft Word seriously.

About This Book

This book is not meant to be read from cover to cover. If that were true, the covers would definitely need to be put closer together. Instead, this book is a reference. Each chapter covers a specific topic in Microsoft Word. Within a chapter, you find self-contained sections, each of which describes how to do a Microsoft Word task relating to the chapter's topic. Sample sections you encounter in this book include

- Saving your stuff
- Cutting and pasting a block
- Making italicized text
- Creating a hanging indent
- Printing envelopes
- Cobbling tables together
- "Where did my document go?"

There are no keys to memorize, no secret codes, no tricks, no pop-up dioramas, and no wall charts. Instead, each section explains a topic as if it's the first thing you read in this book. Nothing is assumed, and everything is cross-referenced. Technical terms and topics, when they come up, are neatly shoved to the side where you can easily avoid reading them. The idea here isn't for you to learn anything. This book's philosophy is to look it up, figure it out, and get back to work.

How to Use This Book

This book helps you when you're at a loss over what to do in Microsoft Word. I think that this situation happens to everyone way too often. For example, if you press Ctrl+F9, Word displays a {} thing in your text. I have no idea what that means, nor do I want to know. What I do know, however, is that I can press Ctrl+Z to make the annoying thing go away. That's the kind of knowledge you find in this book.

Microsoft Word uses the mouse and menus to get things done, which is what you would expect from Windows. Yet there are times when various *key combinations,* several keys you may press together or in sequence, are required. This book shows you two different kinds of key combinations.

This is a menu shortcut:

   Alt,I,L

This means that you should press and release the Alt key, press and release the I key, and then press and release the L key. Don't type the commas or any period that ends a sentence.

This is a keyboard shortcut:

   Ctrl+Shift+P

This means that you should press and hold Ctrl and Shift together, and then press the P key, and release all three keys.

Any details about what you type are explained in the text. And, if you look down at your keyboard and find ten thumbs — or scissors and cutlery — instead of hands, consider reading Chapter 2, "Word Keyboard 101," right now.

This book tells you the easiest and best way to perform tasks and offers you alternatives when appropriate. Sometimes it's best to use the mouse — sometimes the keyboard. This book also presents the best keyboard shortcuts and inserts toolbar icons in the margin for those who like to use the toolbar.

Menu commands are listed like this:

File⇨Open

This means you open the File menu (with the mouse or the keyboard — it's your choice) and then choose the Open command.

If I describe a message or something you see on-screen, it looks like this:

    This is an on-screen message!

This book never refers you to the Microsoft Word manual or — yech! — to the Windows manual. Even so, it helps if you have a good Windows book as a reference. My favorite is *Real Life Windows 95,* published by IDG Books Worldwide.

What You're Not to Read

Special technical sections dot this book like mosquito bites. They offer annoyingly endless and technical explanations, descriptions of advanced topics, or alternative commands that you really don't need to know about. Each one of them is flagged with a special icon or enclosed in an electrified, barbed wire and poison ivy box (an idea I stole from the Terwilliker Piano Method books). Reading this stuff is optional.

Foolish Assumptions

Here are my assumptions about you: You use a computer. You use Windows, specifically Windows 95. Microsoft Word is your word processor. Anything else involving the computer or Windows is handled by someone whom I call your *personal guru*. Rely on this person to help you through the rough patches; wave your guru over or call your guru on the phone. But always be sure to thank your guru. Remember that computer gurus enjoy junk food as nourishment and often accept it as payment. Keep a bowl of M&Ms or a sack of Doritos at the ready for when you need your guru's assistance.

Beyond you, your PC, and the guru, you also should have a computer worthy of running Windows 95. That means you need color graphics, preferably of the VGA or SuperVGA variety. You also need a computer mouse. We make no bones about it: Without a mouse, Microsoft Word cannot be done. (By the way, when this book says to click on the mouse button, I mean the left button — unless your mouse is set up differently in some way.)

One more thing: I call Microsoft Word by its affectionate short form, *Word*. This name is completely unofficial and even the publisher made me (through the miracle of the R̲eplace command) change Word to "Microsoft Word" in this introduction. Face it, the program is Word. That's what I call it in the main body of this text.

How This Book Is Organized

This book contains seven major parts, each of which is divided into three or more chapters. The chapters themselves have been Ginsu-knifed into smaller, modular sections. You can pick up the book and read any section without necessarily knowing what has already been covered in the rest of the book. Start anywhere.

Here is a breakdown of the parts and what you find in them:

Part I: The Basic Word Stuff

This is baby Microsoft Word stuff — the bare essentials. Here you learn to giggle, teethe, crawl, walk, burp, and spit up. Then you can move up to the advanced topics of moving the cursor, editing text, searching and replacing, marking blocks, spell-checking, and printing. (A pacifier is optional for this section.)

Part II: Formatting — or Making Your Prose Look Less Ugly

Formatting is the art of beating your text into typographical submission. It's not the heady work of creating a document and getting the right words. No, it's "You will be italic," "Indent, you moron!" and "Gimme a new page *here*." Often, formatting involves a lot of yelling. This part of the book contains chapters that show you how to format characters, lines, paragraphs, pages, and entire documents without raising your voice (too much).

Part III: Strange Things Living under the Hood

This part covers some general and miscellaneous topics, items that in previous editions of this book were considered to be too esoteric to be put in chapters on their own. My, how times have changed. Thanks to many readers' responses, I've added three new chapters in this part, covering outlining, macros, and a few other topics people apparently were hungry for.

Part IV: Working with Documents

Document is a nice, professional-sounding word — much better than *that thing I did with Microsoft Word. Document* is quicker to type. And you sound important if you say that you work on documents instead of admitting the truth that you sit and stare at the screen and play with the mouse. This part of the book tells you how to save and shuffle documents.

Part V: Working with Graphics

Graphics play a major role in Windows, and Microsoft Word is geared toward having many interesting graphical bits and pieces. This part of the book discusses how graphics can work in your documents, how you can use Microsoft Word's own *applets* to create your own graphics, and how to do some things that previously required a knowledge of desktop publishing (or at least knowing what a Mergenthaller was). The idea here is to make your document look o' so purty.

Part VI: Help Me, Mr. Wizard!

One school of thought is that every copy of Microsoft Word should be sold with a baseball bat. I'm a firm believer in baseball-bat therapy for computers. But before you go to such an extreme, consider the soothing words of advice provided in this part of the book.

Part VII: The Part of Tens

How about "The Ten Commandments of Microsoft Word" — complete with Bill Gates (the president of Microsoft, as if you didn't know) bringing them down from Mt. Redmond. Or consider "Ten Features You Don't Use but Paid for Anyway." Or the handy "Ten Things Worth Remembering." This section is a gold mine of tens.

Icons Used in This Book

This icon alerts you to overly nerdy information and technical discussions of the topic at hand. The information is optional reading, but it may enhance your reputation at cocktail parties if you repeat it.

This icon flags useful, helpful tips or shortcuts.

This icon marks a friendly reminder to do something.

This icon marks a friendly reminder not to do something.

Where to Go from Here

You work with Microsoft Word. You know what you hate about it. Why not start by looking up that subject in the table of contents and seeing what this book says about it? Alternatively, you can continue to use Microsoft Word in the Sisyphean manner you're used to: Push that boulder to the top of the hill, and when it starts to roll back on you, whip out this book like a bazooka and blow the rock to smithereens. You'll be back at work and enjoying yourself in no time.

Part I
The Basic Word Stuff

The 5th Wave   **By Rich Tennant**

"My gosh, Barbara, if you don't think it was worth selling the Harley so we could upgrade to Word for Windows 95, just say so."

In this part...

When the Smith-Corona typewriter company collapsed recently, they tried real hard not to blame their demise on The Computer. All sorts of reasons were dreamt up, everything from "You know, pencils aren't obsolete" to "Computers take longer to start" and finally "Many people prefer using a typewriter because of that satisfying feeling they get from ripping out a piece of paper and crumpling it up to start over." But will mankind miss the typewriter? Doubt it.

The truth is that a word processor is just a much better way to compose your thoughts and get them down — maybe not on paper, but somewhere. Sure, we can tearfully miss our bottles of White Out, grieve over the absence of the warbling electronic typewriter motor, and lament the clack-clack of the hammer whacking the paper. But let's get real. A typewriter is a pogo stick compared to a word processor. I'm certain people also missed chiseling words into stone when paper was developed, but after a few years, who cared?

If you've lived in typewriter hell, then welcome to word processing heaven. This part of the book describes some of basic word processing things you can do with Microsoft Word. Everything is explained in a clear, clever manner that will make you soon forget the joys of ripping a sheet of paper out of a typewriter (which generally meant you didn't like what you had written, anyway).

Chapter 1

The Whirlwind Word Tour
(Basic Stuff)

● ●

In This Chapter

▶ Starting Word

▶ Reading the Word screen

▶ Entering text

▶ Editing a document on disk

▶ Getting Help

▶ Printing

▶ Saving your stuff

▶ Closing a document

▶ Moving on

▶ Exiting Word

● ●

*W*elcome to the basic stuff! This chapter contains a brief description of how Word works, taking you from starting the program, writing something, this and that type of stuff, to turning off Word and doing something else with your computer. More specific stuff happens in later chapters and is cross-referenced here for your page-flipping enjoyment.

Two Simple Ways to Start Word

In Windows, there are about a gazillion different ways to start your work. I won't go into all of them here. Instead, to save wear and tear on your brain, the following sections outline the two most common, painless ways to start your word processor.

The first and best of a gazillion ways to start Word

Here is the way you should start Word if you don't want to go crazy:

1. **Prepare yourself.**

   Physically, are you seated in a comfy chair? Are your hands properly poised over the keyboard — high enough so that your old typing teacher, Mrs. Lattimore, won't whack you with a ruler should your wrists drop a millimeter below your palms? Good.

   Mentally, ponder what you're about to do. "Will I become a computer nerd this way? And how would I look with that pocket protector and cellophane tape around the nose bridge of my glasses? Gosh, I don't even wear glasses! Okay. Deep breath. I will be brave."

2. **Turn on the computer, the monitor, and anything else of importance.**

   The important stuff can usually be identified by the number of blinking lights it has — a kind of status symbol in the computer community, you know.

3. **Fuss with Windows.**

   Be happy that Bill Gates has decided that this is how you're supposed to use a computer. Remember, he uses the same thing. And he's a bazillionaire. Maybe it will work for you too? Naaa . . .

4. **Locate the Start thing button.**

   It's that thing that says Start in the lower-left corner of the screen (see Figure 1-1). Point the mouse at that thing and click the mouse's left button once.

   If you can't see the *Start* button, press the Ctrl+Esc key combination (the Ctrl and Esc keys together).

5. **Choose <u>P</u>rograms⇨Microsoft Word.**

   Point the mouse at the word *Programs* on the Start Thing menu. Soon a submenu appears. (You don't have to click the mouse, just point.)

   Look for the line on the *Programs* submenu that says *Microsoft Word*. Click the mouse on that line. (Now you have to click.)

Watch in amazement as your computer whizzes and whirs. Before too long, you see a screen that looks like Figure 1-3 (look ahead a few pages). It's Word stumbling into town! The whatzits of the screen are discussed in the section "A Quick, Cursory Glance at the Word Screen," a few inches from this spot.

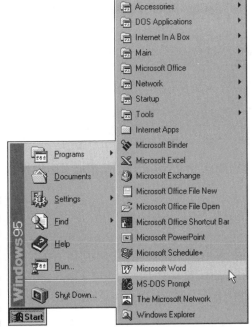

Figure 1-1:
Here is
where you
might find
Word on the
Start Thing
menu.

▶ If you don't see *Microsoft Word* right there on the menu (like in Figure 1-1), then look for a menu item that reads *Microsoft Office*. Point the mouse at that item and up pops another sub-menu, where you'll find *Microsoft Word* lurking.

▶ Your computer can be set up to automatically run Word every time you turn it on. Think of the time that would save! If you want your computer set up in this manner, grab someone more knowledgeable than yourself — an individual I call a *computer guru.* Tell your guru to "make my computer always start in Word." If your guru is unable, frantically grab other people at random until you find someone bold enough to obey you.

▶ I prefer to run Word *full screen*, maximizing its window so that nothing else bugs me when I'm writing. To do this, click the box button (the middle one) in the upper-right corner of the window. This button *maximizes* Word to fill the entire screen. If Word is already maximized, two overlapping boxes appear on the button; no need to click anything in that case.

The Microsoft Office bar way to start Word

If you're forced to use Word as part of the Microsoft Office, then you can quickly start Word using the Microsoft Office bar — which is *not* where the guys and gals of Microsoft go after a hard day of programming (no, that's the Microsoft Office Espresso Bar).

The Office Bar is one of those numerous things hanging onto your Windows desktop. This thing can usually be found along the upper edge of the screen, toward the right (see Figure 1-2).

Click the mouse on the *W* thing — the Word button. This starts Word lickety-split.

Figure 1-2:
Word is the
W button on
the Office
Bar.

A Quick, Cursory Glance at the Word Screen

After Word starts, you are faced with the electronic version of "The Blank Page." This is the same idea-crippling concept that induced writer's block in several generations of typewriter users. With Word, it's worse; the screen is not only mostly blank, it is surrounded by bells, whistles, switches, and doodads that would be interesting if only they were edible.

Figure 1-3 shows the typical, blank Word screen. A few things are worth noting:

- Several separate strips of stuff: bars, ribbons, rulers, and other horizontal holding bins for horrendous heaps of hogwash. Each strip performs some function or gives you some information. I warn you not to memorize this list: the *title bar,* the *menu bar,* the *Standard toolbar,* the *Formatting toolbar* (also known as the ribbon), and the *ruler* (who thinks he's the king or something). Refer to the nearby, easily avoidable technical information box, "Forbidden information about strip bars," if you want to load your brain with the details of these strips and bars.

- A large empty space. This is where any text you type and edit appears. Somewhere in this empty space is the flashing *insertion pointer* — looks like a blinking toothpick — that tells you where the text you type appears.

Here's a handy tip

Nestled amongst the various strips and bars on Word's screen you find the *Tip of the Day*. This is where Word attempts to impart some of its silicon-based wisdom on you. The value of its advice varies from the obscure ("You can use the style gallery to preview how using a different template will change your document's formatting"), to the inane ("You can undo most actions by clicking on the Undo button on the Standard toolbar"), to the truly useful ("You can hurt yourself if you run with scissors").

The Tip of the Day will also relate information regarding various word processing tasks as you fumble about doing your word processing chores. This can be sweet if you feel the help is useful. If you don't, click on the light bulb "Tip Wizard" button to make the Tip of the Day box go away.

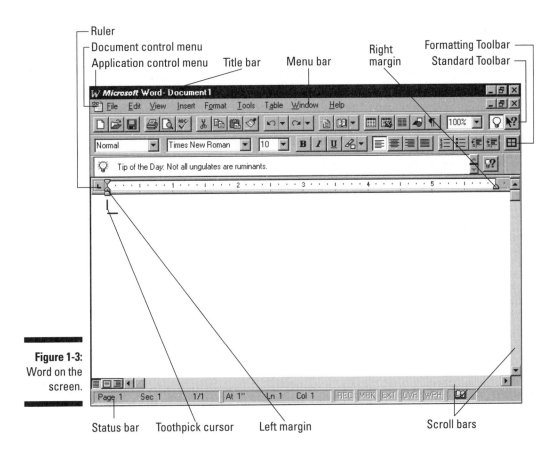

Figure 1-3:
Word on the screen.

Ruler

Document control menu

Application control menu   Title bar   Menu bar   Right margin   Formatting Toolbar   Standard Toolbar

Status bar   Toothpick cursor   Left margin   Scroll bars

✔ The bottom of Word's screen contains the *status bar*. No, this is not a yuppie hang-out. It contains a great deal of information that would impress a bureaucrat but that, frankly, makes my eyes glaze over. The gibberish that is usually there explains "where you are" in your document. Several word fragments are always followed by numbers (like a tenth-grade algebra problem). Table 1-1 explains what this stuff means.

✔ The final doojobbie on the bottom of your screen is Windows' own taskbar, which is used to hop, skip, and flop between various Windows programs or windows on the screen. Cheerfully ignore this thing while you're using Word.

Table 1-1	Stuff lurking on the status bar
Algebra problem	*What it means*
Page *xx*	The page you're editing: 1 = the first page, 8 = the eighth page, and so on.
Sec *xx*	The section of the document you're editing (sections are something just about everyone ignores): 1 = the first section, 8 = the eighth, and so on. This number will almost always be 1 for section 1.
x/x	The page of the document you're editing *over* the total number of pages in the document. So, 1/8 means that you're on page one of an eight-page document. (This is not a math problem; 1/8 does not mean .125 here.)
At *x.xx″*	How far from the top of the document your text is in inches. At 4.89″ means that the line you are editing is 4.89 inches from the top of the page. Like you would care.
Ln *xx*	What line you're editing. Ln 5 means that you're working on line 5, the fifth line down where line 1 is the first line on the page.
Col *xx*	What column you are in (columns being those vertical support structures for Greek-style architecture). In Word, the first column starts on the left side of the page, and the Col (column) numbers get bigger as you type toward the right side of the page. It's usually the number of characters and spaces you are over from the left margin.
TLA boxes	These boxes contain various TLAs (three-letter acronyms or abbreviations or what-have-you). Odd things to stick at the bottom of the screen, anyway. They appear "dimmed" when the option they represent isn't active. Check out the techy sidebar ("What those TLAs mean") for the obscure function each of them may serve.

Algebra problem	What it means
`Mr. Dictionary`	This guy looks like a book with a "magic pen" writing something down. Actually, it's Word's on-the-fly spell checker in action — a truly annoying piece of software engineering you can read about in Chapter 7.

- My advice? Ignore the weird numbers on the status bar; concentrate instead on your writing. After all, only the truly disturbed would whip out a ruler and measure a piece of paper in a typewriter as they go along. (The numbers come in handy later to tell you how much stuff you've written or to find your way to a particular spot in a long document. Pretend that they don't exist for now.)

- There are also three buttons in the lower-left corner of your document, just above the status bar. Call them Larry, Moe, and Outline. They control how you see your document on-screen, a subject dealt with at length in Chapter 27.

- Any weird stuff you see on-screen (a ¶, for example) is a Word secret symbol. Refer to "Out, Damn Spots!" in Chapter 27 for additional information.

- The exact spot where the text appears is called the *cursor*. Normally it's also called an *insertion pointer* because traditional computer cursors are underlines that slide under what you type. I prefer the term *toothpick cursor* because "insertion pointer" is just too medically geometric for my tastes. Characters you type appear immediately to the left of where the toothpick cursor is flashing, and then the cursor moves forward and waits for the next character.

- The bold horizontal line at the end of your text is the End-of-Text marker. Below it is a vast, vacuous, void of a place. Nothing exists in the white space below this marker, not even blank pages. Only infinite nothingness. The End-of-Text marker is the steel beam that supports your text, holding it from harm's way, in the evil nothingness that exists below your text.

- The *mouse pointer* is different from the toothpick cursor. Normally it's an arrow pointer-like thing. But if you move the mouse around the writing part of the screen, the pointer changes. Over your text, the pointer becomes what's commonly called an *I-beam*. The I-beam means "I beam the insertion pointer to this spot when I click the mouse."

- The status bar on the bottom of the screen tells what some Word menu commands do. To see how this feature works, click a menu command with the left mouse button. As long as you press and hold the mouse button, the status bar tries to explain what the command does.

- ✔ The status bar also tells you the function of some toolbar buttons. No need to click anything this time — just hover the mouse pointer over the button and voilà! Instant information crystals.

- ✔ The visibility of the Standard and Formatting toolbars is controlled by selecting the Toolbar option from the View menu. There you'll discover many more toolbars in addition to these two "standards." Don't bother goofing with this stuff until you read Chapter 27.

- ✔ The ruler's visibility is controlled by selecting the Ruler command from the View menu and clicking its check mark on and off. It's there. It's gone. It's there. It's gone.

Entering Text

To compose text in Word, use your *keyboard* — that typewriter-like thing sitting in front of your computer and below the monitor. Go ahead, type away; let your fingers dance upon the keycaps! What you type appears on-screen, letter for letter — even derogatory stuff about the computer. (Your PC doesn't care, but that doesn't mean that *Word* lacks feelings.)

What those TLAs mean

The status bar contains five boxes with strange letter combinations in them. This list tells you what they mean:

REC: Someone, possibly you, is recording a macro. The word REC lets you know that you're recording the macro, which is better than repeating, "OK, I'm recording a macro" over and over in your head. Macros are such an obtuse subject that they're not covered until Chapter 19.

MRK: The Revision Marking feature is on. This feature enables you to see where someone else has made changes — revisions — to your document. See Chapter 17 for information about revision marks.

EXT: Text is being selected, or blocked off, by using the F8 key. Handy thing to know. For more, see Chapter 6.

OVR: Overtype mode is on. Refer to your orthodontist for correction (or look in Chapter 4 for information about deleting text).

WPH: For some silly reason, WordPerfect Help is on. As if anyone ever learned all those cryptic WordPerfect commands in the first place. Refer to Chapter 3 for information about this abnormality. When the letters appear "dim," the option is off. Black letters mean that the option is on.

Incidentally, you can switch any option on or off by double-clicking its cryptic TLA with your mouse. Better refer to the chapters mentioned above before you mess with such a trick.

Forbidden information about strip bars

This section has nothing to do with strip bars. Instead, the topic here is the information you get from those strips of information on the Word screen. Some of them may be visible — others may not show up at all. Turning them on or off is discussed in Chapter 27.

Title bar: The first strip shows the name of your document. Every window in Windows has a title bar as well as the various buttons and gizmos Windows is famous for: the Control menu, the Maximize and Minimize buttons, the Close button, and the scroll bars you may see on the right and bottom sides of a window. (Please refer to your favorite book on Windows for an explanation of how all this stuff works and what relevance it has.)

Menu bar: The second strip contains a list of menus, each of which disguises a pull-down menu you use to select the many Word commands at your beck and call.

Standard toolbar: The third strip has lots of tools you can click to quickly use some of the more common Word commands. This strip may or may not be visible on your screen, depending on how Word is setup. The setup is discussed in Chapter 27.

Formatting toolbar: The fourth strip probably has the word Normal in it, on the left side. As with the Standard toolbar, this strip is optional. On the Formatting toolbar, you find the commands that apply styles, type sizes, fonts, attributes (bold, italics, and underline), justification choices (left, center, right, and full), tabs, and other fun formatting frivolity. Again, see Chapter 27 for more information about the toolbars.

Tip Wizard bar: A potential strip bar below the formatting toolbar is the tip-o-day toolbar, also known as the Tip Wizard bar. When you start Word, this thing shows you your tip of the day (see Figure 1-3). As you use Word, it may (or may not) offer suggestions about what to do next. (Personally I hide this bar, as described in the sidebar "Here's a handy tip," earlier in this chapter.)

Ruler: The fifth strip looks like a ruler. It is. And as with the toolbar and ribbon, your screen may not show the ruler — especially if the country you're in despises monarchy.

New text is inserted right in front of where the toothpick cursor is blinking. For example, you can type this line:

```
Stop, Uncle Cedric! That's the baby's diaper cream.
```

If you want to change the tone of the sentence, move the toothpick cursor to just before the T in *the*. Type in the following text:

```
not toothpaste! It's
```

The new text is inserted as you type, with any existing text marching off to the right (and even to the next line), happily making room.

You may need to type an extra space after *It's* to separate it from the next word.

The whole sentence should now read:

```
Stop, Uncle Cedric! That's not toothpaste! It's the baby's
diaper cream.
```

- ✔ You compose text on-screen by typing. Every character key you press on the keyboard produces a character on-screen. This holds true for all letter, number, and symbol keys. The other keys, mostly gray on your keyboard, do strange and wonderful things, which the rest of this book tries hard to explain.

- ✔ If you make a mistake, press the Backspace key to back up and erase. This key is named Backspace on your keyboard, or it may have a long, left-pointing arrow on it: ←.

- ✔ There is no cause for alarm if you see spots — or dots — on-screen when you press the spacebar. These special doohickeys let you "see" spaces on-screen. See Chapter 27 for the lowdown.

- ✔ Moving the toothpick cursor around the screen is covered in Chapter 3, "Getting Around Your Document."

- ✔ No, we don't call it *diaper cream* around our house.

- ✔ The Shift key produces capital letters.

- ✔ The Caps Lock key works like the Shift-Lock key on a typewriter. After you press that key, everything you type is in ALL CAPS.

- ✔ The Caps Lock light on your keyboard comes on when you're in All Caps mode.

- ✔ The number keys on the right side of the keyboard are on the *numeric keypad.* To use those keys, you must press the Num Lock key on your keyboard. If you don't, the keys take on their "arrow key" function. See Chapter 3, "Getting Around Your Document."

- ✔ The Num Lock light on the keyboard comes on when you press the Num Lock key to turn the numeric keypad on. Most PCs start with this feature activated.

- ✔ If you're a former typewriter user, please type 1 for the number one (not an I or a little L), and please type 0 for the number zero, not a capital letter O.

- See Chapter 2, "Word Keyboard 101," for some handy tips on typing and using your keyboard.

- No one needs to learn to type to become a writer. But the best writers are typists. My advice is to get a computer program that teaches you to type. It makes a painful experience like Word a wee bit more enjoyable.

Typing away, la la la

Eons ago, a word processor was judged superior if it had the famous *word-wrap* feature. This feature eliminated the need to press the Enter key at the end of each line of text, which is a requirement when you're using a typewriter. Word and all other modern word processors have this feature. If you're unfamiliar with it, you should get used to putting it to work for you.

With Word, when the text gets precariously close to the right margin, the last word is picked up and placed at the start of the next line. There's no need to press Enter, except when you want to end a paragraph.

- Press Enter to create a new paragraph. If you want to split one paragraph into two, move the toothpick cursor to the middle of the paragraph, where you want the second paragraph to start, and press Enter.

- You have to press the Enter key only at the end of a paragraph, not at the end of every line.

- There is nerdy variant of the Enter key-at-the-end-of-a-paragraph, which is called the *line break*. You get this by pressing the Shift+Enter key combination and, honestly, I can't think of any place you'd want to use it other than in a table. So see Chapter 12 if you really care.

- Don't be afraid to use your keyboard! Word always offers ample warning before anything serious happens. A handy Undo feature recovers anything you accidentally delete. See Chapter 2, "Word Keyboard 101."

That annoying line of dots

Occasionally, you see a row of dots stretching from one side of the screen to the other — like a line of ants, ants in military school, marching straight across your screen. Don't swat at it! That thing marks the end of one page and the beginning of another, called a *page break*. The text you see above the ants, er, dots, is on the preceding page; text below the dots is on the next page.

✔ You cannot delete the line of dots. C'mon — what good would it even do? Think picnic: You sweep one trail of the little pests away and another trail instantaneously appears. It's insect magic!

✔ You can see how the line of dots works by looking at the scrambled statistics on the status bar. For example, when the toothpick cursor is above the dots, it says Page 5 for page 5. When the cursor is below the dots, you see Page 6 for page 6.

✔ A row of dots close together — very friendly ants — marks a *hard page break*. It even says Page Break right in the middle of the line. This is a definite "I want a new page now" command given by the person who created the document. See Chapter 11, "Formatting Pages and Documents."

Editing a Document on Disk

You use Word to create *documents*. The documents can be printed or saved to disk for later editing or printing. When a document has been saved to disk, it's considered a *file* "on" the disk. (You can still refer to it as a document.)

There are several ways to load and edit a document already on disk. Because this is Windows, why not use the mouse-menu method?

1. Choose the File⇨Open command.

Using the mouse, click the word File on the menu bar, and a drop-down menu, well, drops down. Click the Open menu command, and the Open dialog box appears, as shown in Figure 1-4. (You also can click the Open tool, pictured to the left.)

2. Select the name of the document (or file) you want to open and edit.

Find the document name in the list and double-click it with the left mouse button. You can use the controls in the Open dialog box to whisk yourself around your disk drive and scout out files. Using the Open dialog box is standard Windows stuff. When you find your file, highlight it and click the OK button in the Open dialog box; or just double-click the filename with the left mouse button.

✔ If the cat is playing with your mouse, you can open the Open dialog box by pressing Alt,F,O, the menu shortcut, or use the keyboard shortcut Ctrl+O. Then you can use the keyboard to type a filename — although this method is so primitive that you had better lock the door first. No one wants to be seen using a *keyboard* in Windows!

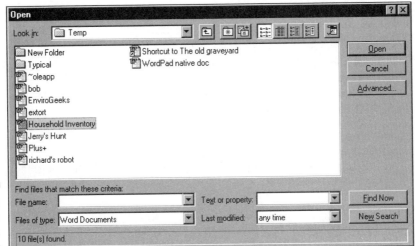

Figure 1-4:
The Open
dialog box.

✔ If you do end up typing the name of the document you want to load, make sure that everything is spelled right; Word is finicky about filename spelling. You can type it in either upper- or lowercase letters; it's all the same. Or you can simply select the name with the mouse by clicking on it. That way, you don't have to worry about spelling.

✔ The term *editing* means to read, correct, or add to the text you have composed and saved to disk. This process involves using the cursor keys, which are covered in Chapter 2, "Word Keyboard 101." Also see Chapter 4, "Deleting and Destroying Text"; Chapter 5, "The Wonders of Find and Replace"; and Chapter 6, "Playing with Blocks."

✔ If you want to edit a file you recently had open, pull down the File menu and look at the list on the bottom of the menu to see whether it is listed. Word "remembers" the last few documents you worked on. If you see what you want there, click on the file's name to open it.

✔ When you finish editing a document, you print it, save it back to disk, or do one and then the other. Printing is covered later in this chapter, in the section "Getting it Down on Paper (Printing)"; saving a document to disk is covered in the section "Save Your Stuff!"

✔ Documents you save to disk are given their own, special name. This name — a filename — can be from 1 to 255 characters long, can contain spaces, periods, and all sorts of other hogwash. Honestly, you're better off if you keep your filenames short and to the point. Chapter 22 discusses this in lurid detail.

✔ Also see Chapter 22 for more information on working the Open dialog box.

Getting Help

That group of latte-slurping, bespectacled, Birkenstock-wearing programmers up at Microsoft can make some delightful blunders every once in a while. However, no matter what else they do, they are forgiven. They put a wonderful, new and improved, technologically advanced, super-duper, ultra-brightening Help system into Word.

Well, actually Word's Help system is the same help system you find in just about every Windows program. It's activated by pressing the F1 key, and you can search for helpful topics or, if you're in the middle of something, grab help on only that one topic.

The Word Help menu

If you click <u>H</u>elp on the menu bar, you open the Word Help menu. The only menu item worth bothering with is the first one, <u>M</u>icrosoft Word Help Topics. This displays the multipaneled Word help dialog box, shown in Figure 1-5. The rest of the menu items in the Help menu can be cheerfully ignored.

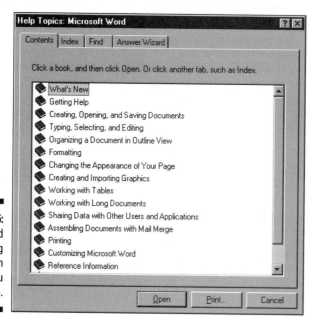

Figure 1-5:
The Word Help dialog box. From here, you get help.

- ✔ The Help Contents panel basically shows you what would have (should have) been the Word manual. Topics are displayed like chapters in a book; double-click on one of the li'l book icons to open that chapter and see the document — or even more chapters — nestled inside. Some of the information actually borders on being useful.

- ✔ The index panel contains an alphabetical list of topics related to word. To see it, click on the *Index* tab. You can search through the list of topics alphabetically, or type in whatever you're interested in to move through the list a tad bit more swiftly. Personally, I prefer this method since it gets me right to where I want to go.

- ✔ After choosing a topic from the index panel, you'll probably see another dialog box with even more choices; choose the one that best applies to whatever it is you need help with.

- ✔ You also can access the Help Index by pressing the F1 key while you're editing.

- ✔ When you press F1 while you're doing something else, such as being mired in a dialog box, you see helpful information about that topic only. Click the Help Topics button in the Help system to see the Index panel again.

 ✔ When you're done with Help, you must close its window. Click the X close button in the Help window's upper-right corner.

Help me Mr. Answer Wizard!

When Word happens to be in a very good mood, it may slip into Answer Wizard mode, displaying a series of interactive dialog boxes that hopefully help you solve a problem one step at a time.

Word has two ways to wake up the Answer Wizard. The first is to choose the Answer Wizard panel from the help dialog box; the second happens when you stumble upon it while looking for help elsewhere. I'll assume you're being deliberate and clicking on the Answer Wizard panel in the Help dialog box here (see Figure 1-6).

1. **Choose Help⇨Microsoft Word Help Topics.**

   The Help dialog box splashes on the screen.

2. **Click on the Answer Wizard panel.**

   This brings that panel forward, looking something like Figure 1-6.

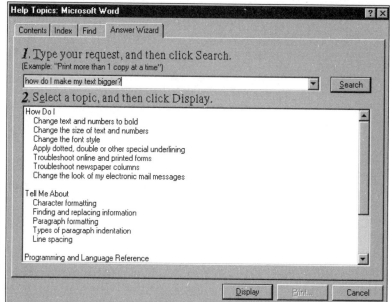

Figure 1-6:
The Answer
Wizard
braces itself
for your next
inquiry.

3. Type your request into the first box.

Just type it in like you would ask your computer guru: "How do I make my text bigger?" Don't try to be cryptic or use big words you don't understand like people who testify before Congress do.

4. Press the Enter key.

Word goes to work and displays related topics it thinks may help you. Scour the list and you may find one of them — such as the item reading `Change the size of text and numbers`, the third line down in the bottom half of Figure 1-6.

5. Double-click the mouse on the solution topic.

Click-click.

Now the Answer Wizard takes over, guiding you through the steps necessary to complete your task. Along the way you'll be asked to do various things, point and click the mouse, maybe type. (This is not a look-only operation.)

✓ If you see a dialog box displayed, read all the contents. Then click the Next button to move on to the next step.

✓ The Answer Wizard may choose menu items for you. Don't be alarmed; your computer is not possessed.

- If your computer ever does become possessed, most priests will gladly perform an exorcism for you. I had this done once to my PC. After a nervous hour of sweating and coaxing, we finally got the computer to spit out an old WordPerfect diskette.

- Answer Wizard may display a pop-up bubble help telling you what to type or which options to select. Do so.

- Sometimes the bubble help merely directs you to where in Word you need to be to carry out some task. For example, to change the size of your text, you use the text size thingy on the formatting toolbar. (See Chapter 9 for more information.)

Context-sensitive help

The spiffiest thing about Word's Help capability is that it can give you help with what you're doing when you're doing it. If you hold down the Shift key while you press the F1 key (that means when you press Shift+F1), the mouse pointer changes into a question mark or arrow. Or just click the question mark/arrow button on the left side of the Standard toolbar for an instant metamorphosis.

 Point the question mark/arrow thing at what you want help with and click the mouse button. For example, point the arrow at the scissors on the toolbar and click the mouse. You'll find out that the scissors are used to cut text, not to give you a haircut (though the help you'll read on the screen says that in a typically nerdy way). This button works with just about anything you see on the Word screen — even the really weird stuff.

- For a briefer, more simplistic, and generally less helpful explanation of what some of the doodads on-screen do, hover the mouse pointer over the icon in question. In a moment, a cryptic couple of words appear, which unfortunately tell you only what the button or tool is and not what it does.

- A slightly more intelligible explanation simultaneously appears on the status bar.

- If the computer rudely beeps at you when you click, assume that no help is available for that item.

 - Some dialog boxes have a question mark button in their upper-right corner. Click on this button, then click on any item in the dialog box to see what it does. Hopefully.

- Yet another way to get help on something in a dialog box is to right-click the mouse on it. This typically displays a pop-up box telling you what it is you're pointing at and how it works.

- Click the question mark/arrow thing or press the Escape key to change the mouse pointer back to normal.

Getting it Down on Paper (Printing)

After entering what you feel is the best piece of written work since Lincoln wrote the Gettysburg Address, you decide that you want to print it. After all, dragging the computer around and showing everyone what your prose looks like on-screen just isn't practical.

To print your document in Word — the document you see on-screen, all of it — do the following:

1. **Make sure that your printer is on and ready to print.**

   Refer to Chapter 8 for additional information about preparing the printer if you need it.

2. **Open the File menu and then choose the Print command. (You also can choose the Print tool from the Standard toolbar, depicted at the left.)**

   The Print dialog box opens. This is the place where printing and related activities happen.

3. **Click the OK button with the mouse.**

   Zip, zip, zip. The document comes out of your printer. Or whir, crunch, flap-blap-blap, the document comes out of your laser printer all nice and toasty.

   ✔ When you print, the little dictionary on the status bar changes to a wee li'l printer spewing out pages. Out of what you paid for Word, you probably paid $2.56 for that trick.

   ✔ You also can summon the Print dialog box by pressing Alt,F,P or Ctrl+P. This method is more desirable if you have long fingers or do needlepoint or if the mouse is off eating the cheese again.

   ✔ There is no need to click the OK button when you click the Print tool on the Standard toolbar; your document instantly prints.

   ✔ Detailed information about printing is provided in Chapter 8, including information about making sure that your printer is ready to print.

   ✔ To print only part of your document — a paragraph, page, or "block" — refer to Chapter 6, "Playing with Blocks."

Save Your Stuff!

Word doesn't remember what you did the last time you used the computer. You must forcefully tell it to *save* your stuff! The document on-screen must be saved in a file on disk. To do this, you have to use Word's Save command.

To save a document to disk, choose the File⇨Save command, Alt+F, S. (You also can click the Save button on the Standard toolbar, which looks like a wee li'l disk.) This step saves your document to disk. Or if the file hasn't yet been saved, a Save As dialog box appears. In that case, type a name for the file. Click the *Save* button when you're done.

✔ If the document you created hasn't yet been saved to disk, you have to give Word a filename to remember it by. The name is how you recognize the file later, when you want to edit or print it again. Type the document's name in the dialog box. If you make a mistake typing, use the Backspace key to back up and erase. Click *Save* to save the file.

 ✔ The fastest way to save a file is to use the keyboard. The Save file key combination is Ctrl+S. Press and hold the Ctrl (Control) key and press the S key. If you can't pick up a basketball with one hand, you can also use the Shift+F12 key combo.

✔ When you save a document, watch the status bar — it is temporarily replaced with a message that Word is saving your document (or fast saving, for our Frequent Fliers).

✔ If you entered a forbidden filename, Word just sits there and acts stubborn. Stab! Stab! Stab at the Save button. Nothing happens. Try again with a new filename (and read the nearby Technical Stuff box about filenames).

✔ Save your documents to disk so that you can work on them later! The documents can be reloaded into Word the next time you start it. Refer to the section "Editing a Document on Disk" earlier in this chapter.

✔ After the document has been saved to disk, you see its name displayed on the window's title bar. This is your clue that your document has been saved to disk.

 ✔ If you're not in a clever mood, you may decide to name your file with the name of a file already on disk. This is a boo-boo because the newer file "overwrites" the other file with the same name already on disk. For example, if you decide to save your new letter by using the LETTER filename and LETTER already exists on disk, the new file overwrites the old one. There is no way to get the original back, so use another, more clever name instead. Word warns you with this message:

```
Do you want to replace the existing whatever?
```

Click the No button. Use another name.

✔ See Chapter 22, "Managing Files," for more information about filenames and such.

TECHNICAL STUFF

Complicated — but important — information about filenames

You must name your file according to Window's loving, yet firm, file-naming rules. This isn't as tough as memorizing stuff for a DMV test, and it's not as horrid as things were in the ancient days of DOS — but it's darn close:

- ✔ A filename can be up to 255 characters long, so just about anything you want to type in is okay.

- ✔ Even so, try to keep your filenames short and descriptive.

- ✔ A filename can include letters, numbers, spaces and can start with a letter or a number.

- ✔ The filename cannot contain any of the following characters:

    \ / : * ? " < > |

- ✔ Don't bother typing a three letter extension — .DOC — on the end of any of your Word files.

Here are some sample filenames that are OK:

LETTER: A prim and proper filename, though it lacks passion, like a salad without the garlic. A better and more descriptive example would be:

LETTER TO MOM: This filename actually describes the type of document and what it's about — and it does it all without requiring a lot of extra typing.

CHAPTER 1: Another OK filename. Notice how numbers and letters can be mixed — no oil and vinegar here!

941 FORM: A fine, upstanding filename; numbers are okey-dokey.

M*A*S*H: Oops! The forbidden * (asterisk) character has been used. Shame, shame, shame.

I.LOVE.YOU: While this is okay, it looks stupid. Probably someone who used to work on a mainframe thunk up this one. The alternative, however, is correct and looks a lot better:

I LOVE YOU: Aw, shucks. I love you, too.

Closing a Document

If you're finished with a document, you can make it vanish from your screen by "closing" it, which is similar to ripping a sheet of paper out of your typewriter — without the satisfying sound it makes.

To close a document, choose the File⇨Close command (Alt,F,C). This step closes the document window and makes it vanish from the screen. Zzzipp! (although you have to say "Zzipp!" when you do this; Word is mute on the point.)

- Why close a document? Because you're done working on it! Maybe you want to work on something else or quit Word after closing. The choices are yours, and they're explained in the next section.

- If you try to close a document before it has been saved, Word displays a warning dialog box. Click the Yes button to save your document. If you want to continue editing, click the Cancel button.

- If you were working on one document and you close it, Word looks like it's vacated the premises: ribbons and menus disappear, as do scroll bars and other screen debris. Don't panic; you've just closed a document and Word has little else to do. Word sits patiently and waits for your next command.

- If you're working on other documents, another one appears on-screen in place of the document you just closed. See Chapter 20 for information about working with multiple documents.

Moving Right Along . . .

When the document is closed, and Word has gone into comatose mode, you have several options for what to do next. I won't mention the "take a break" or "play with the mouse pointer" options. And if you know how to switch over and play Solitaire for a few eyeball-glazing hours, that's up to you as well. But within Word, you have several options.

First, you can start working on another document on disk. Refer to "Editing a Document on Disk," earlier in this chapter.

 Second, you can start working on a new document. Do this by pressing the Ctrl+N key combination, or choose the File menu, choose the New command, and click OK, or click the "I wanna blank sheet o' paper" button on the Standard toolbar. This starts you off again with a clean, blank sheet of "electric" paper. Now it's up to the word-processing muse to get you going again. (You also can click on the New tool on the toolbar.)

Third, you can quit Word and do something else in Windows. Refer to the next section.

 You don't have to quit Word when you just want to start working on a new document.

Exiting Word

It is the height of proper etiquette to know when to leave. For example, your twin two-year-olds have just discovered that Aunt Winthorp's crystal figurine collection cannot survive the drop from the second story banister. So before the cat or her even smaller dog starts walking around with bloody footprints, you should discover something else you need to do and leave quickly. It's just proper. Leaving Word is properly accomplished by using the Exit command. This common Windows command is used to quit all Windows applications and programs.

To politely excuse yourself, get up and leave Word and choose the File menu by clicking it once with the mouse. Then, near the bottom of the list, look for the word Exit. Click that with the mouse. Poof! Word is gone.

- ✔ If you haven't yet saved your document, Word asks whether you want to do so before it quits. Again, this is just being polite. A dialog box appears, asking whether you want to save any changes to your file. Click Yes to save them. This part is important. Then, Word peaceably steps aside and lets you do something else in Windows, possibly something fun. (If the document doesn't yet have a name, Word asks you to think up a name to save your document; refer to "Save Your Stuff!," earlier in this chapter.)

- ✔ The File➪Exit command (Alt,F,X or Alt+F4) is the proper way to exit Word. Do not, under any circumstances, reset or turn off your PC to "quit" Word. This is utterly irresponsible and you'll go to Computer Etiquette Jail for life if you're ever caught — and that's in Redmond, Washington! You also run the very real risk of scrambling stuff on your disk so well that you won't ever get it back.

- ✔ Suppose that you don't want to quit, but instead you just want to get rid of a document and start on a new one. Refer to "Closing a Document," earlier in this chapter. Then refer to "Moving Right Along," for information about starting over with a new document for editing.

- ✔ Exiting Word returns you to the Windows desktop. If you want to turn your machine off, choose the *Shutdown* command from the *Start* button's menu; press Ctrl+Esc, U, and then click on the *Yes* button. Only turn off your computer when Windows says that it's "safe" to do so.

Chapter 2

Word Keyboard 101

. . . .

In This Chapter

▶ Using the keys on your keyboard

▶ Pressing and releasing

▶ Inserting and overwriting

▶ Knowing when to press the Enter key

▶ Knowing when to use the spacebar

▶ Using the Undo keys

▶ Using the Kindergarten Keys: Cut, Copy, and Paste

▶ Using the Help key

▶ Using the Repeat key

. . . .

*Y*ou wouldn't think using a keyboard in Windows would be that important. But the truth is, a lot of what you do in a word processor relies more upon the keyboard than the mouse. And the biggest problem I've encountered in 15 years of writing about word processors is that too many people are timid about using their computer keyboards. It's like there are land minds under half the keys. Let me reassure you: The thing won't explode, no matter how fast you type or how big your thumbs are.

If this chapter had a theme, it would be "Be bold!" Word doesn't do anything perilous unless you tell it to. Even then, you are asked a yes/no question before the dangerous-something happens. You can press the handy Esc key to cancel just about anything before you do it (that's why it's called "escape"), and the Edit➪Undo command undoes your last action. (You also can click the Undo tool or press the Ctrl+Z shortcut.) Consider these options to be similar to wearing little high-density uranium thimbles to protect yourself against those keyboard land mines.

Know Your Keyboard

Take a look at your keyboard and then at Figure 2-1.

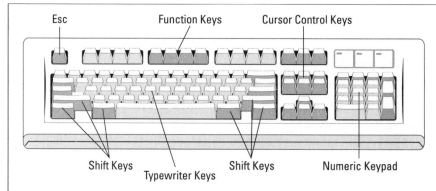

Figure 2-1:
Key
locations on
the
keyboard.

See how the keyboard is divided into separate areas, each of which has a special function? These are keys you use in Word, either alone or in combination with other keys:

Function keys: Along the top row of the keyboard, labeled F1 through F12. These keys are used alone or in cahoots with the Ctrl, Alt, and Shift keys.

Typewriter keys: Standard *alphanumeric* keys you find on any typewriter: A through Z, 1 through 0, plus symbols and other exotic characters.

Cursor keys: Arrow keys that move the toothpick cursor around the screen. Also lumped in are the Home, End, PgUp or Page Up, PgDn or Page Down, and the Insert and Delete keys. Oh, and the big plus and minus keys on the keypad are counted as well.

Car keys: Don't leave these in the car, nor should you have any exposed valuables lying about. Buy the Club.

Numeric keypad: These keys toggle between cursor keys and numbers. The split personality is evident on each key cap, which displays two symbols. The Num Lock key and its corresponding light are on if the numeric keypad (1, 2, 3) is active. If the cursor keys (arrows, Home) are active, Num Lock is off.

Shift keys: These keys don't do anything by themselves. Instead, the Shift, Ctrl, and Alt keys work in combination with other keys.

These two individual keys are worth noting:

Enter: Marked with the word Enter and sometimes a cryptic, curved arrow-thing: ⏎. You use the Enter key to end a paragraph of text.

Escape: The Escape key may be labeled Esc on your keyboard. It's a handy key to use in Word, but its location may vary. Sometimes Escape is next to the Backspace key. Find its location on your keyboard.

- ✔ Be thankful: A piano has 88 keys, black and white with no labels. It takes years to master. A computer, by comparison, is easy.

- ✔ Antique PC keyboards have a layout that is different from the currently popular, 101-key "enhanced" PC keyboard. Some older models have the function keys to the side of the keyboard; some are lacking the separate cursor keys. They all work the same under Word, but this book assumes that you have the 101-key keyboard. (Go ahead and count 'em; there are 101 keys.)

- ✔ Laptop keyboards are all goofed up. Primarily, they lack the numeric keypad. This is okay, but you'll miss the gray plus and minus keys, which can be used for some special formatting commands, divulged in Chapter 9.

Press and Release!

Welcome to Word Aerobic Mania! And press and release and one and two and down on the floor to tighten that tush! Okay, lift and squeeze and . . . oh, wait, that's another book. The title of this section is "Press and Release!" and it helps tone those flabby fingers for some fancy Word key combinations.

Word uses key combinations to represent some commands. For example:

Ctrl+P

Or if you can lift a basketball with one hand, you can try:

Ctrl+Shift+F12

Both commands open the Print dialog box — which isn't really important right now. Instead, what that key combination tells you is to press and hold the Ctrl and the Shift key and then press the F12 key. Release all three keys. Or press and hold the Ctrl key while you press P, and then release both keys.

These key combinations appear all the time. Always press and hold the first key (or keys) and then press the last key. Press and release.

- This works just like pressing Shift+F to get a capital F. It's the same thing, but with the odd Ctrl (Control) and Alt (Alternate) keys.

- Yeah, you have to really reach to get some of those key combinations.

- There's no need to press hard. If you're having trouble working a command, pressing harder doesn't make the computer think, "Oh, Lordy, she's pressing really hard now. I think she means it. Wake up, wake up!" A light touch is all that's required.

- Remember to release the keys: Press and hold the Ctrl key, press P, and then release both keys. If you don't know which one to release first, release the second key and then the Shift key (Shift, Ctrl, Alt) last.

- Ahhh! Feel the burn!

- There also are menu-key shortcuts, which aren't the same as function-key combinations. For example, Alt,F,P chooses the File⇨Print command, the same as Ctrl+Shift+F12. However, Alt,F,P is a menu shortcut, not a function-key combination. Notice that commas separate the keys instead of + signs adding them together. This means that you press and release each of them alone. For example, to print by using the menu-key shortcut, press and release Alt, press and release F, and then press and release P. Of course, Ctrl+P is still the easier keyboard option.

When to Press the Enter Key

On an electric typewriter, you press the Return key when you reach the end of a line. With a word processor, you should press the Enter key only when you reach the end of a paragraph.

For example, type in the following text. Just type it all in and don't bother pressing the Enter key, nope, not at all:

```
Lacking a flashlight (and a lot of common sense), Carla lit a
match and peered into the gas can to see just how empty it was.
```

You'll notice the text *wraps*, putting the last part of the text on the next line. There was no audible *ding* when you hit the right margin, and you didn't have to press Enter at the end of the line.

Word *word-wraps* any words hanging over the right margin and moves them down to the next line on the page. Therefore, you have to press Enter only at the end of a paragraph, even a short paragraph that is just a line of text by itself.

Ignore this info on WordPerfect's awful key combos

To convince (or dupe) WordPerfect users into switching over to Word, Microsoft has a special WordPerfect key command option. When it's switched on, old WordPerfect hands will have no trouble with Word because Word will understand and obey WordPerfect's ugly horde of keyboard commands. Needless to say, this is madness. Madness!

I recommend avoiding the WordPerfect "emulation mode." Golly, this is Word and you should use it that way. If you see the WPN three-letter-acronym highlighted on the bottom of your Word screen (on the status bar), double-click it with the mouse. That brings up the Help for WordPerfect Users dialog box. There, you click the Options button and the Help Options box appears. Finally, click the X by the item titled Navigation Keys for WordPerfect Users. That shuts off the WordPerfect keys and returns you to normal Word operation (which is what's covered in this book). Click the OK button and then the Close button to return to your document.

- Some people end a paragraph with two presses of the Enter key; others use only one press.

- If you want to indent the next paragraph, press the Tab key after pressing Enter. This technique works just like it does on a typewriter.

- If you want to double-space a paragraph, you have to use a special line-formatting command, covered in Chapter 10, "Formatting Sentences and Paragraphs." You do not use the Enter key to double-space lines.

- If you press the Enter key in the middle of an existing paragraph, Word inserts a new paragraph and moves the rest of the text to the beginning of the next line. This works like any other key inserted in your text. The difference is that you insert an Enter character, which creates a new paragraph.

- You can delete the Enter character by using the Backspace or Delete keys. Removing Enter joins two paragraphs together or, if you press Enter more than once, cleans up any extra blank lines.

- The word *Carla* may appear on your screen with a wavy red underline. That's Word's annoying real-time spell checker in action. Turn to Chapter 7 to learn the secret way to turn it off.

When to Use the Spacebar

A major vice committed by many Word users is mistakenly using the spacebar rather than the Tab key. Allow me to clear the air on this one.

Trivial information about the Enter and Return keys

Enter or Return? Some keyboards label the Enter key "Return." Most PCs use the word "Enter"; even so, some yahoos call it the Return key. Why? (And you really have to be hard up for trivia if you're continuing to read this.)

The reason has to do with the computer's background. On a typewriter, the key is named Return. It comes from the pre-electric days of typewriters when you had to whack the carriage return bar to move the paper over to the other margin and continue typing. From the computer's calculator background, the Enter key was pressed to enter a formula into the calculator. This is the reason that some computers can't make up their mind whether it's the Enter or Return key. My keyboard says Enter on it — and in two places. So that's what I use in this book.

Use the spacebar to insert space characters, such as you find between words or between two sentences. You have to press the spacebar only once between each word or sentence, although some former touch typists (myself included) put two spaces between two sentences. That's fine.

To indent, align columns of information, or organize what you see on-screen, you have to use the Tab key. The Tab key indents text to an exact position. When you print, everything is lined up nice and neat. This doesn't happen with the space characters.

- ✔ Use the Tab key to indent; use the spacebar only when you're putting spaces between words and paragraphs. I'm serious: Do not use the spacebar to indent or line up your text. Your stuff will look tacky, tacky, tacky if you do.

- ✔ It is okay, however, to hold your clothes together with safety pins (underwear excluded).

- ✔ As an old touch typist, I'm used to sticking two spaces between a sentence. Period-space-space. This isn't necessary with a word processor; type only one space after a sentence. (I gleaned this information from my managing editor, Mary "the bee" Bednarek, who bulged her eyes out at me one day and screamed, "Stop putting double spaces between your sentences! It takes me hours to delete them all!")

- ✔ In fact, I'll make up a new rule right now: Anytime you're tempted to use more than two spaces in a row, use a Tab instead. The word processing gods will bless you.

- ✔ To set the tab stops in Word, see Chapter 10, "Formatting Sentences and Paragraphs."

The Undo Keys

Be bold! Why not? Word has a handy Undo command. It remembers the last several things you did or deleted and unravels any mistakes you made quite easily. Furthermore, there's a Redo command, which is essentially Undo-Undo, though that's too much mental work to bother with right now.

"Now mark me how I will undo myself." — *Richard II, William Shakespeare*

What thoust do, thou canst undo

To undelete any text you just accidentally zapped, do any of the following:

- ✔ Press Ctrl+Z.

- ✔ Choose Edit⇨Undo with the mouse.

- ✔ Press Alt,E,U.

- ✔ Click the Undo tool on the toolbar.

- ✔ The quickest way to undo something is to press Ctrl+Z. This is the handy undo key combination used in almost all Windows applications.

- ✔ When you choose Edit⇨Undo, the last action you did is undone; if you choose Edit⇨Undo again, you undo whatever you did before that.

- ✔ The Undo item in the Edit menu changes to pertain to whatever needs undoing: Undo Bold, Undo Typing, Undo Boo-boo, and so on.

- ✔ To undo an Undo, select Redo. See the section "Redo, or Take Two" a couple of sections from now.

- ✔ Yabba-dabba-do.

- ✔ Because the Undo command remembers several things you just did, you can select any one of them individually for undoing. You do this by clicking the down arrow next to the Undo button on the standard toolbar. There you find a brief and terse list of actions (up to 99) Word remembers and can undo. Select any one of them for undoing, but keep in mind that they're out of sequence. To undo everything up to a point, select the action that you want as well as everything above it. Or just keep whacking Ctrl+Z until something looks familiar to you.

Can't Undo? Here's why. . . .

Sometimes it eats you alive that Word can't undo anything. On the menu bar, you even see the message `Can't Undo`. What gives?

Essentially, whatever it was you just did, Word can't undo it. This can be true for a number of reasons: There is nothing to undo; there isn't enough memory to undo; Word can't undo because what you did was too complex; Word just forgot; Word hates you; and so on.

I know that it's frustrating, but we all have to live with it.

Redo, or Take Two

If you undo something and — whoops! — you didn't mean to, you must use the Redo command to set things back. To undelete any text you just accidentally zapped, do any of the following:

- ✔ Press Ctrl+Y.

- ✔ Choose Edit⇨Redo with the mouse.

- ✔ Press Alt,E,R.

- ✔ Click the Redo tool on the toolbar.

- ✔ You can't use the Undo command to undo an Undo. (Huh?) This message can be ignored by anyone who never used the ancient version of Word that used to print on stone tablets.

- ✔ Like the Undo command, the Redo command remembers several things you just undid. You can select any one of them by clicking the down arrow next to the Redo button on the standard toolbar.

- ✔ If there's nothing to redo, the Redo command becomes the Repeat command. See the section "The Repeat Key," just a few paragraphs away in this chapter.

The Kindergarten Keys: Cut, Copy, and Paste

Cutting, copying, and pasting text are covered in Chapter 6. Three of the keys you use to perform those feats are covered here, however, because by the time you get to Chapter 6, this stuff won't make any sense. The three keys are shown in this list:

Cut   Ctrl+X

Copy   Ctrl+C

Paste   Ctrl+V

Now, I can understand Copy as Ctrl+C. *C* is Copy. And Cut is Ctrl+X. Sorta like X-ing something out, it disappears from your document right there. But Paste — well, he is a little more complicated.

Paste is Ctrl+V. V for what? Vomit? How about the word *weld* with a German accent? Veld? Does that make sense? Whatever. But what does make a modicum of sense is that these keys — X, C, and V — are all nestled close together on your keyboard (see Figure 2-2). Even the Z key, for Ctrl+Z Undo, is right there. I bet Mr. Qwerty never assumed that the day he designed the keyboard layout in 1870-something.

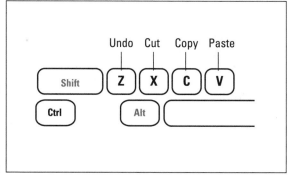

Figure 2-2:
How the kindergarten keys line up.

✔ The Cut, Copy, and Paste (and Undo) keys are all related to commands living in the Edit menu.

✔ Once you get the hang of them, you'll use these keys often to save time.

✔ Kindergarten is one of only a handful of German words used in English. You'd think there'd be more, but there aren't. (Now French words . . . Oo, la-la!)

The Help Key

No key on your keyboard is labeled *Help*. PCs just aren't that nice. The closest you'll come to a help key is the F1 key — which is the Windows help key, by the way. Here are some tips for using it in your fleeting moments of panic:

✔ Press F1 when you're doing something to display help and options available for that something. If you're just editing text, F1 displays the Help Index or the Answer Wizard, from which you can select a topic you're interested in, or just waste time using the Help system.

✔ Press Shift+F1 to get context-sensitive help. The mouse pointer changes to the question mark/arrow thing. Point and shoot for help!

✔ Getting help in Word really means that you're running another program — the Windows Help engine. You must quit the Help program when you're finished. Do this by clicking on the X close button in the upper-right corner of the Help window or by clicking on the Cancel button near the bottom of the Help screen.

The Repeat Key

Here's a good one: The F4 key in Word is known as the repeat key, and it can be a real time-saver. If you press a Word command, cursor key, or character and then press the F4 key, that command, cursor key, or character is repeated. (You also can choose the Edit⇨Repeat Typing command or press Ctrl+Y.)

For example, type the following lines in Word:

```
Knock, knock.
Who's there?
Miss Emmerson.
Miss Emmerson who?
```

Now press the F4 key. Word repeats the last few things you typed, which includes the hours of entertainment from these lines plus anything else you typed before them.

✔ Ctrl+Y, the Redo command, also acts as the Repeat command — but only when there's nothing to redo (meaning nothing left to undo-undo). For certain, F4 is the repeat key.

✔ A practical use of this command is creating forms. Type a bunch of underlines on-screen — your form's blank lines — and then press Enter. Press the F4 key a few times and the page is soon filled with blank lines.

✔ F4 not only echoes text, it's also especially useful when you issue the same command over and over, like when you are doing a find-and-replace, inserting the date, inserting special characters, or extensively formatting a document.

✔ If you use the F4 key along with the Shift key, as in Shift+F4, Word repeats your last Find or Go To command (see Chapter 5, "The Wonders of Find and Replace").

✔ The F4 key isn't your only access to the Repeat command. It also lives on the Edit menu, although it may be listed as Repeat Typing, Repeat Format-ting, or any of a number of Repeat-*blank* options.

Chapter 3

Getting Around Your Document

· ·

· ·

*Y*ou know those people who write the 23rd Psalm on a postage stamp? They don't really need a handy way to move from one part to another of their document. On the other hand, if you're told to write a four-page report but have only 1½ pages of text, then you learn to stretch things out. In those cases, Word's navigation keys come in handy. These keys are the nautical commands that move you from one part of your prose to another, up or down a paragraph, back and forth a word, even leapfrogging over dozens of pages at a time. Word can do it, and you don't ever have to memorize terms such as bow, stern, port, starboard, or adrift.

Your Basic Arrow Keys

The most common way to move about your document is to press the arrow keys, which are called the *cursor-control keys* because they control the toothpick cursor on-screen.

On your keyboard you can find the cursor-control keys on the numeric keypad, and they are duplicated between the keypad and the typewriter keys. The location of these cursor-control keys is shown in Figure 3-1. This duplication enables you to activate the numeric keypad by pressing the Num Lock key and still have access to a set of cursor-control keys.

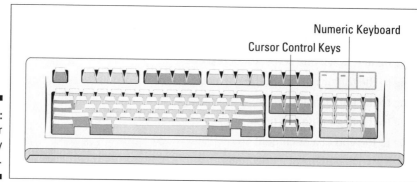

Figure 3-1:
Cursor
control key
locations.

The four basic cursor-control keys are the up-, down-, left-, and right-arrow keys. On the numeric keypad, they are on the 8, 2, 4, and 6 keys:

↑	Moves the cursor up to the preceding line of text
↓	Moves the cursor down to the next line of text
→	Moves the cursor right to the next character
←	Moves the cursor left to the preceding character

✔ The cursor-control keys on the numeric keypad and the separate cursor-control keys work in the same way; you can use either set. But keep your eye on that Num Lock light! It must be off for the keypad cursor-control keys to work.

✔ The mouse provides a quick and easy way to move the toothpick cursor: First spy a new location for the cursor on-screen. Then move the mouse pointer to where you want the cursor to be and click the left mouse button. The cursor is instantly relocated.

✔ If the cursor is on the top line of the document window (the top line of text) and you press the up-arrow key, the document scrolls to reveal the preceding line of text, if there is one. If not, the computer beeps at you and the cursor stays in place and blinks with that special look it reserves for the mentally impaired.

✔ When the cursor is on the last line of the screen and you press the down-arrow key, the document scrolls up to reveal the next line of text, if there is one. If not, the cursor stays in place and blinks at you with that special look it reserves for the soon-to-be-institutionalized.

✔ Moving the cursor does not erase characters.

Using Ctrl with the Arrow Keys

If you press and hold the Ctrl (Control) key and then press an arrow key, the toothpick cursor jumps more than one character. This is *cursor afterburner* mode (rumor has it that this is the *only* cursor mode Arnold Schwarzenegger uses):

Ctrl+↑	Moves the cursor up one paragraph
Ctrl+↓	Moves the cursor down to the next paragraph
Ctrl+→	Moves the cursor right one word
Ctrl+←	Moves the cursor left one word

Press and hold the Ctrl key and then press an arrow key. Release both keys. You don't have to press hard; use the Ctrl key the same as you use the Shift key.

✔ Ctrl+→ and Ctrl+← always move the cursor to the first letter of a word.

✔ Ctrl+↑ and Ctrl+↓ always move the cursor to the beginning of a paragraph.

✔ If you press Ctrl and click the mouse, you highlight, or *select,* a sentence in your document. Click again (without the Ctrl key) to move the cursor or to unhighlight the sentence (see Chapter 6 for information about selecting blocks).

Moving by Great Leaps and Bounds

You could just use the simple cursor keys and, Lordy, it would take you weeks to get around a long document. Besides that, you'd have to poke your finger at the keys and risk contracting Woodpecker Pointy Finger Syndrome. Instead, heed the advice in the following sections for moving around your document in great leaps and bounds.

Moving up and down one screenful of text

No need to adjust your chair here. The screen does not show you the entire document — usually not even a whole page (unless you're working on another 23rd Psalm on a postage stamp project). To see the next or preceding screen, press the PgUp and PgDn keys. These keys move you or your document (I can't tell which) around by the screenful.

PgUp: Moves the cursor up one screen. Or if you're at the tippy-top of your document, it moves you to the top of the screen.

PgDn: Moves the cursor down one screen or to the end of the document, if you happen to be there.

It's funny how PgUp and PgDn, where Pg is rumored to be short for *page,* moves you up and down a *screen* at a time. You get used to this illogic, if you're not already.

Moving to the top or bottom of the current screen

There are times when you want to zip to the top or bottom of the current screen. This is easy to do:

Ctrl+PgUp	Moves the cursor to the top of the current screen
Ctrl+PgDn	Moves the cursor to the bottom of the current screen

Moving to the end of a line

To get to the end of a line of text, press the End key.

- ✔ To move to the end of a paragraph, press Ctrl+↓ and then ← . Pressing Ctrl+↓ actually moves to the beginning of the *next* paragraph. Pressing the ← key moves you back to the end of the current paragraph.

- ✔ Moving to the beginning of a line is accomplished with the Home key, which is covered . . . well, here it is:

Not-so-moving information about moving the cursor

As you move the cursor around, look at the status bar on the bottom of your screen. It gives you some valuable information about your location within a document:

```
Page 2 Sec 1 2/6 At 2.5" Ln 6
Col 42
```

The status bar shows which page you are on, which section you are in, your position with regard to the total number of pages in your document, how far down the document you are in inches, the slope of your biorhythm, and number of past lives. Nah, those Microsoft techies aren't that progressive. Actually, the Ln and Col values tell you which line (from line 1 at the top of the page) and column (from the left margin) the cursor is on — useless stuff, but informative.

Moving to the beginning of a line

To get to the beginning of a line of text, press the Home key.

- ✔ There's no key like Home.
- ✔ To move to the beginning of a paragraph, press Ctrl+↑.

Moving up and down one page at a time

You knew that there had to be a way to do this. Whereas the obvious PgUp and PgDn keys move you up or down a *screen* at a time, the able assistance of the Ctrl *and* Alt keys is required in order to move you around a page at a time:

Ctrl+Alt+PgUp   Moves the cursor to the beginning of the current page

Ctrl+Alt+PgDn   Moves the cursor to the beginning of the next page

A page is actually a printed page of text, which you can see on-screen by a line of dots marching from left to right. The Pg thing to the left of the status bar (on the bottom of the screen) also tells you which page you're looking at.

Moving to the end of a document

If you use the Ctrl key with the End key, as in Ctrl+End, you're whisked to the end of your document.

You can use this command to get a feel for how big your document is. Press Ctrl+End and then look at the numbers on the status bar. You can see which page you are on, how far down the page you are, which line you are on, and which column you are in. Feel satisfied. Feel accomplished. Take a moment to gloat.

Ctrl+End is an easy key combination to mistakenly press. It throws you — literally — to the end of your document. If you do this and feel that you have boo-booed, press Shift+F5, the Go Back command, to return from whence you came. (Also see "Going Back," later in this chapter.)

Moving to the beginning of a document

To go to the beginning — nay, the tippy top — of a document, press the Ctrl and the Home keys: Ctrl+Home.

Using the Go To Command

The Ctrl+Home and Ctrl+End key combinations let you fly to the beginning and end of a document, but what if you want to go off somewhere in the middle? The Go To command in Word is what you need.

Go To, as in the Shakespearean "Getteth thee outta hereth," enables you to go directly to just about wherever in the document you want to be. To do so, choose the Edit➪Go To (Alt,E,G) command and the Go To dialog box appeareth before thine eyes (see Figure 3-2).

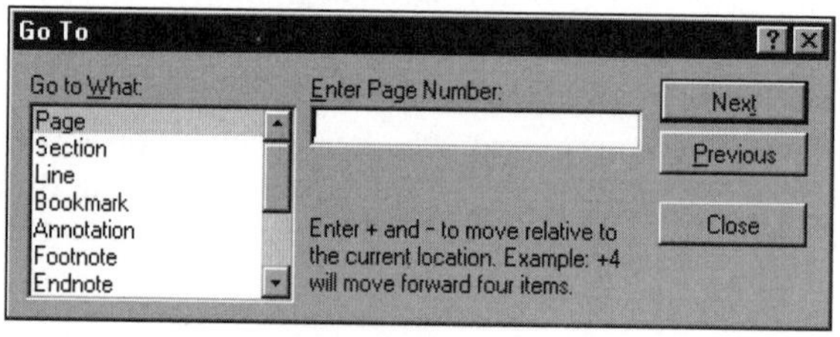

Figure 3-2:
The Go To
dialog box.

You can type a number of things in the Go To dialog box. The most effective use is typing a page number; Word instantly beams you to the top of that page. For example, type **14** in the box and press Enter, and you go to page 14.

- ✔ You also can press the F5 key to open the Go To dialog box.

- ✔ Heck, you can also press the Ctrl+G keyboard shortcut. (Makes more sense than F5, anyway.)

- ✔ If you click twice on the page number on the status bar (muttering "Change, you idiot. Change, change," while you do this helps), the Go To dialog box appears like a genie out of a lamp.

- ✔ To be even more specific in your Go To commands, see "Using the Highly Useful Bookmark Command," later in this chapter.

The Go to Underline What part of the Go To dialog box enables you to select a specific whatzit in your document in order to relocate yourself. It's an ugly assortment of items in there, most of which pertain to advanced Word formatting. But if you are inserting graphics or footnotes or using the useful Bookmarks, you can select them from the list, type the proper number or name in the box, and press Enter and you're there. Needless to say, this feature is only for the truly bold.

Sailing with the Scroll Bars

If you love your mouse, you can use the power of Windows to help you traverse your documents. You use the vertical scroll bar to the right of your document. It looks like a one-lane highway, but it is really used like an elevator shaft (see Figure 3-3).

- ✔ To scroll your document up one line of text, click the mouse on the up scroll arrow at the top of the scroll bar.

- ✔ To scroll down one line of text, click the mouse on the down scroll arrow at the bottom of the scroll bar.

- ✔ In the middle of the scroll bar is a scroll box or elevator button. It gives you an idea of which part of your document you're looking at; if the box is at the top of the scroll bar, you're near the top of your document, and vice versa.

- ✔ To see the previous screen of text, click the scroll bar just above the elevator button.

- ✔ To see the next screen of text, click the scroll bar just below the elevator button.

Vertical scroll bar ———
Up-down elevator button ———
Up scroll arrow ———

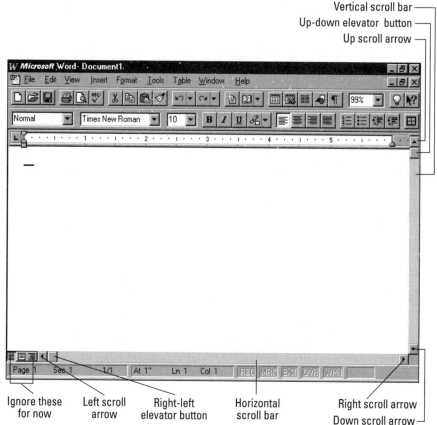

Figure 3-3:
The scroll
bars on the
Word
screen.

Ignore these | Left scroll | Right-left | Horizontal | Right scroll arrow
for now | arrow | elevator button | scroll bar | Down scroll arrow

✔ To move to a specific position in the document, use the mouse to *drag* the elevator button up or down. The elevator button's position indicates which portion of the document you want to see. Also, a pop-up bubble tells you approximately which page you'll be looking at when you release the mouse button (see Figure 3-4).

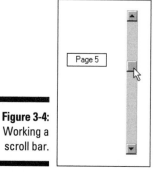

Page 5

Figure 3-4:
Working a
scroll bar.

> ✔ The scroll bar is not where Greek philosophers went to get drunk. Well, okay, maybe they had a *few drinks* there.

Going Back

They say that once you commit, there's no going back. Boy, are they wrong. If you go anywhere you don't want to be, press Shift+F5 and Word carries you back to where you started.

The Shift+F5 key command works only in Word; you can't try this command in real life.

If you keep pressing Shift+F5, you return to where you were before; if you press it again, you're back to where you were before that. This works about three times before it starts repeating itself.

Using the Highly Useful Bookmark Command

Have you ever done this: You're working away on great stuff, but occasionally you need to zip off elsewhere in your document? So you try to fold down the edge of the screen — *dog-ear* it, if you will — to remember where you were? I do it all the time. Fortunately, Word has a command that helps save wear and tear on your monitor. It's the highly useful Bookmark command.

Setting a bookmark

To set a bookmark in your document, follow these steps:

1. **Put the toothpick cursor where you want to place a bookmark.**

2. **Select the Edit⇨Bookmark command (or use Ctrl+Shift+F5).**

   The Bookmark dialog box opens, as shown in Figure 3-5.

3. **Type a name for the bookmark.**

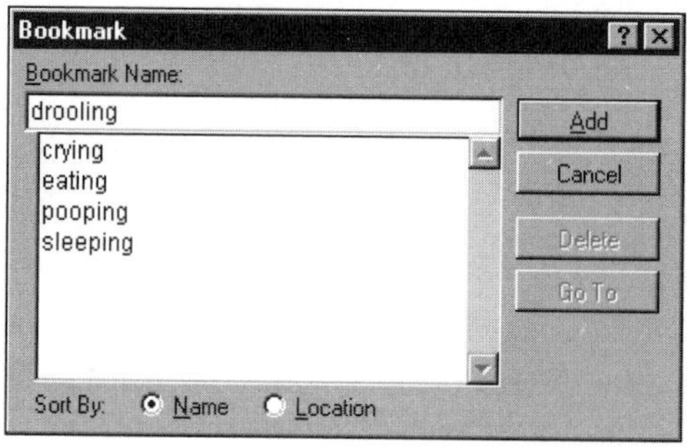

Figure 3-5:
The Bookmark dialog box.

Be clever! The name reminds you of where you are in your document. So if you're writing a report on things babies can do, the bookmark name *drooling* would be appropriate.

4. Press Enter or click the Add button with the mouse.

Finding a bookmark and moving to that spot in your document

To return to a bookmark, you use the Go To command, as covered in "Using the Go To Command," earlier in this chapter. These steps keep you from turning the page and losing your train of thought:

1. Press the F5 key.

The Go To dialog box splats across your screen.

2. Highlight Bookmark in the Go to What list.

It's the fourth item down.

The Enter Page Number box changes to read Enter Bookmark Name. Your most recent bookmark appears in that space.

If you don't see your bookmark, click the down arrow and you'll see a long list of bookmarks in your document. Click the one you want by using the mouse.

3. Click the Go To button.

You're there!

4. Click the Close button to get rid of the Go To dialog box and return to editing your document.

Chapter 4
Deleting and Destroying Text

● ●

In This Chapter

▶ Using Insert and Overtype modes

▶ Using your basic delete keys: Backspace and Delete

▶ Examining the "Backspace-blip" phenomenon

▶ Deleting a word

▶ Deleting a line of text

▶ Deleting odd shapes with blocks

▶ Undeleting

● ●

*T*he first thing you'll never miss about your old typewriter was it's crummy ability to erase text. Remember correction ribbons? Remember gloopy globs of White Out? Or worse, remember having "erasable bond" and getting eraser stubble inside the works? The lines of people screaming from their Smith-Coronas running into the computer stores should have been the signal to sell that stock years ago. But I digress. . . .

Nothing gives you that satisfying feeling like blowing away text — especially if it's someone else's document you're "editing." Of course, most of the destroying and deleting that goes on in Word is minor stuff: You snip out a letter here, slay a word here, yank out a sentence there. It's much easier than using a typewriter (major "DUH" to you ex-SC corporate types out there), and because you delete text *on-screen*, it happens quickly and painlessly in the electronic ether. And if you change your mind, you can press Ctrl+Z, the Undo shortcut key (or click the Undo tool) to bring your text back to glowing phosphorescent perfection.

Insert and Overtype Modes

The Insert key on your keyboard controls Word's two methods of putting text on-screen. Normally, new text is inserted just before the blinking toothpick cursor. New text pushes any existing text to the right and down as you type. This is *Insert mode.*

If you press the Insert key, you enter *Overtype mode.* The letters OVR in the lower-right section of the status bar become bold, indicating *over,* as in *Overtype mode* or "all of this is over your head." Any text you type next over-writes existing text on-screen.

If you press the Insert key again, the OVR returns to its wallflower-gray color and you're back in Insert mode.

✔ The Insert key appears in two places on the 101-key keyboard. The word Ins appears on the zero key on the keypad, and Insert appears just to the right of the Backspace key. Both keys perform the same function.

✔ The new characters you type in Insert mode appear right in front of the flashing toothpick cursor. Then the cursor moves to the right, awaiting the next character you type.

✔ The OVR in the status bar indicates that you are in Overtype mode. Any new text you type overwrites existing text. I point this out because a stray elbow can press the Insert key and put you in that mode when you don't want it. This is a good reason not to type with your elbows. But if you are typing along and suddenly notice that part of your text seems to be missing, check your status bar to see whether you're in Overtype mode.

✔ Leaving Word in Insert mode all the time is a safe bet. If you want to overwrite something, just type the new text and then delete the old.

Your Basic Delete Keys: Backspace and Delete

You can use two keys on the keyboard to delete single characters of text:

Backspace key: Deletes the character to the left of the toothpick cursor

Delete key: Deletes the character to the right of the toothpick cursor

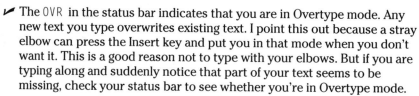
```
I can't eat an|other thing. Except for maybe that last piece
of Heath Crunch pie.
```

In the preceding line, the toothpick cursor is "flashing" between the *n* and the *o* in "another." Pressing the Backspace key would delete the *n* in "another"; pressing the Delete key deletes the *o*.

- ✔ After deleting a character, any text to the right or below the character moves up to fill the void.

- ✔ If you're in Overtype mode, the Backspace key still pulls the rest of the text to the right.

- ✔ Backspace works like the Backspace key on a typewriter. The difference is that when you press Backspace in Word, the cursor backs up and erases. (The Word equivalent of the typewriter's Backspace key is the left-arrow key.)

- ✔ You can press and hold Backspace or Delete to continuously "machine-gun delete" characters. Release the key to stop your wanton destruction.

The Backspace-Blip Phenomenon

Word's childlike reaction to something it doesn't like is the *blip,* a nice and brief beep from your PC's speaker. Sometimes you may hear the blip when you press Backspace to delete. Nothing is deleted; you hear the blip, blip, blip only once for each desperate stab at the Backspace key.

The blipping is Word's way of warning you. What you're trying to do is delete one of the secret, hidden codes littered about the document — codes that change paragraph formatting and other covert stuff. You can't indiscriminately delete this stuff with the Backspace key.

- ✔ If you really want to delete the codes, press the ← key and then press the Delete key. No blip.

- ✔ Whenever you want to hear the blip, press the End key more than once. Keep holding down the End key to hear Word's equivalent of a raspberry.

- ✔ The blip can really scare the pee out of you if you have a sound card and external speakers set up with Windows.

- ✔ Don't be surprised by the mystery codes in your document. You put them there as you create and format your text.

- ✔ If you want your old formatting back, choose Edit⇨Undo or press Ctrl+Z before you do anything else (or click the Undo tool).

Deleting a Word

Word lets you gobble up entire words at a time by using one of two "delete word" commands:

Ctrl+Backspace   Deletes the word that is in front (to the left) of the cursor

Ctrl+Delete   Deletes the word that is behind (to the right) of the cursor

To delete a word by using Ctrl+Backspace, position the cursor at the last letter of the word. Press Ctrl+Backspace and the word is gone! The cursor then sits at the end of the preceding word or the beginning of the line (if you deleted the first word in a paragraph).

To delete a word by using Ctrl+Delete, position the cursor at the first letter of the word. Press Ctrl+Delete and the word is gone. The cursor then sits at the beginning of the next word or the end of the line (if you deleted the last word in a paragraph).

- No mere pencil can match Ctrl+Delete or Ctrl+Backspace for sheer speed and terror.

- If the cursor is positioned anywhere in the middle of a word, Ctrl+Backspace deletes everything from where the cursor is to the last letter of the preceding word.

- If the cursor is positioned anywhere in the middle of a word, the Ctrl+Delete command deletes everything from where the cursor is to the first letter of the next word.

- To delete a word, position the mouse pointer on the offending critter and double-click the mouse button. The word is highlighted, and pressing the Delete key erases it.

Deleting a Line of Text

Word has no single command for deleting a line of text from the keyboard. But with the mouse, it is only a matter of a click and a key press. Follow these steps:

1. Move the mouse into the left margin of your document.

 The cursor changes into an arrow pointing northeast rather than northwest. The winds of change are a-blowin'. . . .

2. **Point the mouse pointer arrow at the line of text you want to obliterate.**

3. **Click the left mouse button.**

   The line of text is highlighted, or *selected.*

4. **Press the Delete key to send that line into the void.**

When the mouse cursor is pointing northeast, you can drag it down the left margin and select as many lines of text as you care to. They all can then be deleted with one stroke of the Delete key.

Also see Chapter 6 on marking text as a block and then blowing it to Kingdom Come.

Deleting Paragraphs

To mark a complete paragraph for destruction, give it the symbolic kiss on the cheek and click three times (quickly) on any word in the paragraph. This action highlights the paragraph as a block. Now press either the Backspace or Delete key and — presto! — vaporized text!

 If you're fond of the northeast-pointing mouse, move the mouse pointer into the left column on the page (where it turns into the northeast pointer) and then double-click it. The paragraph to the right of the mouse cursor is selected and primed for deletion.

Deleting Odd Shapes with Blocks

Word can delete characters, words, and lines all by itself. To delete anything else, you have to mark it as a block of text and then delete the block.

To delete a block of text, follow these steps:

1. **Mark the block.**

   The block can be highlighted by using the mouse; click the mouse at the beginning of the block and then drag it to the block's end. Using the keyboard, you move the toothpick cursor to the beginning of the block; then press F8 and press the cursor keys to highlight the block.

2. **Press the Delete key to remove all the highlighted text.**

Chapter 6 contains more information about selecting, highlighting, and other-wise playing with blocks.

Undeleting

Deleting text can be traumatic, especially for the timid Word user. But editing is editing, and mistakes happen. If you want some of your freshly deleted text back, you can use the Undo command, Ctrl+Z, to undelete text. It usually works like this:

1. Panic!

"Whoops! There went my letter to the editor, the best one I've written, the one I got down to four pages, the one I'm certain they'll print."

2. Press Ctrl+Z.

See? Communists don't live in your computer after all.

✔ Don't forget the Undo command in the Edit menu — first item, by the way. If you can't remember Ctrl+Z or if you find yourself pressing other keys by mistake, just select Edit⇨Undo *whatever* (or click the Undo tool).

✔ You can be sloppy with the Undo shortcut because Undo remembers the last several things you just did. But don't get lazy! If you delete it and want it back, press Ctrl+Z without thinking about it.

Chapter 5

The Wonders of Find and Replace

- -

In This Chapter

▶ Finding text

▶ Finding secret codes

▶ Using Find and Replace

▶ Using Find and Replace spaces

▶ Using Find and Delete

- -

*P*oor little Bill has lost his marbles! Too bad he doesn't know about Word's Find and Replace commands. He could locate the little round rocks — and maybe his sanity, too! But not only that, Bill could use Find and Replace, maybe replacing all his marbles with his own fleet of zeppelins. It's all really cinchy when you force the various purposes of the Find and Replace commands into your head. Sadly, only words are replaced. If Word could find and replace real things, there would be at least one more wonderful house with a swimming pool and sauna in this world, I bet you.

Finding Text

Word can locate any bit of text anywhere in your document, from a bombastic oratory down to the tiniest iota of plot. The command used to find text is called, surprisingly enough, the Find command. It dwells in the Edit menu. Follow these steps to use the Find command and locate text lurking in your document:

1. Think of some text you want to find.

For example, "marbles."

2. Choose the Edit⇨Find command.

You see the Find dialog box, shown in Figure 5-1.

Find	? ✕
Find What:	[▼]	Find Next
		Cancel
Search: [All ▼] ☐ Match Case		
☐ Find Whole Words Only		Replace...
☐ Use Pattern Matching		
☐ Sounds Like		
☐ Find All Word Forms		
─ Find		
[No Formatting] [Format ▼] [Special ▼]		

Figure 5-1:
The Find
dialog box.

3. Type the text you want to find.

Enter the text into the box titled Fi**n**d What. For example, **sheep**. Type lowercase letters.

4. Click the **F**ind Next button to start the search.

Or you can press Enter.

If any text is found, it's highlighted on-screen. The Find dialog box does not go away until you click the Cancel button or press the Escape key. (This allows you to keep searching for more text, if you're so inclined.)

✔ The quick shortcut key for finding text is to press Ctrl+F (the F stands for Find, in this case).

✔ Type the text you want to find exactly. Do not end the text with a period unless you want to find the period, too.

✔ If the text isn't found, you see this message:

```
Word has finished searching the document. The search item
was not found.
```

Oh, well. Try again and check your typing.

✔ To find any additional occurrences of the text, click the **F**ind Next button.

✔ After you close the Find dialog box, you can use the handy Shift+F4 key to repeat finding the next matching bit of text in your document. This keystroke saves time over using the full-on **F**ind command again.

✔ You can search for a variety of things by using the **F**ind command: text, spaces, the Enter character, and formatting codes. This subject is covered in "Finding secret codes," later in this chapter.

✔ Typing lowercase letters helps you find just about any text in the document. But when you want to find text that matches uppercase and lowercase the way you type it, be sure to select the Match Case check box. This box makes the Find command know the difference between Marbles and marbles.

✔ You may also select the nifty Sounds Like option so that Word notifies you of all instances in the document where anything sounding like the text you're looking for occurs. So if Bill loses focus and, for some reason, decides to find any *Zeplins*, Word will magically locate and match *Zeppelins* (as well as *Zeplins*).

Searching up, down, left, and right

Word typically looks for text everywhere in a document. It starts from the toothpick cursor's position to the end of the document, but then jumps up hither to the top of the document and keeps on searching. Even so, you can force Word to look in only one direction or the other, putting blinders on the Find command in a manner of speaking. To do this, click the Search drop-down box in the Find dialog box (see Figure 5-1). There you find three options:

Down: Searches from the toothpick cursor to the end of the document

Up: Searches from the toothpick cursor to the beginning of the document

All: Damn the toothpick cursor — searches the *entire* document!

I was just kidding about searching left and right in this section's title. Left is actually "up" or before the toothpick cursor; right is "down" or after the toothpick cursor. And starboard is right and port is left, if you happen to be using Word on a laptop somewhere in the ocean.

TIP

Finding or not finding bits and pieces of words

Word finds any matching text in your document. It can find things so well that it can drive you crazy. Suppose Bill cashes in his marbles for zeppelins and then, on a whim, decides he wants to become a shipping magnet (magnetically attracted to ships). So he searches his document for the word *ship* and, lo, Word will show him ships in places he hadn't yet thought of: friend*ship*, court*ship*, relation*ship*, not to mention the *ship*shape *ship*ment of *ship*mates waiting down at the *ship*yard.

To make Word more precise — to locate only a whole *ship*, for example, the type that sails on the ocean blue — select the Find Whole Word Only check box in the Find dialog box. When that box is checked, the Find command logically locates only words and not things nestled in other words.

Finding secret codes

Laced throughout a document are secret codes and printing instructions. You don't see these codes on-screen, but they affect the way your document looks and prints. Basically, the secret commands — bold, underline, center, and special paragraph formatting — can be searched for just like text can.

To search for a secret code, choose Edit⇨Find and then click the Format button to open a menu asking whether you want to search by Font, Paragraph, Tabs, Language, Dopey, Sneezy, or Doc. Oops! Wrong seven dwarfs. The other three secret things you can search for are Frame, Style, or Highlight. In real life, however, you'll probably only use the Font and Paragraph items, maybe Style, too.

For example, choose Font to open the Find Font dialog box, as shown in Figure 5-2. You can find a bunch of character-related stuff with this dialog box. If you want to search a document for italicized words in a 9-point Roman font, for example, select each of these things from their menus and click OK. The dialog box closes and you can then select Find Next to look for any of this highly stylized stuff.

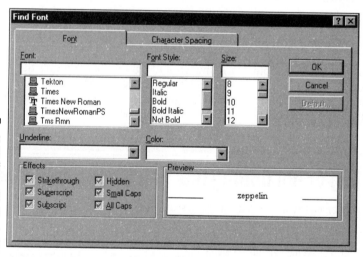

Figure 5-2: You can find a bunch of character-related stuff by using this dialog box.

✔ You can use this box to look for specific occurrences of a font, such as Courier or Times New Roman, by selecting the font from the selection list. Scroll through the font menu to see what you can choose.

✔ You can look for a particular size of type (24 point, for example) by selecting it from the Size selection list. See Chapter 9, "Formatting Characters," for information about character formatting.

✔ You can look for occurrences of anything shown in this box (or any combination of things) by putting in what you want to look for.

✔ You also can search for paragraph formatting by selecting P̲aragraph rather than F̲ont from the F̲ormat menu in the Find dialog box. See Chapter 10, "Formatting Sentences and Paragraphs," for information about paragraph formatting.

✔ You also can search for styles by selecting S̲tyle rather than F̲ont from the Find dialog box. Refer to Chapter 14, "Formatting with Style," for a discussion of styles.

✔ For those of you who often find yourselves slipping back and forth between more than one language (it's tough being fluent in so many different tongues, I'm sure), you can also search for text by the language in which it is written. Word even discriminates between the English used by Aussies, the Brits, and us Yanks. Woo-hoo.

✔ No, there is no language called "Texan" known to Word.

✔ An invisible-looking box below both the Fi̲nd What and the S̲earch boxes is named Format. It contains formatting information, such as fonts and things you may have just searched for. Word doesn't forget this information, and it's possible for a whole mess of formatting stuff to accumulate. So if Find refuses to locate some text that you *know* is in your document, click the No Formatting button. That way, Word finds only text and forgets about any formatting stuff.

Finding unprintable, unmentionable characters

No, this isn't a censorship issue. There are just some characters you can't properly type in the Fi̲nd What part of the Find dialog box. Try finding a Tab character, for example; press the Tab key and — whoops! — nothing happens. That's because the Tab character, plus a few others, are special, and you must force-feed them into the Find dialog box.

To find a special, unprintable character, click the Sp̲ecial button. You see a pop-up list of various characters Word can search for but that you would have a dickens of a time typing. Click one of them, and a special, funky shorthand representation for that character appears in the Fi̲nd What box (such as ^t, for Tab). Click the F̲ind Next button to find that character.

✔ The special characters appear in the Fi̲nd What box in secret code. That code starts with a caret (^) and then a letter of the alphabet. Please don't try to make sense of it.

✔ The Paragraph Mark special character is the same as the Enter character — what you press to end a paragraph.

✔ Any Character, Any Digit, and Any Letter represent, well, just about anything. These buttons are used as wildcards for matching lots of stuff.

✔ The caret (^) is a special character. If you want to search for it, be sure to select Caret Character from the Special button's pop-up list.

Find and Replace

Find and replace is the art of finding a bit of text and replacing it with something else. This happens all the time. For example, you can replace the word *marble* with *igneous sphericus*. Word does it in a snap, by using the Replace command:

1. **Choose Edit⇨Replace.**

   The Replace dialog box, shown in Figure 5-3, appears on-screen. It looks seriously like the Find dialog box, but with an extra box for the replacement text.

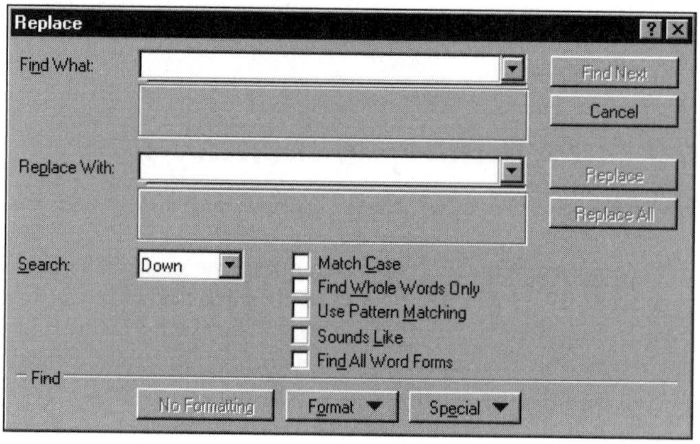

Figure 5-3:
The Replace
dialog box.

2. **In the Find What box, type the text you want to find.**

   This text will be found and replaced with something else. For example, you could type **marble**. Press the Tab key when you're done typing.

3. **In the Replace With box, type the text that you want to use to replace the original text.**

   For example, type **igneous sphericus**, which is a fancy-schmancy, geologically dooded-up term for a marble.

4. Choose a direction from the <u>S</u>earch drop-down list.

Choose *All* to search and replace everything in your document, top to bottom; *Down* merely to replace from the toothpick cursor's position to the end of your document; *Up* to replace in the other direction only.

5. Ask yourself, "Do I want the chance to change my mind before replacing each bit of found text?"

If so, select the <u>F</u>ind Next button. This is a good idea. If not, you can select the Replace <u>A</u>ll button; text is found and replaced automatically, giving you no chance to change your mind.

6. If you selected <u>F</u>ind Next, Word pauses at each occurrence of the text.

The found text is highlighted on-screen just like in the regular Find task. When this happens, you can click the <u>R</u>eplace button to replace it or click <u>F</u>ind Next to skip and find the next matching bit of text. Click the Cancel button or press the Escape key when you tire of this.

✔ When the Replace operation is over, Word announces that it's done by displaying this message:

```
Word has finished searching the document.
```

The gist of this message varies depending on which direction you're searching in. For example, if you just looked from hither down, Word may beg you to continue searching at the top of the document.

✔ Word replaces the same way it finds text: either up or down or all over the document. If you want to replace every instance of some text in your document, click the <u>S</u>earch button's drop-down list and select All.

✔ If you select Replace <u>A</u>ll, Word displays a dialog box telling you how many items were replaced. Interesting trivia.

✔ Always type something in the Re<u>p</u>lace With box. If not, you systematically delete all the text found in a wanton round of wholesale slaughter. This process is called "Find and Delete," and it's covered later in this chapter, in a section by the same name.

✔ The quick shortcut key for the <u>R</u>eplace command is Ctrl+H. Uh-huh. H means what? Hunt and replace?

✔ My advice is to select <u>F</u>ind Next most of the time. Only if you're replacing something and you're certain (a rare occurrence, at least in my travels) should you select Replace <u>A</u>ll.

✔ The <u>U</u>ndo command restores your document to its previous condition if you foul up the Replace operation. Refer to Chapter 4 for more information about undoing things.

✔ Dear Mr. Corona: Typewriters were lousy at Find and Replace. So there!

Find and Replace Spaces

Here's a practical use for the Replace command. Too many Word users litter their documents with excessive spaces. The most harmless of all these spaces come at the end of a line of text, after the period but before you press Enter. I do this, too. Yet the extra spaces serve no purpose. These steps show you how to get rid of them:

1. **Choose the Edit⇨Replace command.**

   Or just press Ctrl+H. Either way, the Replace dialog box appears.

2. **Open the Special menu from the Replace dialog box.**

   Click the Special button at the bottom of the dialog box.

3. **Select White Space from the pop-up list.**

   If you can't find *White Space* in the list, click in the Find What box first, and then click the Special button.

4. **Repeat steps 2 and 3 and select Paragraph Mark instead of White Space.**

   This step tells the Replace command that you're looking for a space followed by the Enter key. The following characters appear in the Find What box:

   ```
   ^w^p
   ```

   These characters are the secret codes for a space and the Enter key — essentially, extra space (that no one needs) at the end of a paragraph.

5. **Press the Tab key to move to the Replace With box.**

6. **Click the Special button and select Paragraph Mark.**

   So you're replacing ^w^p with ^p, which is just getting rid of the ^w — excess spaces — which is the end to this madness.

7. **Click Replace All.**

   It's okay to click Replace All here. Or if you're not the daring type, select Find Next. You're telling Word to replace the space-Enter with just Enter. The end result is to remove the spaces before the Enter key in your document.

   ✔ To confirm whether any spaces exist before trying this exercise, use the Find command to search for space-Enter (the ^w^p thing again).

   ✔ To replace double spaces between sentences with single spaces, stick two White Space characters in the Find What box (^w^w) and only one (^w) in the Replace With box. Then try to wean yourself from the double-spacing-after-period habit they taught you in typing class.

✔ A quick way to transform extra spaces into a Tab character is to search for five spaces in a row and translate them into tabs. In the Find What box, enter White Space five times (^w). In the Replace With box, select Tab Character (^t). Those spaces are replaced with tabs, which are much easier to align. See Chapter 10 for more information about using and setting tabs.

Find and Delete

If you don't type anything in the Replace With box, Word's Replace command systematically deletes all the Find Whats. This process can be a scary thing, so be sure to select Find Next. Otherwise, you may zap parts of your document and, boy, would you be bummed (until you used the Undo command).

Suppose, however, that Bill wanted to get rid of his marbles. Instead, he wants to be the president of a major software concern in the Northwest. These steps show you how to delete the *marbles* from a Word document:

1. **Choose Edit⇨Replace.**

   Or type Ctrl+H (if that ever makes sense to you).

2. **In the Find What box, type the text you want to find.**

   For example, **marbles**. Enter the text exactly. Any previously searched for text appears at the prompt. Edit it or type new text, secret codes, or whatever to search for.

3. **Don't type anything in the Replace With box; leave it blank.**

   You're deleting text here and replacing it with nothing — a bold concept Rod Serling touched upon a few decades back in some "Twilight Zone" episodes.

4. **Click the Replace All button.**

   In moments, your text is gone. It's as if Bill got into a marble game with Mr. Thumbs, the 12-year-old marble champion of the world (who you can see on ESPN 2 on one of the slow days). If you were timid and selected the Find Next button instead of Replace All, it takes a bit longer because you have to squint at the screen and then press the Replace button at each occurrence.

Let's all wish Bill the best of luck in his new profession.

Chapter 6

Playing with Blocks

· ·

· ·

A major advantage of a word processor over, say, a typewriter is that you can work with blocks of text. The closest you can come to blocks of text in a typewriter is to cut and paste — literally. All that glue and Scotch tape is so *très gauche*. Hand such a thing with a report on it to your boss and he'll shake his head and mutter, "Tsk, tsk, tsk. This is tacky, Jenson."

A block in a word processor is a marvelous thing. You can rope off a section of text — any old odd section, a letter, word, line, paragraph, page, or a rambling polygon — and then treat the text as a unit — a *block*. You can copy the block, move it, delete it, format it, spell-check it, use it to keep the defensive line from getting to your quarterback, and on and on. Think of the joy: Years after childhood, Word has made it okay for us to play with blocks again.

Marking a Block

You can't do anything with a block of text until you *mark* it. Marking a block is telling Word, "Okay, my block starts here. No, *here!* Not over there. Here, where I'm looking, where the cursor is." You can mark a block two ways in Word: by using the mouse or by using the keyboard.

Marking a block with your mouse

To mark a block with the mouse, follow these rodent-like steps:

1. **Position the mouse pointer where you want the block to start.**

2. **Hold down the left mouse button and drag the mouse over your text.**

   As you drag, the text becomes highlighted, or *selected,* as shown in Figure 6-1. Drag the mouse from the beginning to the end of the text that you want to mark as a block.

3. **Release the mouse button — stop the dragging — to mark your block's end.**

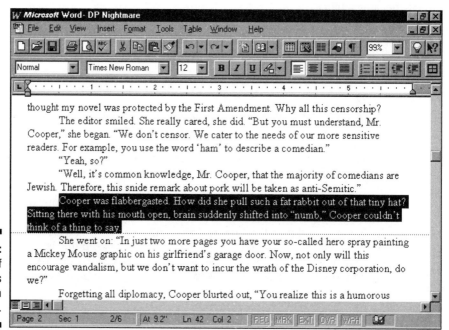

Figure 6-1:
A block of text is marked on the screen.

- If you continue dragging above or below the text that appears on-screen, the screen scrolls up or down.
- To quickly mark a word, position the mouse pointer over that word and double-click.
- To quickly mark a sentence, press and hold the Ctrl key while clicking the mouse.
- To mark a line of text, move the mouse pointer to the left margin. The pointer becomes an arrow that points northeasterly. Click the mouse to highlight one line of text, or drag the mouse to select several lines at a time.
- To mark an entire paragraph, place the insertion pointer anywhere in the paragraph and click three times.

Marking a block with your keyboard

Dragging over the screen with the mouse is great for selecting small portions of text. Marking anything larger than a screenful, however, can get a bit out of hand with the mouse — which tends to think that there's a cat around or something whenever you scroll-drag and move too fast to control. In those instances, it's much better to mark text by using the keyboard. Follow these steps:

1. **Press the F8 key.**

   This is the Start Block command. The F8 key "drops anchor" by marking one end of the block.

2. **Use the cursor navigation keys to move to the other end of the block.**

   The navigation keys are discussed in Chapter 3.

Word highlights text from the point where you dropped anchor with F8 to wherever you move the toothpick cursor (refer to Figure 6-1). Text appears in white-on-black. After the block is marked, you're ready to do something with it.

- After you press the F8 key, you see EXT (for Extend Selection) on the status bar. The block-marking mode is active until you type a block or formatting command or press Escape to cancel.
- To quickly mark a word, position the toothpick cursor on the word and press the F8 key twice.
- To quickly mark a sentence, position the toothpick cursor somewhere in the sentence and press the F8 key three times.
- To quickly mark a paragraph, position the toothpick cursor in the paragraph and press the F8 key four times.

- ✔ To quickly break your keyboard, press the F8 key 100,000 times.

- ✔ To mark your whole do-dang document, press the F8 key five times, or press Ctrl+5 (the 5 key on the numeric keypad).

- ✔ Press the Escape key to cancel the block-drop-and-chop F8 method of marking text. The block still is marked; move the cursor to unhighlight it.

- ✔ You can use the mouse *and* the F8 key to get real fancy. Position the cursor at either end of the block you want to mark and press the F8 key. Then position the mouse cursor at the other end of the block and press the left mouse button. Everything from there to there is marked.

- ✔ After a block has been marked, you're ready to type a block command. You can copy the block, cut it, paste it elsewhere, format the block, print it, spell-check it, or a dozen more interesting things, all covered in this chapter. Refer to the appropriate section later in this chapter for the next step.

- ✔ Rather than press the cursor keys to mark a block with the keyboard, you can type a character. Word locates the next occurrence of that character and includes all the text between it and the beginning of the block inside the block. You can do this several times to make the block as large as you want.

- ✔ Get used to using the keyboard commands to block your text and you will be much happier, believe me.

Another keyboard way: The Shift key

If you use the Shift key in combination with any of the cursor-movement keys, that also marks a slab of text on-screen. Refer to Chapter 3 for information about keys that you can use to move around your document. Just press and hold the Shift key with those keys to mark text as you move the cursor. (This method may tie your fingers in knots, so be careful.)

Marking a block with the Find command

Marking a block can get sloppy with the mouse or the cursor-navigation keys — especially if you're pressing the PgUp or PgDn keys to mark large acres of text. A better way is to use the Find command to locate the end of the block. Do this:

1. **Position the toothpick cursor at the beginning of the block.**

   The cursor must be blinking right before the first character to be included in the block. Be precise.

2. Press the F8 key.

This step turns on the EXT word-fragment message on the status bar. You're in block-marking mode.

3. Choose Edit⇨Find.

You see the Find dialog box open on-screen. Yes, you're still in block-marking mode, but now you can use the Find command to locate the end of your block.

4. Type the text that you want to locate, which marks the end of the block.

After typing the text, press Enter. Word stretches the block highlight down to that point in the text and includes the found text in the block.

When the cursor is at the end of the block, you're ready to use a block command. Refer to the proper section later in this chapter for additional details.

- Until you type a block command, the block remains highlighted and EXT continues to stare at you from the status bar. Remember to press the Escape key to cancel block-marking mode.

- If text isn't found by using the Find command, you see an appropriate not found error message box displayed — but you're still in block-marking mode. Click the OK button to tell Word what a good little program it is and that you are sorry it was unsuccessful.

- To find the next occurrence of the matching text, you can click the Find Next button in the dialog box. Or . . .

- If you don't see the dialog box on-screen, pressing the Shift+F4 key combination does a Find Next for you.

- Although you're using the Find command to help mark your block, you still can use the cursor-navigation keys. Heck, you can even use the mouse if you press and hold the Shift key first. Blocking is a liberal thing here; you're not limited to using only the cursor or Find command methods to mark a block.

- More details about the Find command are in Chapter 5, in the section "Finding Text."

Marking the whole dang-doodle document

To mark everything, choose the Select All command from the Edit menu. The commonly accepted Windows key equivalent for the Select All command is Ctrl+A.

Copying and Pasting a Block

After a block is marked, you can copy and paste that block into another part of your document. The original block remains untouched by this operation. Follow these steps to copy a block of text from one place to another:

1. Mark the block.

Locate the beginning of the block and select text until you've highlighted to the block's end. Detailed instructions about doing this task are offered in the first part of this chapter.

2. Conjure up Edit⇨Copy.

Choose Copy from the Edit menu. Or if you're adept at such things, press Ctrl+C for the Copy shortcut (or click the Copy tool).

Word places a copy of the marked block in the Windows Clipboard — a storage area for text or graphics that you've cut or copied and are about to paste back into your document.

3. Move the cursor to the position where you want the block copied.

Don't worry if there isn't any room there; Word inserts the block into your text just as though you had typed it there manually.

4. Do Edit⇨Paste.

Pressing Ctrl+V is the Paste shortcut (or click the Paste tool).

You now have two copies of the block in your document.

- ✔ You also can copy blocked text with the mouse. Position the mouse cursor anywhere in the blocked text, hold down the Ctrl key and the left mouse button while you drag the block to the location where the copy will be placed. The mouse pointer changes to an arrow-with-square-lasso design while you're dragging. Release the mouse button to paste in the block copy.

- ✔ After a block has been copied, you can paste it into your document a second time. This subject is covered in "Pasting a Previously Cut or Copied Block," later in this chapter.

- ✔ You can also copy or drag a block of text to Windows' desktop for long-term storage. This weird activity is discussed in "Odd Blocks and the Desktop," later in this chapter.

Cutting and Pasting a Block

Cutting a block is like deleting it — but nothing is really gone. Instead, as you snip out an article in the newspaper, the cut block can be pasted into your document at another location. This process is technically called a *move;* you move a block of text from one spot to another in your document. (Talk about writing moving text!)

Cutting a block of text works like copying a block. Follow these steps:

1. **Mark the block of text you want to move (cut).**

   Locate the block's start by using the cursor; press the F8 key and press the cursor keys or use the mouse to highlight the block.

2. **Choose the Edit➪Cut command.**

   You also can press Ctrl+X, the Cut shortcut (or click the Cut tool). Either way, the block disappears. That's okay — it's been stuffed into the Windows Clipboard, an electronic storage place nestled deep in your computer's memory.

3. **Move the toothpick cursor to the position where you want the block pasted.**

   Don't worry if there isn't any room for the block; Word makes room as it inserts the block.

4. **Summon the Edit➪Paste command.**

   You also can press Ctrl+V to paste in your block (or click the Paste tool).

   ✔ Additional information about marking a block is in the first two sections of this chapter.

   ✔ Copying a block works just like moving a block, although the original isn't deleted. Refer to the preceding section, "Copying and Pasting a Block."

   ✔ Moving a block is not the same as deleting a block; the block can be recovered only by positioning the cursor and pasting it in with the Ctrl+V key combination.

   ✔ The Ctrl+Z Undo shortcut undoes a block move.

   ✔ After a block has been cut and moved, you can repaste it into your document a second time. This subject is covered in the next section, "Pasting a Previously Cut or Copied Block."

✔ You also can move blocked text by dragging the mouse — although I recommend using this tip only when the move is just a short distance away. (Scrolling the screen while dragging with the mouse can be unwieldy.) Position the mouse cursor anywhere in the blocked text and hold down the left mouse button while you drag the bar-looking cursor to the location where the block is to be moved. This dance step is particularly useful when you are rearranging stuff on a page.

Pasting a Previously Cut or Copied Block

Whenever a block of text is cut or copied, Word remembers it. You can re-yank that block into your document at any time — sort of like repasting text after it's already been pasted in. You use Ctrl+V, the Paste shortcut.

To paste a previously cut block of text, follow these exciting steps:

1. **Position the toothpick cursor in the spot where you want the block of text to be pasted.**

   This step should always be done first. The block appears right at the cursor's position as though you typed it in yourself.

2. **Choose the Edit⇨Paste command.**

    You also can press Ctrl+V, the Paste shortcut. Ctrl+V equals paste? Uh-huh. (Or click the Paste tool.)

Zap. There it is on your screen.

✔ If nothing has been copied or cut by using the other block commands, nothing is pasted by this command. Duh.

✔ Word has a small brain. It remembers only the last cut or copied block. Anything cut or copied before that is gone, gone, gone.

Odd Blocks and the Desktop

Since this is Windows 95 you're dealing with, there are a few Windows 95-like things you can do with a Windows 95-happy program like Word 95. One of these is taking advantage of the desktop — that background thing upon which Windows' icons float.

- ✔ If you're following my suggestions, then you're using Word at full-screen strength. In that maximized mode you cannot see the desktop. So if you want to see the desktop and take advantage of its cut-and-paste block action, you'll need to click on the restore button in the upper-right corner of Word's window.

- ✔ You may also need to restore or minimize other windows that may also be blocking your view of the desktop.

- ✔ If you find all this window rearranging a pain, then just don't bother with this stuff.

Dragging a block out to the desktop

When you drag a block to the desktop, you're copying it to something called the *scrap*. That's a little icon that sits on the desktop until you drag it somewhere else — a completely strange Windows 95 concept that no one will ever get used to. But since I started discussing it, here are the steps you'd take to make it happen:

1. **Mark the block you want to fling onto the desktop.**

   Obey the proper block marking instructions located near the beginning of this chapter.

2. **Point the mouse at the block.**

3. **Drag the block out of Word's application window and onto the desktop.**

   You'll see the mouse pointer change. A fuzzy box and plus sign will appear, which indicates that you're dragging, copying, and pasting something to the desktop, as shown in Figure 6-2.

4. **Release the mouse button.**

   This ends the drag and places a copy of the block on the desktop.

The pasted block is given the name *Document Scrap*, followed by the first few bits of text in the document. You can change the icon's name to something else using the proper Windows 95 "I wanna change an icon's" name command.

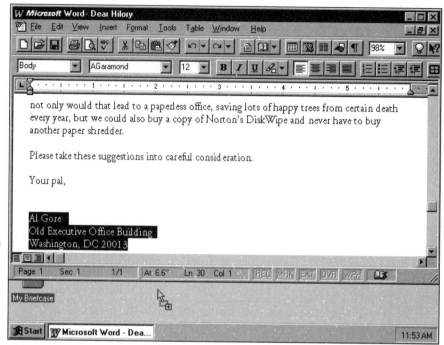

not only would that lead to a paperless office, saving lots of happy trees from certain death every year, but we could also buy a copy of Norton's DiskWipe and never have to buy another paper shredder.

Please take these suggestions into careful consideration.

Your pal,

Al Gore
Old Executive Office Building
Washington, DC 20013

Figure 6-2:
A block is dragged out to the desktop.

✔ This operation can be done a number of times. Unlike copy or cut, where only the last thing you've copied or cut is remembered, you can drag any number of blocks to the desktop for long-term storage.

✔ As in the figure, the text you want to drag to the desktop should be something you'll be using over and over — your address, for example. Or it can be a block you'll want to repaste into a document several times — typical "use-over" stuff.

✔ If you want to cut the block, you're out of luck. This technique only *copies* something to the desktop.

✔ To rename an icon in Windows, click on the icon once with the mouse. This highlights it. Then press the F2 key and type in a new name. Be sure to be descriptive about what the scrap icon contains. Press the Enter key to lock the new name into place.

✔ Whenever you drag a block, the mouse pointer grows a little fuzzy rectangle. When you drag a block to the desktop, it also grows a little plus sign. And if you drag the block off the screen, it grows teeth and will eventually eat you.

Dragging a block in from the desktop

If you're a drag-em-to-the-desktop pro, then you'll eventually want to use all those little bits of scrap blocks, pasting them back into your document at some point or another. To do so is really cinchy. Follow these steps:

1. **Locate the spot where you want to paste the block.**

    For example, suppose you have a scrap block of text on the desktop that contains your name and address to close a letter. If so, then you'll want to make sure that part of your document is visible in Word's application window. (You don't need to be fussy with the toothpick cursor here; just ensure that the proper part of your document is visible on the screen.)

2. **Locate the scrap icon.**

    Scrap icons live on the desktop. If Word's window covers the icon, then drag the icon to a spot where it will be visible when you're in Word.

3. **Drag the icon up into your text.**

    Drag the icon from the desktop up into your document: Point the mouse at the icon. Press and hold the mouse's button (the left button). Roll (drag) the mouse up into your document's window. Release the mouse button.

    ✔ Be careful where you release the mouse button. It's at that exact spot where the block of scrap text will be pasted into your document.

    ✔ This is a copy-only operation. The scrap icon will still live on your desktop after you drag it into a document. The only way to rid yourself of a scrap icon is to drag it into the Windows Recycle Bin.

    ✔ Since the scrap icon lives (It lives! It lives!), you can use it over and over.

    ✔ Not every bit of scrap you drag into Word will be text. Sometimes those scrap icons contain graphics, spreadsheets, or any of a number of low-life characters. Hopefully, whoever put them there will have properly named them. Hopefully.

Deleting a Block

There are two ways to delete a block: the complex way and the easy way. How about the easy way, eh?

1. **Mark the block.**

    Refer to the first section of this chapter for the best block-marking instructions in any computer book.

2. Press the Delete key.

Thwoop!

✔ You also can press the Backspace key to delete the block.

✔ Additional and detailed information about marking a block is covered in the first section of this chapter.

 ✔ This time, the block can be recovered by using the Edit⇨Undo command (or the Undo tool). This step is what makes deleting a block different from cutting and pasting a block. When you Undo, however, the block appears in the same position from where it was deleted.

✔ Chapter 4 covers the vast subject of deleting and destroying text. Turn there to quench your destructive thirsts.

Formatting a Block

When you've roped off a section of text as a block, you can format the text and characters as a single unit. Formatting is covered in detail in Part II of this book, "Formatting — or Making Your Prose Less Ugly." So instead of going over the details, here are the various things you can do to a block for formatting:

✔ You can make the text bold, underlined (two different flavors), italicized, superscripted, or subscripted by using various Ctrl-key combinations, all of which are detailed in Chapter 9.

✔ You can change the font for the block's text, which also is covered in Chapter 9.

✔ Any formatting changes affect only the text roped off in the block.

✔ Information about changing the text style, bold, underlining, italics, and all that is offered in Chapter 9. Information about shifting between uppercase and lowercase is presented in the same chapter.

✔ Information about changing the position of a block — its *justification* — is covered in Chapter 10.

Spell-Checking a Block

If you want to spell-check a small or irregularly sized part of your document, you can block it off and then use Word's Spelling command. This command is much quicker than going through the pains of using the full spell-check.

To see whether your spelling is up to snuff, follow these steps:

1. **Mark the block.**

   Refer to the first section in this chapter.

   The highlighted area marked by the block is the only part of your document that is spell-checked.

2. **Select the <u>T</u>ools⇨<u>S</u>pelling command.**

   No muss, no waiting — the block is spell-checked. (You also can click the Spelling tool.)

3. **Word compares all words in the block with its internal dictionary.**

   If a misspelled or unrecognized word is found, it is highlighted and you are given a chance to correct or edit it. If you tire of this, click the Cancel button.

4. **After the block has been spell-checked, Word asks whether, by the way, you want to continue checking the rest of your document. Press N.**

   Or press Y if you really want to see how poor your spelling has gotten outside the block.

   ✔ I often use this technique to look up the spelling of a single word I don't trust: Just double-click on the word to select it and then click on the Spelling tool.

   ✔ Word's on-the-fly spell checker has more-or-less made this function unnecessary. However, if you're like me, you'll turn that annoying little sucker off. In that case, spell-checking a block makes a lotta sense.

   ✔ Chapter 7 covers using Word's spell checker in glorious detail. Refer there for additional information about changing or correcting your typos.

Using Find and Replace in a Block

You cannot find text in a marked block, but you can use Word's <u>R</u>eplace command. When a block is on, Replace finds and replaces only text in the marked block. The rest of your document is unaffected (unless you tell Word to replace outside the block when it's done).

✔ A full description of this operation is offered in the Chapter 5 section "Find and Replace." I'm too lazy to rewrite all that stuff here.

✔ The <u>F</u>ind command cannot be used in a block because the <u>F</u>ind command is used to mark the block; see "Marking a block with the <u>F</u>ind command," earlier in this chapter.

Printing a Block

Word's Print command enables you to print one page, several pages, or an entire document. If you want to print only a small section of text, you have to mark it as a block and then print it. Here's the secret:

1. **Make sure that your printer is on and ready to print.**

   See Chapter 8 for additional printer setup information.

2. **Mark the block of text that you want to print.**

   Move the cursor to the beginning of the block and press F8 to turn on block-marking mode; move the cursor to the end of the block or use the mouse for wrist-action block marking.

3. **Choose the File⇨Print command.**

   You also can press Ctrl+P or qualify for the Finger Gymnastics event at the next Olympics and press Ctrl+Shift+F12.

4. **Tickle the button by the word Selection.**

   Press the Alt+S key or click the word Selection with your mouse. (Selection is located in the *Print range* area of the dialog box.) This step tells Word that you want to print only your highlighted block.

5. **Click the OK button or press the Enter key.**

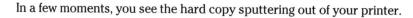

In a few moments, you see the hard copy sputtering out of your printer.

- ✔ The Print tool on the standard toolbar is used only to print the entire document, not your selected block. Use Ctrl+P to print your block instead.

- ✔ Additional information about marking a block of text is in the first section of this chapter.

- ✔ The full subject of printing is covered in Chapter 8. Look there for information about printing options and setting up your printer.

- ✔ The Selection item in the Print dialog box is available only when you have a block selected.

Chapter 7

The Logical Spelling Solution

For all of English's popularity, it's biggest fault is spelling. It's almost laughable: The Chinese have no idea what a spelling bee is. And I seriously doubt if anyone in France or Germany really needs Word's Spelling command to figure things out for them. Heck, many languages solve the problem right up front by omitting those offensive vowels. Think about it: If there weren't any A, E, I, O, or U in the alphabet, spelling would be a lot easier. (But then you'd have to contend with things like C sounding like both S and K; the GH phenomena; and when you need double S or double D. Oh, bother.)

I could go on and on about English spelling, and maybe I will: Our spelling is based on a dialect of English that isn't spoken anymore. In those days, they actually pronounced all the letters in *knight*. Had they nailed down spelling 20 years later, it would have probably been spelled *nite*. But one thing our spelling does afford us is commonality. You may say *for* or *foor* or *fowa*, but *four* is how you spell it.

Honestly, English spelling is so utterly illogical you need a computer to tell you how to spell anything. And that's exactly what you've got in the form of Word's spell checker. It can even be rude, just like Mrs. Bradshaw, your old fourth-grade teacher.

Word's Amazing, Annoying On-the-Fly Spell-Checking

This was something that was bound to happen sooner or later. As computers get faster, they're capable of more and more things. Word processors don't really work very fast since they spend a lot of time waiting for you to type. So they sit and spin, wasting a lot of the computer's power.

"But, ah-ha!" they said at Microsoft one day. "We can use all that extra time floating around inside the computer to correct users' spelling as they type!" Cries of "Amazing! Fantastic! Applaudable!" rose in the room. Of course, at the time, no one knew how annoying it would be to have your spelling checked as you type it. It's like having Mrs. Bradshaw, your fourth-grade teacher and goddess of English spelling, standing over your shoulder telling you things were wrong as you typed them in. What a great way to break your concentration!

Anyway, given all that, the following sections discuss (and cuss) Word's on-the-fly spell checker, which I strongly urge everyone to switch off immediately.

You misspelled another one. You misspelled another one. You misspelled another one.

Word automatically checks everything you type as you type it. Make a booboo, Word lets you know. It does this by underlining the word using a red zig-zag pattern. See Figure 7-1 for a sampling.

The second you press the spacebar or type some punctuation character, Word examines what you typed and immediately flags it as *wrong, wrong, wrong!*

If you're mentally fit, you can go on typing. Otherwise, you should point the mouse at the word and click the right mouse button (a right-click) to get further instructions.

You can select a new spelling word from those listed (see Figure 7-1), or you can click on Ignore All so that Word won't bug you when you type that word again.

- ✔ Right-click on a red-underlined word to see possible correct spellings.

- ✔ Word flags as wrong anything it doesn't recognize. This includes the five million-or-so words not represented in Word's electronic dictionary. Among them will probably be your name, street name, city name, and favorite ice cream.

✓ Personally, I'd rather concentrate on my writing than worry about mis-spelled words as I'm composing my thoughts.

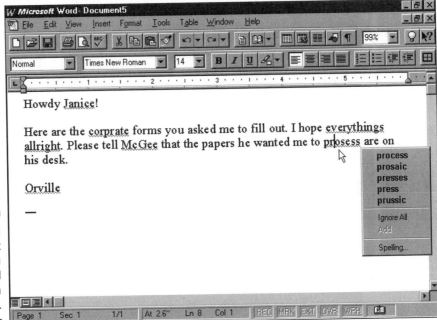

Figure 7-1:
Word rubs it
in that you
cannot spell
worth a
darn.

Turning the bloody thing off

If you find the on-the-fly spell-checking as annoying as I do, be thankful that you can turn it off. Follow these blessed steps:

1. **Choose Tools⇨Options.**

   The Options dialog box flashes on the screen.

2. **Click on the Spelling tab.**

   This brings the Spelling panel forward for your viewing pleasure.

3. **Remove the check mark from the Automatic Spell Checking item.**

   Just press Ctrl+A or click on the box by Automatic Spell Checking item to remove the check mark. This disables Word's annoying habit of ringing out misspelled words on the screen.

4. **Click the OK button.**

   This closes the Options dialog box and makes your settings known to Word and mankind.

This book assumes you *do not* have the automatic spelling option on. Why? Because that's the way I use my computer. So there.

- ✔ You can always switch automatic spell-checking back on by going through the above steps again and putting the check mark back into the box.

- ✔ So how do you check that horrid English spelling? Keep reading in the next section.

- ✔ The on-the-fly spelling option is actually good, but only under one circumstance: If you're using Word as your e-mail editor, then it's kind of nice to have something flag your spelling as you type. This is sort of acceptable since e-mail tends to be more spontaneous than the stuff you really care about in Word.

Checking Your Spelling

Forget arguing about it: The computer knows English spelling better than you do. Thank goodness. I really don't know how to spell. Not at all. The rules are obtuse and meaningless. There are too many exceptions. But thank the guardians of fourth-grade golden rules: With Word, you don't have to worry about being accurate. Just be close enough and the Spelling command does the rest.

To check the spelling of the words in your document, use the Spelling command in the Tools menu. Follow these steps:

1. **Get the Tools⇨Spelling command.**

   You also can choose the Spelling tool or press F7, the Spelling shortcut.

   Word scans your document for offensive words that would debun your fourth-grade teacher's hair.

   A misspelled word is found!

   The Spelling dialog box appears and the misspelled or unknown word appears highlighted in your text on-screen. The dialog box displays the misspelled word and suggests alternative spellings — most of them correct. Figure 7-2 shows an example.

2. **Pluck the correctly spelled word from the list.**

   Highlight the correct word and click the Change button. If the word isn't in the list, you can type it in the Change To box. Or if the word is okay, you can click the Ignore button to skip over the word without making any changes.

3. **Word continues to check every word in your document.**

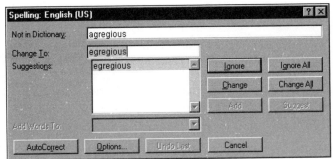

Figure 7-2:
A misspelled
word is
spied.

When it's done, you see a dialog box proclaim:

The spelling check is complete.

Okay, it's complete.

✔ Click the Ignore All button if your word is really a word (such as your name) and you don't want to be stopped every time Word encounters it in this document.

✔ Select Change All if you want to change every instance of a misspelled word to whatever is in the Change To box. If you have the annoying habit of typing *breif* rather than *brief*, for example, you can click Change All so that Word automatically makes the substitution without bothering you every time.

✔ If you find yourself making a large number of consistent mistakes — *teh* for *the, fi* for *if; alright* for *all right* — take advantage of Word's AutoCorrect tool. Refer to "Correcting Stuff As You Type," later in this chapter.

✔ You can click the Add button to place words Word doesn't know into its dictionary. For example, your last name, street name, city, and other frequently used words probably aren't in Word's dictionary. When the word is flagged as "misspelled," click the Add button and it becomes a part of Word's dictionary for life.

✔ If the Add button appears dimmed, see "What? The Add Button Is Dimmed!," later in this chapter.

✔ Undo Last undoes your last spelling change, most of the time. This option is great for those sleepy nighttime spell checks when you quickly select the wrong replacement word and aren't sure. Just click Undo Last and check out the last word again. (Undo Last may not work all the time; don't count on it.)

✔ To check the spelling of only one word — which does come in handy — see the next section in this chapter, "Checking Only One Word."

✔ To check the spelling of a paragraph or irregularly shaped block of text, refer to "Spell-Checking a Block" in Chapter 6.

✔ The Word dictionary is not a substitute for a real dictionary. Only in a real dictionary can you look up the meaning of a word, which tells you whether you're using the proper word in the proper context. No computer writer works with an electronic dictionary alone; there's usually a good, thick Webster's sitting right within arm's reach.

✔ If two identical words are found in a row, Word highlights them as a `Repeated Word`. Error, error! Click the Ignore button to tell Word to forget about the double word, or click the Delete button to blow the second word away, or click the Suggest button if you meant to type something similar but your fingers didn't respond.

✔ My, but this is a long list of check marks.

✔ The Spelling command also locates words with weird capitalization. For example, `bONer`. You're given an opportunity to correct the word to proper capitalization just as though it were misspelled.

✔ The Word dictionary is good but definitely not as good as your fourth-grade teacher. For one thing, it doesn't check your words in context. For example, *your* and *you're* can be spelled correctly in Word's eye, but you may be using them improperly. The same thing goes for *its* and *it's*. For that kind of in-context checking, you need something called a *grammar checker*. It's discussed later in this chapter.

✔ The word *spell* here refers to creating words by using the accepted pattern of letters. It has nothing to do with magic. Many people assume that a spell check instantly makes their document better. Wrong! You have to read what you write and then edit, look, and read again. Spell-checking doesn't fix things up other than finding rotten words and offering suggested replacements.

Checking Only One Word

There's no need to spell-check an entire document when all you want to check is one teeny weenie word. Actually, this is a great way to mentally deal with English spelling: Go ahead and spell the word how you think that it *should* be spelled. Then check only that word. Word looks up the accurate, wretched English spelling and you're on your way. And the cool part is that you don't have to learn a thing!

To check the spelling on a single, suspect word, do the following:

1. **Put the cursor somewhere on the word or just before it.**

2. **Highlight the word.**

Press F8 twice or double-click the word with the mouse and you can skip steps 1 and 2.

3. Spell-check it!

Choose the Tools⇨Spelling command. Better yet, click your Spelling tool or press F7, the Spelling shortcut.

4. Word checks that word.

If you spelled the word correctly (and the way I spell, the odds are 50-50), Word reports that it has finished checking the selection and politely, with a great deal of reverence and respect, asks whether you want it to check the remainder of the document. If your first attempt is not correct, however, Word sighs that exhausted sigh of saints, martyrs, and elementary schoolteachers everywhere and presents you with the Spelling dialog box, which lists possible alternative spellings and suggestions.

5. Click a word from the suggested spellings.

6. Press the Change button.

Word replaces the word you thought was spelled correctly with its proper and nonintuitive English spelling.

✔ Refer to the first section of this chapter for additional information about working with Word's Spelling feature.

✔ Single-word checking is often a good way to immediately tackle a word you know is hopelessly wrong. Of course, my philosophy (or "filosofy") is to spell any old which way and then use a document spell check to catch everything at one time.

✔ Granted, if you're going to be checking a lot of words individually, you might as well struggle with the on-the-fly spell checker. See the very first section in this chapter.

Adding Words to the Dictionary

Some common words don't appear in the dictionary — my last name, for example. Perhaps your last name is as unique as mine or maybe your first name, city, business name, and so on, are all spelled correctly yet are unknown to Word. This means that every time you spell-check your document, it will come up with alternative suggestions for those words. You have two options for avoiding this tautological conundrum:

The first, and most stupid option, is to press the Ignore button when the spell checker finds the word. Word then ignores that word during the spell check. But next time you spell-check, you have to do the same thing. Dumb, dumb, dumb.

The second, and wiser, option is to <u>A</u>dd said word to your custom dictionary. This dictionary is a list of words Word keeps and skips every time you spell-check because you've told it that they're all okay. Follow these steps:

1. **Start your spell check as you normally do.**

   Refer to the first section of this chapter for the persnickety details.

2. **Lo, you stumble upon a word unbeknownst to Word yet beknownst to you.**

   It's spelled just fine.

3. **Select the <u>A</u>dd button.**

   This step stuffs the word into the custom dictionary, and you never have to mess with it again.

✔ When a word is in the custom dictionary, Word knows and recognizes it as it does the words that come in the real dictionary — the one your fourth-grade English teacher wrote.

✔ Be careful when you decide to add a word to the custom dictionary, because it isn't easy to un-add a word from the dictionary. This is something you may want to do when you commit a flub and inadvertently put a seriously misspelled word in the dictionary. (I once added "fo" to the dictionary and spent three weeks in the Word penalty box — and that's in Seattle, of all places!) You can get the word out again, which is covered in the nearby technical information box (optional reading).

✔ You actually can maintain several custom dictionaries on disk. To select or create a new dictionary, select the Add <u>W</u>ords To text box in the Spelling dialog box and give the new dictionary a name. Word adds the word and uses the custom dictionary (along with the real one) for the spell check.

What? The Add Button Is Dimmed!

This happens because you haven't set up a custom dictionary. To do so, follow these steps:

1. **Fire up the <u>O</u>ptions for the Speller.**

   If you're in the Spelling dialog box, click the Options button. Otherwise, select the <u>O</u>ptions command from the bottom of the <u>T</u>ools menu and then click the word *Spelling* located on one of the tabs in the top of the Options dialog box.

2. **Click the Custom <u>D</u>ictionaries button to create your own dictionary.**

   The Create Custom Dictionary dialog box is displayed.

The first item in the list of custom dictionaries should be CUSTOM DIC. That's the one you want.

3. Click in the box by CUSTOM DIC.

This puts a check mark in that box, telling Word that you want to use it as your own, personal, custom dictionary.

4. Click the OK button in the Custom Dictionaries dialog box.

It goes away.

5. Click the OK button in the Options dialog box.

Poof!

You can now use the <u>A</u>dd button in the Spelling dialog box to stick words into your own personal dictionary.

Correcting Stuff As You Type

One of the handy things Word can do is correct your foul spelling as you type. No, this isn't the same as on-the-fly spell-checking. Unlike that monstrosity, this time Word actually *corrects* your boo-boos, sometimes so fast you don't even see it.

Word's AutoCorrect feature is amazing stuff. You type *teh* and Word quickly and quietly corrects it. So if you know how to spell a word but find out that your fingers just don't have a clue, AutoCorrect comes to your rescue.

No need to bother with this trivial drivel about the custom dictionary

The custom dictionary is a text document on disk. It contains, in alphabetical order, all the words you added. And as a special bonus, you can edit the list and remove any deleterious words you may have added.

To remove nasty words, follow steps 1 and 2 in "What? The Add Button Is Dimmed!" Then click on the dictionary you want to edit (if there are more than one) to highlight it. Then click on the <u>E</u>dit button. This opens the dictionary as a document in Word, where you can go about your business removing any mistakes you've added.

For example, suppose that you accidentally stuck "fo" in the dictionary. Only by editing the CUSTOM.DIC file can you get "fo" out of there.

Activating AutoCorrect

To ensure that AutoCorrect is on, select the AutoCorrect item from the Tools menu (Alt,T,A). The AutoCorrect dialog box is displayed, as shown in Figure 7-3.

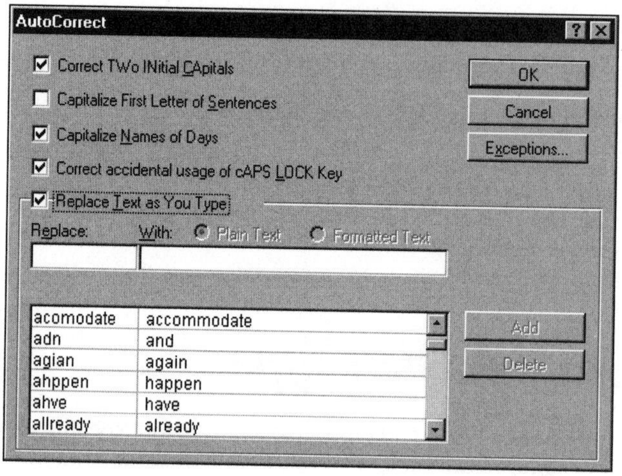

Figure 7-3: The AutoCorrect dialog box.

About midway down the left side of the box, you see the Replace Text as You Type item with a wee box by it. If the box is empty, click it (or press Alt+T). That sticks a check mark in the box, which means that AutoCorrect is on and ready to work while you type.

Click the OK button to close the AutoCorrect dialog box.

- AutoCorrect's main role in life is to replace words that you commonly goof automatically. It also has four other functions, each of which is listed at the top of the AutoCorrect dialog box. These functions are described in the following check mark items. To activate or deactivate any item, click it with the mouse. A check mark in an item's box means that it's on and working.

- The Correct TWo INitial CApitals item directs Word to correct this common typing faux pas by switching the second capitalized letter back to lowercase.

- The Capitalize First Letter of Sentences item controls whether Word automatically capitalizes the first letter in a sentence when you forget to. e. e. cummings should leave this item unchecked.

✔ The Capitalize Names of Days item capitalizes Monday, Tuesday, and so on, as they should be capitalized. Of course, if you weren't asleep in class that day in the fourth grade, you'd remember this tiny bit of English trivia.

✔ The Correct accidental usage of cAPS LOCK Key item fixes a minor, yet annoying problem: When you unwittingly type with the Caps Lock key on, your text looks very bizarre. Checking this item tells Word to fix it automatically. I suppose this is primarily intended for those who don't look at the screen as they type.

Adding words to AutoCorrect's repertoire

The bullies at Microsoft have already inserted a few common typos into AutoCorrect's brain. These are listed at the bottom of the AutoCorrect dialog box, in a scrolling list. The dojabbie on the left is the way you often spell something. The whatzis on the right is what Word replaces it with.

From Figure 7-3, you can see the common adn-and combination; type **adn** in Word and it automatically is corrected to *and*. (It's those three-letter-words that get you.)

To add a new item to the list, follow these steps:

1. **Choose the AutoCorrect command from the Tools menu.**

   Use your mouse or press Alt,T,A. The AutoCorrect dialog box appears.

2. **Focus in on the Replace box, where you type a common goof.**

   Click the mouse in the Replace box or press Alt+E on your keyboard.

3. **Type the word you often goof.**

   Don't worry if you can't think of words to add; it's also possible to add words to AutoCorrect's repertoire by using the Spelling command. See the following checklist for information.

4. **Press the Tab key.**

   This step moves you over to the With box, where you type the proper way the word goes.

5. **Type the proper way the word goes.**

6. **Click the Add button when you're done.**

7. **To add more AutoCorrect words, repeat steps 2 through 6.**

   Or

   Click the OK button after you're done.

- You can remove words from AutoCorrect that you don't want repaired automatically. Just highlight the word in the list and click the Delete button. Poof! It's gone.

- You may notice the (r) thing in AutoCorrect's word list. That's an abbreviation for a special symbol AutoCorrect automagically inserts into your document. To specify a special symbol, type that character in the With box. For example, to assign the em dash (a longer dash than a hyphen) to the -- (double hyphen) characters, type two hyphens in the Replace box and press Ctrl+Alt+- (the minus key on the keyboard's numeric key pad) in the With box. (See the Chapter 9 section, "Inserting Oddball and Special Characters," for more information about such characters.)

- You can also add graphical characters to AutoCorrect. You'll see an arrow and happy face in the list at the bottom of the AutoCorrect dialog box.

- It's entirely possible to be cruel with AutoCorrect. For example, inserting a meanie like **thier** for **their** would drive some people nuts. Remember, AutoCorrect is subtle. If you type looking at the keyboard, you never know what it's up to.

- An easier way to get words into AutoCorrect's list is to click the AutoCorrect button in the Spelling dialog box (refer to Figure 7-2). But be careful! Clicking the AutoCorrect button sticks the misspelled word and the highlighted replacement into AutoCorrect's list. Make sure that you have the proper replacement word highlighted *before* you click the AutoCorrect button.

Checking Your Grammar (Woe Is I)

Word's grammar checker is a wonderful tool, and I hate it. It keeps telling me how far I have strayed from the boring writing style that the folks who gave the checker life think is the "one true path." Don't get me wrong — it does a great job of distinguishing between *I* and *me, neither* and *nor,* and other similar stuff. I just think it's snooty.

For example, I think we would all agree that Henry David Thoreau was no slouch as a writer. Aaah, but check out the dialog box in Figure 7-4; perfect little Word can assume an air of condescension even with one of America's great literary treasures. Obviously, the grammar checker values a senseless adherence to the narrow strictures of socially ordained dialogue over the untamed spirit of inspired prose.

Anyway, regardless of the results, if diagramming sentences didn't burn out enough of your creative brain cells, select Grammar from the Tools menu. Your document is spell-checked (because the grammar checker has a sense of spell), and then the Grammar dialog box opens — unless you're computer perfect.

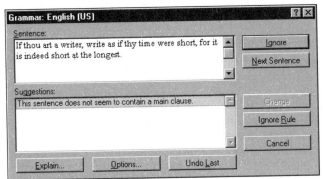

Figure 7-4:
The grammar checker doesn't get Thoreau.

✔ If you're going to run the grammar checker, don't bother manually running the spell checker first. The grammar checker checks your spelling as well as your grammar.

✔ The grammar checker works much like the spell checker; it tells you what's wrong and then suggests, in a patronizing tone, how to fix it.

✔ You can select buttons to ignore the suggestion, make the changes, move on to the next sentence, ignore the offending rule (my favorite), demand an explanation about why it didn't like what you did, or get out.

✔ You can select the Options button to set the way the grammar checker works. This feature sets some rather rough parameters, enabling you to select between three sets of writing rules: Strict, Business, and Casual.

✔ You can turn off the Check Spelling button so that Word doesn't tell you that, yes, once again, you misspelled February when all you really wanted to know was whether that preposition could live at a sentence's end.

✔ If you really want to get into the grammar thing, open the Grammar dialog box, click the Options button, and then click the Customize Settings dialog box. Yea, verily, although you're several dialog boxes in the thick of things, the one you see on-screen contains many switch-offable things that you can set or reset to control the grammar checker's level of fastidiousness.

Using the Thesaurus

If you think that I'm smart enough to use all the big words in this chapter, you're grievously mistaken. Witness *grievous*. That's just another word for *badly*. Behold! It's Word's thesaurus in action. An amazing tool, astounding utensil, or marvelous implement. You get the idea. The thesaurus helps look up synonyms or other words that have the same meaning but more weight or more precision.

Here's how to instantly become a master of big, clunky words in English:

1. **Hover the cursor on a simple word, such as _big_.**

   Adjectives are best for the thesaurus, although the Word Statistical Department tells me that the thesaurus contains more than 120,000 words.

2. **Do the <u>T</u>hesaurus command.**

   Choose <u>T</u>ools⇨<u>T</u>hesaurus or press the Thesaurus shortcut, Shift+F7. Instantly, the Thesaurus dialog box opens (see Figure 7-5). Word displays several alternatives for the word. They're grouped into categories by meanings on the left and synonyms on the right.

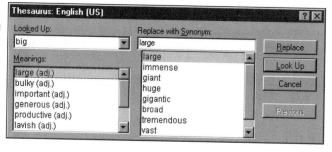

Figure 7-5:
The
Thesaurus
displays
other terms
for _big_.

3. **To replace the word in your document, highlight your choice and select <u>R</u>eplace.**

   After selecting a word, you return to your document. If you don't find a word, select Cancel to return to your document.

   ✔ A thesaurus is not a colossal, prehistoric beast.

   ✔ If one of the words in the left column is close but not exactly what you want, select it and click the <u>L</u>ook Up button. The new word's synonyms appear in the right column.

   ✔ If the word that you select has no synonym, the thesaurus displays an alphabetical list of words. Type a new, similar word or select Cancel to get back to your document.

   ✔ After inserting a new word, you may have to do a bit of editing: add "ed" or "ing" to the word or maybe replace "a" with "an" in front of it. A bit of editing is usually required whenever you replace one word with another.

Pulling a Word Count

One of the silliest writing assignments you probably ever got in school was the "I want you to write a five-page dissertation on why ketchup isn't green" type of project. Five pages! Are they nuts? Didn't Strunk and White stress brevity and clarity of thought over ghastly verbiage? I mean, if you can offer a lucid argument in a single seven word sentence, why not do it? But I digress.

Then there are those of us who get paid by the word. "Dan, write a 1,000-word article on Windows registration editor." I need to know when to stop writing. Also, curiosity generally gets the best of any writer, and you want to get a good feel for how many words and such you have in your document. To do that, select the Word Count command from the Tools menu.

The Word Count dialog box displays a summary of your document's pages, words, characters, paragraphs, and lines. Figure 7-6 shows the stats for this document (before my editor got his blue ink-stained hands on it.) How impressive. Okay. Click the Close button to get back to work.

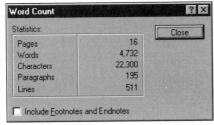

Figure 7-6:
Gonna count
me up some
words.

The Word Count command is far more accurate than a page count. Pages can be fudged. Larger fonts and narrower margins have saved many a student from the perils of turning in too short a paper.

The 5th Wave

Chapter 8
Send *This* to the Printer!

· ·

In This Chapter

▶ Getting your printer ready

▶ Selecting a printer

▶ Printing a whole document

▶ Printing a specific page

▶ Printing a range of pages

▶ Printing a block

▶ Printing several documents

▶ Printing envelopes

▶ Canceling a print job

· ·

*Y*ou sure didn't need a printer if you were "word processing" on a Smith-Corona typewriter; writing and printing happened at the same time. It works the same way with a pencil, too. Obviously you're being silly by using a computer with word processing software and a printer. Look at the cost! Then again, look at the fine output from a printer. And if you tame Word, that output will be close to perfection. No dollops of White Out, no eraser smudges. (Yes, Mr. Corona, it was time for you to go. . . .)

Of course, making everything turn out so splendidly requires that you get your printer to work. And no single device in your entire computer system deserves a good flogging like the printer. If you've been messing with your printer for a while, you'll discover that it's a stubborn little guy, rarely cooperative and hard to tame. This chapter should give you some tips for using your printer with Word, hopefully making what it prints look exactly like you imagined — or close enough to amaze all those Smith-Corona executives who are still baffled by all this technology.

Getting the Printer Ready

Before printing, you must make sure that your printer is ready to print. This involves more than flipping on its power switch.

Start by making sure that your printer is plugged in and properly connected to your computer. A cable connects the computer and your printer. It should be firmly plugged in at both ends. (This cable needs to be checked only if you're having printer problems.)

Your printer should have a decent ribbon installed. Old, frayed ribbons produce faint text and are bad for the printing mechanism. It will cost you more later in repair bills if you're trying to save a few bucks now by using a ribbon longer than necessary. Laser printers should have a good toner cartridge installed. If the laser printer's "toner low" message appears or a "toner low" light is on, replace the toner at once!

There must be paper in the printer for you to print on. The paper can feed from the back, come out of a paper tray, or be fed manually one sheet at a time. However your printer eats paper, make sure that you have it set up properly before you print.

Finally, your printer must be *on-line* or *selected* before you can print anything. Somewhere on your printer is a button labeled *On-line* or *Select,* and it should have a corresponding light or display. You have to press that button to turn the option (and the light) "on." Although your printer may be plugged in, the power switch on, and doing its warm-up stretching exercises, it doesn't print unless it's on-line or selected.

✔ Before you can print, your printer must be plugged into the wall; plugged into your computer; turned on; full of paper; and *on-line* or *selected*. (Most printers are in the *on-line* or *selected* mode when you turn them on.

✔ Never plug a printer cable into a printer or computer that is on and running. Always turn your printer and computer off whenever you plug anything into them. If not, you may damage the internal electronic components.

✔ If you're printing to a network printer — and it makes me shudder to think of it — *someone else* is in charge of the printer. It should be set up and ready to print all for you. If not, there's usually someone handy to whom you can complain.

✔ The printer you use affects the way Word displays and prints your document, so before you do a lot of formatting, check to be sure that you have the correct printer selected. For help in installing your printer and connecting it to your computer, refer to your favorite book on Windows, such as *Real Life Windows* written by myself and available from IDG Books Worldwide.

✔ Some additional information about setting up, or *installing*, your printer for
use with Word is covered in Chapter 28, "The Printer Is Your Friend." That
chapter also contains troubleshooting information and a detailed anatomi-
cal guide to popular printers that tells you where to shoot the printer for a
quick death or a lingering, slow, and painful one.

Plucking Out Printer

One of the joys of printing with any Windows application is its capability for
using many different printers. Word even remembers the capabilities of several
different printers and automatically formats your work to show you, on-screen,
what it will look like when it gets to paper. This feature is called *WYSIWYG*,
("wizz-i-wig") or *what you see is what you get* (more or less).

After the joy, depression sets in when you realize that you can only select a
printer that has been installed in Windows. This is definitely Windows Guru
time, although you should rest happy in the knowledge that if your printer
works with other Windows programs, it works swell in Word, too. This feature
more than makes up for the fact that Windows is painfully slow, even on the
fastest computer.

To select a printer — if you *really* want to — follow these steps:

1. Choose the File⇨Print command.

Or, better yet, press Ctrl+P, the Print shortcut. The Print dialog box is
displayed, looking an awful lot like Figure 8-1.

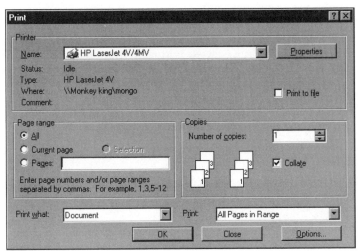

Figure 8-1:
The Print
dialog box.

The top area of the dialog box describes your current printer, called the *default printer* by those who really don't know what the word default means.

2. Click the down arrow on the Name list box.

The Name list box is at the top of the Printer area. When you click on the down arrow, a list of the printers Windows knows about is displayed.

3. Select the printer that you want to use and then click OK.

Click once on the printer's name and then click the OK button.

Instantly, Word is alerted to your new printer. You're done. That's it.

- ✔ Selecting a printer is necessary only if you have more than one printer connected to your PC.

- ✔ You can also select a Fax card from the Print Setup dialog box, which is one way you can send faxes with Word.

- ✔ If you're using a network printer, an appropriate section for your needs is hidden in Chapter 28, "The Printer Is Your Friend."

Preview Your Printing

Printing something 1,000 times to get it right sure doesn't make Mr. Bunny feel good. Not that I have anything against slaughtering trees. I own a few myself. It's a cash crop! But that's not an excuse to waste paper. Instead you can take the more environmentally conscious route — and save yourself time as well — by employing Word's fancy Print Preview command. That lets you see what your document will look like printed before you print it.

To sneak a preview of how your document will print, choose File⇨Print Preview or click on the handy Print Preview button on the Standard toolbar. That switches Word's display to a rather standoffish look at your document.

- ✔ I don't really use Print Preview much for standard fair. But if I'm really formatting something heavily — with footnotes, strange columns, and stuff like that — Print Preview can be a godsend.

- ✔ Click on the Close button if you want to return to your document for editing.

- ✔ Use the Page-Up and Page-Down buttons to peruse various pages of your document in print preview mode.

✔ Click on the Print button to print your document right here and now! See the next section for the details.

   ✔ No, you can't edit anything in Print Preview mode. Sniff.

Printing a Whole Document

If you think that your work is worthy enough to be enshrined on a sheet of paper, follow these steps. To print your entire document, from top to bottom, head to toe, from *Once upon a time* to *happily every after:*

1. **Make sure that the printer is *on-line* and ready to print.**

   What's that noise? Is Bobby at it again with the Playskool Li'l Plumber Kit? No, it's the printer humming its ready tune.

2. **Summon the <u>P</u>rint command.**

   Choose the <u>F</u>ile⇨<u>P</u>rint command. (You also can click the Print tool or press Ctrl+P.) The Print dialog box magically appears (see Figure 8-1).

3. **Click OK or press the Enter key.**

   No need to do this if you click the Print tool.

4. **The printer warms up and starts to print.**

   Printing may take some time. Really. A long time. Fortunately, Word lets you continue working while it prints in "the background." To ensure that it works this way, refer to the techy sidebar, "Printing and getting on with your life."

   ✔ If nothing prints, don't hit the Print command again! There's probably nothing awry — the computer is still thinking or sending (downloading) fonts to the printer. If you don't get an error message, everything will probably print, eventually.

   ✔ If you have a manual feed printer, the printer itself will beg for paper. Your printer says, "Beep, feed me!" You must stand by, line up paper, and then shove it into the printer's gaping maw until your document is done printing. Refer to "Printing Envelopes," later in this chapter, to figure this one out.

   ✔ Before you print, consider saving your document to disk and — if we're talking final draft here — do a spell check. See Chapter 7 and the sections "Checking Your Spelling" and "Saving a document to disk (after that)" in Chapter 20.

✔ It's actually Windows that does the printing. Word simply acts as a messenger. Because of this, you'll see Windows' li'l printer guy appear by the current time on the taskbar whenever something is printing in Word. This isn't very important.

Printing a Specific Page

Follow these steps to print only one page of your document:

1. **Make sure that your printer is on and eager to print something.**

2. **Move the toothpick cursor so that it's sitting somewhere in the page you want to print.**

   Check the Page counter in the lower-left corner of the screen to ensure that you're at the page that you want to print.

3. **Do the Print command.**

   Choose File⇨Print or press Ctrl+P. The Print dialog box appears.

4. **Select Current Page.**

   Click Current Page in the Page Range area in the Print dialog box.

5. **Click OK or press Enter.**

6. **You return to your document when that sole page is printed on your printer.**

   The page should have a header, footer, all formatting — and even a page number — just as though you had printed it as part of the complete document.

Printing and getting on with your life

Word has the capability to print while you do something else. If this capability isn't coddled to life, you may have to wait a dreadfully long time while your document prints. To ensure that it's on, select the Options button in the Print dialog box (press Ctrl+P and then Alt+O to get at the Options button). The Options dialog box appears, with the Print area up front.

In the upper-left corner of the Print area is the Printing Options corral. The last item is Background Printing. Make sure that it has a check mark in its little box. If not, click in the box or press Alt+B. Press Enter or click the OK button when you're done and press the Escape key to banish the Print dialog box.

Printing a Range of Pages

Word enables you to print a single page, a range of pages, or even some hodgepodge combination of random page numbers from within your document. To print a range or group of pages, follow these steps:

1. **Make sure that the printer is on-line, happy, and ready to print.**

2. **Conjure up the Print command.**

   Choose File⇨Print or press Ctrl+P. You see the Printer dialog box.

3. **Choose Pages.**

   Click Pages with the mouse. It's the third item in the Page Range area of the dialog box.

4. **Enter the page numbers and range of page numbers.**

   To print pages 3 through 5, type **3-5**. To print pages 1 through 7, type **1-7**.

5. **Choose OK.**

   Click the OK button or press the Enter key. The pages you specified — and only those pages — are printed.

You can get very specific with the page ranges. For example, to print page 3, pages 5 through 9, pages 15 through 17, and page 19 (boy, that coffee went everywhere, didn't it?), you type **3, 5-9, 15-17, 19**.

Printing a Block

When a block of text is marked on-screen, you can beg the Print command to print only that block. Refer to "Printing a Block" in Chapter 6 for the down-and-dirty details.

Printing Several Documents

It may seem that the best way to print several documents at a time is to load them one at a time and print them one at a time. There is a better way, however, and it's hidden in the Open dialog box, the same one you use to open any old document on disk. You can use this secret command to select documents on disk and do a "gang-print." This process is rumored to be easier than loading each file into Word, printing it, putting the file away, and then loading another file. You be the judge.

To print several files at a time, follow these steps:

1. **Make sure that the printer is on, selected, and rarin' to print.**

2. **Choose File⇨Open.**

   Or you can press Ctrl+O or click on the Open tool. Either way, the Open dialog box appears in all its glory, as shown in Figure 8-2.

3. **Tell Word where to look for your files.**

   Use the controls in the Open dialog box to find the folder on disk containing your documents.

   To open a folder, double-click its folder icon in the Open dialog box's main window. This displays documents in that folder.

   To see what's in the next folder "up," click on the Up One Level tool in the Open dialog box.

   Use the Look in list box to scan for folders on other disk drives and even folders on other computers, should your PC be shackled to a network.

4. **When you find your folder, start selecting documents.**

   To select a document, Ctrl-click it with the mouse. Press and hold the Ctrl key and click on the file. This highlights that document.

   Keep Ctrl-clicking documents until you've highlighted them all.

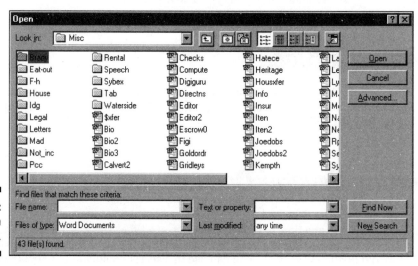

Figure 8-2:
The Open
dialog box.

5. **Click the Commands and Settings button at the top of the Open dialog box.**

   A list of commands appears in a pop-up menu. The one you want is the second one down, Print.

6. **Click the Print command with the mouse.**

7. **The Print dialog box appears.**

   At last, familiar territory.

8. **Click OK to print the many documents.**

   Word happily prints all the documents that you selected.

   ✔ This is perhaps the most obtuse way of printing multiple files that I've ever encountered in any word processor.

   ✔ Yes, as with printing a single document, printing multiple documents takes a while.

   ✔ Finding files in folders and all over your hard drive is covered in Chapter 22, "Managing Files."

Printing Envelopes

Yes, Word can print envelopes. Yes, it can even be a snap. A special Word command is specifically designed for this purpose. (Alas, Word does not print the stamp as well. And if it could, it might as well print money.)

To print an envelope, follow these steps:

1. **Make sure that your printer is oh-so-eager to print something.**

2. **Choose the Tools⇨Envelopes and Labels command.**

   This step opens the Envelopes and Labels dialog box, shown in Figure 8-3. If an address had been selected in your document or if Word has somehow magically located the address near the toothpick cursor, it appears in the Delivery Address box.

   If Word didn't automatically fill in the address, type it now.

3. **Stick an envelope in your printer.**

   I mention this step because most printers must be spoon-fed envelopes one at a time. (Mine works like this.) In some fancy-schmancy offices, printers may have *envelope feeders*. La-de-da.

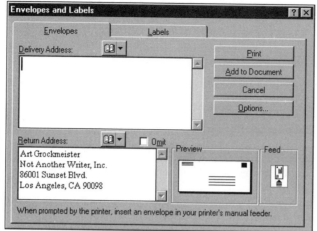

Figure 8-3:
The
Envelope
dialog box,
please.

By the way, you can double-click the Feed part of the Envelope dialog box to tell Word how the envelope will arrive through the printer. This really depends on how your printer sucks in envelopes. Mine has a special slot for them that takes 'em face up in the middle.

4. Choose Print.

Click that button with the mouse. Your printer may beep or otherwise prompt you to insert the envelope or it may just print it right then and there.

✔ Check the envelope to make sure that you didn't address the backside or put the address on upside down — as I so often do. This is an important last step because you can just repeat the above steps to reprint your envelope if you goof.

✔ Place the envelope in your laser printer's manual-feed slot-thing. The envelope goes in face up with the top side to your left. Draw a picture of this or print the preceding two sentences on a piece of paper and tape it to the top of your laser printer for future reference.

✔ On a dot-matrix printer, the envelope goes into the feeder upside-down and faces away from you. It helps to wedge it in there a bit to make sure that the printer grabs it. Or you may have a newfangled printer that has a special envelope slot. And if you do, well, la-de-da.

✔ Printing envelopes on a dot-matrix printer is a study in frustration. They usually look like something that a four-year-old did in preschool, all smeared up and not legible. You may be able to reduce the amount of smear by increasing the distance between the paper and the roller; you have to experiment.

✔ If you don't want the return address to print, check the Omit box in the upper-right part of the return address space in the dialog box. I do this routinely because my printer munges the top part of the envelope and the return address never prints right.

Canceling a Print Job

Sometimes you print something and then change your mind. This happens all the time. (Rumor has it that Gutenberg originally wanted to print a hanging floral wall calendar.) Or maybe your printer is so slow that you repeatedly press Ctrl+P, Enter too many times. Then you find yourself accidentally printing several dozen copies of the same document. Ugh.

Because Word simply passes off its printing jobs to Windows, there is no obvious way to cancel printing. It can be done if you're crafty, however. Follow these steps:

1. Locate the li'l printer dude by the current time on the taskbar.

This little cuss only appears when Windows is sending something to the printer. Depending on how much you're printing and how fast your printer is, you may not even see it at all. If you don't, then you're out of luck and you might as well quit right now and eat some ice cream.

2. Double-click on the little printer guy.

This opens up your printer's window (see Figure 8-4). It displays a list of documents waiting to be printed. The top document in the list is currently printing; other documents are waiting in the queue (which is the way the British say "line").

3. Click on the name of your Word document "job" in the Print Manager's list.

Documents in the list are called *print jobs*. Your task is to fire one of them.

4. Choose Document⇨Cancel Printing.

You may be asked whether you really want to terminate the employee, er, print job. Click the OK button.

If you're using a network printer, you may not be able to cancel the document. Oh well.

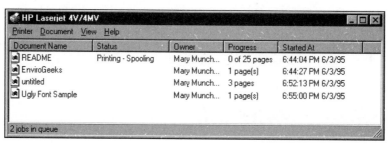

Figure 8-4:
Documents
waiting in
your
printer's
queue.

5. Cancel more print jobs if you feel in an especially vicious mood.

Repeat steps 3 and 4 for each job you want to fire.

6. Close your printer's window when you're done.

Choose Printer⇨Close to remove that window from the desktop. You'll be zapped back to Word, ready for more editing action.

Obviously, canceling a print job is the act of a desperate person. In its efforts to make life easy for computer users, Windows tries hard to help us change our minds. Canceling something that's printing may or may not work as planned. My advice is just to be careful with the Print command in the first place.

Part II
Formatting — or Making Your Prose Look Less Ugly

The 5th Wave — By Rich Tennant

"YES, WE STILL HAVE A FEW BUGS IN THE WORD PROCESSING SOFTWARE. BY THE WAY, HERE'S A MEMO FROM MARKETING."

In this part...

*F*ormatting makes your documents shine. It's what makes you boast when you show your printed labors to a — dare I say it — WordPerfect user, who snivels, "Gosh, how'd you get it to look so good?" Few other things in life make you swell with such pride.

Yet formatting isn't without its dark side. It involves a great deal of key pressing and other secret rituals. This part describes the intricacies of how formatting works in Microsoft Word and how to make your documents look oh-so-purty.

Chapter 9
Formatting Characters

The most basic thing you can format in a document is a character. *Characters* include letters, words, text in paragraphs, and weird Uncle Lloyd, who trims the hair in his ears with a butane lighter. You can format characters to be bold, underlined, italicized, little, big, in different fonts, or in an Easter bunny suit at Thanksgiving dinner. Word gives you a magnificent amount of control over the appearance of your text and enables you to generate documents that are truly professional in quality — and fool everyone in the process.

Making Bold Text

To emphasize a word, you make it bold. Bold text is, well, bold. It's heavy. It carries a lot of weight, stands out on the page, speaks its mind at public meetings, wears a cowboy hat — you know the type.

To make new text stand out, follow these steps:

1. Press the Ctrl+B key combination.

This step activates bold mode, in which everything you type is bold. Go ahead — type away. La-la-la. (You also can click the Bold tool in the Formatting toolbar to turn it on.)

2. Press Ctrl+B again.

This step turns off the bold character format. All your text is then normal. (Click off the Bold tool.)

If you already have text on-screen and you want to make it bold, you have to mark it as a block and then make it bold. Follow these steps:

1. Mark the block of text you want to make bold.

Move the toothpick cursor to the beginning of the block; press F8 to turn on block-marking mode; move the cursor to the end of the block. Or you can use the mouse to drag and select the block. The block appears highlighted on-screen.

2. Press Ctrl+B, the Bold key command.

The block is bold. (You also can click the Bold tool.)

- ✔ Everything you type after pressing Ctrl+B appears in boldface on-screen and in your printed document. However, if you wander with the toothpick cursor, you may turn off the bold command. My advice is to do this: Press Ctrl+B, type bold stuff, press Ctrl+B, and type normal stuff.

- ✔ When the Bold tool is depressed (it's crying or bemoaning something trivial), the text the toothpick cursor is nestled in has the bold attribute. (This feature helps when you can't tell by looking at the screen whether text is already bold.)

- ✔ You can mix and match character formats; text can be bold and underlined or bold and italicized. To do so, you have to press the proper keys to turn on those formats before typing the text. Yes, this means that you may have to type several Word character-formatting commands before typing your text: Ctrl+B, Ctrl+I, and Ctrl+U for bold, italicized, and underlined text all at once, for example. It's a hassle, but everyone has to do it that way.

- ✔ You can turn off all character formatting with one stroke by pressing the Ctrl+spacebar key combination. Granted, it helps to have a block of formatted text marked first.

- ✔ Refer to "Marking a Block" in Chapter 6 for more information on marking blocks.

Making Italicized Text

Italics are replacing underlining as the preferred text-emphasis format. I'm not embarrassed to use italics to emphasize or highlight a title just because it looks so much better than shabby underlined text. It's light and wispy, poetic, and free. Underlining is what the DMV does when it feels creative.

To italicize your text, follow these steps:

1. Press the Ctrl+I key combination.

Italics mode is on! (You also can click the Italic tool.)

2. Type away to your heart's content!

Watch your delightfully right-leaning text march across the screen. Pat Buchanan, eat your heart out!

3. Press Ctrl+I when you're done.

Italic formatting is turned off. (Turn off the Italic tool.)

If the text you want to italicize is already on-screen, you must mark it as a block and then change its character format to italics. Follow these steps:

1. Mark the block of text you want to italicize.

Do the block-marking thing here. Detailed instructions are offered in Chapter 6 and earlier in this chapter.

2. Press the Ctrl+I key combination.

This step italicizes the block. (You also can click the leaning *I* Italic tool.)

✔ If you want to double up on a character font — make something italic and bold, for example — you can press both character-formatting keys while you hold down the Ctrl key. Holding down the Ctrl key and pressing I and then B seems to be easier than doing the Ctrl+I and Ctrl+B dance.

✔ You also can press Ctrl+spacebar to turn italics off, but then you turn off all other formatting as well.

Making Underlined Text

Underlined text just isn't as popular as it used to be. Instead, people now use *italicized* text for subtle emphasis — unless you are writing a paper on <u>War and Peace</u> for that stodgy professor who thinks that all modern influence is of the devil. In that case, underline the title of major literary texts (or at least those by Tolstoy). And always, *always,* italicize titles by Danielle Steele. Everything in between is pretty much a judgment call.

To underline your text, follow these steps:

1. Press the Ctrl+U key combination.

This step turns on the underline character format. (You can also use the Underline tool-button thing on the Formatting toolbar.)

2. Type!

You're now free to type the text you want underlined.

3. Press the Ctrl+U key combination again.

This step returns you to typing normal text. (Or click off the Underline tool button.)

If you already have text on-screen that you want to underline, you have to mark the text as a block and then press the Ctrl+U key combination. Here are the steps you take:

1. Mark the block of text you want to underline.

Refer to Chapter 6 or the first section of this chapter for exciting block-marking rules and regulations.

2. Press the Ctrl+U keys.

The block is underlined. (Or click the Underline tool.)

✔ After you finish typing underlined text, you can press Ctrl+spacebar or Ctrl+U, or click the Underline tool to turn off underlining.

✔ Chapter 6, the king of the block chapters, contains a section called "Marking a Block," which tells you more about — you guessed it — marking blocks.

Text-Attribute Effects

Bold, italics, and underlining are the most common ways to dress up a character. They are each covered in previous sections. However, they are only the beginning of what Word can do for your character formatting. You can use a whole slew of other Ctrl+other key combinations to slap a different look on your text. Most of this stuff is rather esoteric, which is why I stuck it in a boring old table (Table 9-1) rather than write about it with sharp wit in a traditional paragraph.

Table 9-1	Text-format samples and commands
Key Combination	**Applies this Format**
Ctrl+Shift+A	ALL CAPS
Ctrl+B	**Bold**
Ctrl+Shift+D	<u>Double Underline</u>
Ctrl+Shift+H	Hidden Text (it doesn't print — shhh!)
Ctrl+I	*Italics*
Ctrl+Shift+K	SMALL CAPS
Ctrl+U	<u>Continuous underline</u>
Ctrl+Shift+W	<u>Word</u> <u>underline</u>
Ctrl+=	Subscript
Ctrl+Shift+=	Superscript
Ctrl+Shift+Z	Undo character formatting

To apply one of these weird text formats to a character you type or blocked text, refer to the preceding section, "Making Underlined Text," and substitute the proper shortcut from Table 9-1.

Any of these neat-o formatting tricks can also be achieved by opening a dialog box. If you are feeling reckless, powerful, able to leap tall terminals in a single bound, skip ahead to the section "Doing It the Hard Way." Fair warning: Tying your fingers in knots with key combinations is much safer.

Pressing Ctrl+spacebar is the easiest way to recover when your character formatting seems to have gotten rambunctiously encumbered.

Hidden text — what good is that? It's good for you, the writer, to put down some thoughts and then hide them when the document prints. Of course, you don't see the text on-screen either. To find hidden text, you must use the Find command (covered in Chapter 5) to locate the special hidden-text attribute. This information is in the section "Finding secret codes." You have to press the Format button, choose Font, and then click the Hidden box. (This information really should have been hidden to begin with.)

Text-Size Effects

Attributes — bold, italics, underline, and so on — are only half the available character formats. The other half deal with the text size. By using these commands, you can make your text teensy or humongous.

Before getting into this subject, you must become one with the official typesetting term for text size. It's *point.* That's what Word uses: Point instead of text size. It's not point, as in "point your finger" or "point on top your head." It's point, which is a measurement of size. One point is equal to $1/72$ inch. Typesetters . . .

To change the size of text as you type, follow these steps:

1. **Get at the point size box on the Formatting toolbar.**

   Two ways to do this: Click the mouse in the point size box or press Ctrl+Shift+P.

2. **Type the new point size and press Enter.**

   The text you type from that moment on is in the new size.

Here are some things to remember about setting the point size:

- ✔ You can also use the drop-down button next to the point window to display the entire gamut of point options for your current font.

- ✔ Bigger numbers mean bigger text; smaller numbers mean smaller text.

- ✔ The average point size is 12, or sometimes 10.

- ✔ TrueType or Adobe Type 1 fonts can be sized from 1 point to 1638 points.

- ✔ The author is 5,112 points tall.

If you want to apply a size format to text that is already on-screen, you have to mark those characters as a block before modifying the size.

To quickly change the size of a marked block, you can use the following shortcut keys:

Ctrl+] — Makes text one point size larger

Ctrl+[— Makes text one point size smaller

There really is no good mnemonic for this feature; you just have to commit it to memory.

Some fonts look ugly in certain point sizes. To ensure that the font looks good, you can use the following shortcut keys:

Ctrl+Shift+> — Makes the font larger in the next "look good" size

Ctrl+Shift+< — Makes the font smaller in the next "look good" size

Making superscript text

Superscript text is above the line (for example, the 10 in 2^{10}). To produce this effect, press Ctrl+Shift+= (the equal key) and then the text you want to super-script. Or mark a block of text and then press Ctrl+Shift+= to superscript the text in the block.

To return your text to normal, press Ctrl+spacebar.

Some people prefer superscript text that's a tad bit smaller than what Word gives you. Refer to the preceding section for information on changing the size of the text.

Here's a reason to be glad for Pepto-Bismol: Ctrl+Shift+= is the art of pressing the Ctrl and Shift keys at the same time — which anyone can do after a light lunch — and then pressing the equal key. Actually, Shift+= is the plus key. So this key combination is really Ctrl++ or Control+plus sign. Ugh. I bet if they made a bigger keyboard, Microsoft would find things to do with all the keys, no sweat.

Making subscript text

Subscript text is below the line (for example, the 2 in H_2O). To subscript your text, press Ctrl+= (the equal key) and then type away. If you mark a block of text and then press Ctrl+=, all the text in the block is subscript. To return your text to normal, press Ctrl+spacebar (the long, boney key under your thumb).

Making normal text

Sometimes you have so many character attributes going that you don't know what to press to get back to normal text. This situation can be very frustrating. Fortunately, Word has lent a tiny ear to your cries for help. You can use the Reset Character text-formatting command to shut off everything — size and attribute formats — and return the text to normal. Here's how:

Press Ctrl+spacebar, the Reset Character shortcut.

Everything you type from that point on is normal (or at least has the normal attributes).

If you mark a block and then press Ctrl+spacebar, all text in the block is returned to normal. Refer to "Marking a Block" in Chapter 6 for more information on marking blocks of text.

Pressing Ctrl+spacebar does not work on cousin Melvin.

Changing the font

One of the fun things about Word is its capability to use lots of different fonts. Sure, text can be made bold, italic, underlined, big, little, and on and on, but adjusting the font to match your mood takes expression to an entirely new level.

To switch to a different font, follow these steps:

1. **Arouse the font box on the Formatting toolbar.**

   Click the down arrow by the box with the mouse or press Ctrl+Shift+F and then the down-arrow key. This step displays all the fonts that have been installed for Windows (see Figure 9-1).

Figure 9-1:
The list of fonts you can use in Word.

2. **Scroll down to the font you want.**

   They're listed by name in alphabetical order. Any fonts you've recently chosen appear at the top of the list, before the double bar (see Figure 9-1).

3. **Press Enter to choose a font.**

   Or click it once with your mouse.

   ✔ Everything you type after choosing a new font appears on-screen in that font. It should print and look the same as well.

   ✔ If you know the name of the font you want, you can save time by toggling directly to the font window and typing the name of the font in which you want your text to appear. *Caveat:* Word is not lenient on spelling mistakes.

✔ You can change a font for text already in your document by first marking the text as a block (refer to Chapter 6) and then choosing the font you want from the ribbon.

✔ The section "Doing It the Hard Way," later in this chapter, contains information on previewing certain fonts, which enables you to see how they will look before you use them.

✔ The fonts are listed in the font box by name and appear in the drop-down list with little icons before the name. A printer icon identifies a *printer font,* one that's part of your printer. This type of font may not show up on-screen the same as it prints; Windows is odd this way. Fonts with a double T by them are *TrueType fonts,* which look the same on-screen as they print. (If the font has nothing in front of it, it's just a screen font.)

✔ In Word, fonts are the responsibility of Windows alone. You install new fonts by using the Windows Control Panel. Thousands of fonts are available for Windows, and they work in all Windows applications. (Windows users trade fonts like characters in cheesy sitcoms trade insults; contact a local computer club or scour the back of a computer magazine to look for some cool Windows fonts.)

Converting to upper- and lowercase

Upper- and lowercase effects aren't considered part of a font, character attribute, or format. But still, the Word geniuses at Microsoft found room in their bustling bag o' tricks for a two-fingered command that lets you mix around in the case conversion of your text. And it doesn't even sound like procrastination, huh?

To play with, er, I mean convert the case makeup of a block of text:

1. **Mark the text to convert as a block.**

   Refer to Chapter 6 for the best block-marking advice since the ancient Babylonians.

2. **Press Shift+F3.**

   This step capitalizes the first letter of a sentence or capitalizes every character in the block or returns them all to their humble, lowercase origins.

3. **Continue pressing Shift+F3 until you have settled on the case you like most.**

   Yes, a veritable cornucopia of case conversion lies at your fingertips. Genie-in-a-Key-combo, I like to call it.

You don't have to mark a single word as a block of text for this trick: Just put the toothpick cursor somewhere in the middle of a word and press Shift+F3 to change that word's case.

Alas, this trick does not work on single letters you may select as a block (which is kind of silly and requires too many keystrokes as well). Just type in a new capital letter using the Shift key if that's what you want to do.

Inserting Oddball and Special Characters

Look over your keyboard's keys. Yeah, it has the letters of the alphabet plus numbers and some weird symbols. Word can display all those characters just fine; you see them on your screen every day.

But there are several dozen to several hundred additional, interesting characters you can display. These Word oddball characters seem to accumulate like French fries and stray shoes at the McDonaldland play park.

Oddball characters are inserted by using the Insert⇨Symbol command. Here's how you work it:

1. **Position the toothpick cursor where you want the oddball character to appear.**

2. **Choose the Insert⇨Symbol command.**

   Use the mouse or press Alt, I, S. You see the Symbol dialog box, as shown in Figure 9-2. (If the Special Characters panel appears, click the Symbols tab with the mouse.)

3. **Choose the symbol you want.**

   Point the mouse at the symbol that interests you and then double-click that character. Or you can press the cursor keys to move a highlight box around and then press Enter.

4. **The oddball character is inserted into your text.**

   Well, I'll be @#$%&ed!

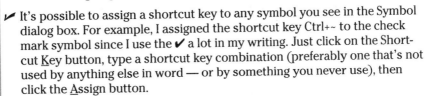
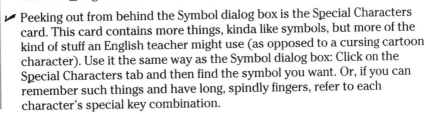

Figure 9-2:
The Symbol
dialog box.

Here are some tips for inserting special characters:

- ✔ To get a good look at a particular symbol, point the mouse cursor at it and press and hold the mouse button. That one symbol is magnified.

- ✔ Just about any font you have installed that has symbols in it appears in the drop-down list at the top of the Symbol dialog box. To look at other symbols, click the down arrow next to the Font box and choose a different symbol set by clicking on its name. The best symbols can be found in the various Wingdings fonts.

- ✔ It's possible to assign a shortcut key to any symbol you see in the Symbol dialog box. For example, I assigned the shortcut key Ctrl+~ to the check mark symbol since I use the ✔ a lot in my writing. Just click on the Shortcut Key button, type a shortcut key combination (preferably one that's not used by anything else in word — or by something you never use), then click the Assign button.

- ✔ Peeking out from behind the Symbol dialog box is the Special Characters card. This card contains more things, kinda like symbols, but more of the kind of stuff an English teacher might use (as opposed to a cursing cartoon character). Use it the same way as the Symbol dialog box: Click on the Special Characters tab and then find the symbol you want. Or, if you can remember such things and have long, spindly fingers, refer to each character's special key combination.

Doing it the hard way: Taking a Yellow Line bus tour of the Font dialog box

Too many choices can overwhelm you. Most people prefer simple, straightforward information — all the options explained right there on the menu, with pictures of what they look like. Or a smell may waft from two tables over and you'll point and say, "I want what the nun is having."

Then again, there are times when — if you know what you're doing — you want all the options right there at once. You know which levers you want pulled — the salad dressing and potato fixings and how burnt the meat should be — all at once. For those times, Word offers the Font dialog box, a place where almost all your character formatting can take place simultaneously. This dialog box is definitely not for the timid. But exciting and exotic things await you.

When you select Format⇨Font, you open up the rather imposing Font dialog box. All sorts of interesting things happen here, depending on at which bus stop you disembark:

Day 1	**Font**	If you click on the drop-down list under the word Font, you see the name of each and every font on your machine. You may have anywhere from a handful to a kabillion of them. If you highlight the name of one, a sample appears in the Preview sneak-peak window.
Day 2	**Font Style**	Choose from Regular, *Italic,* **Bold**, ***Bold Italic,*** and, if you're in Seattle, double-decaffeinated latté!
Day 3	**Size**	If you click on the drop-down list under Size, you see all available sizes of the font in question. The available sizes run from 1 point to 1638 points, or from teensy-weensy to abnormally big.
Day 4	**Underline**	Choose from a Single, continuous underline, underline only the Words themselves, and Double underline, or use a Dotted line to underscore your text.
Day 5	**Color**	Create text in living color by choosing a new color from the Color drop-down list. The color shows on-screen only if you have a color monitor, and it prints only if you have a color printer.
Day 6	**Effects**	You can have ~~Strikethrough~~, Superscript, Subscript, Hidden text, SMALL CAPS, or ALL CAPS.

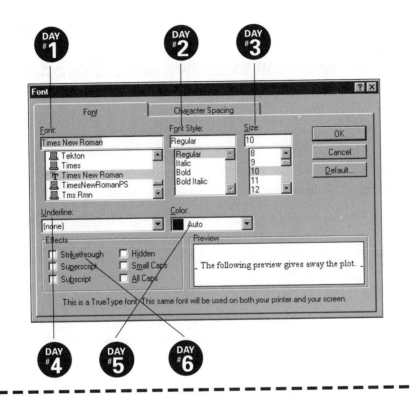

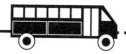

A bonus afternoon excursion to the Character Spacing panel

If you're willing to pay extra, click on the Character Spacing tab to see that panel, which is hiding right behind the main Font panel in the Font dialog box. (This panel stuff is really batty. If you're new to it, get used to it. It's the "future of Windows" — primarily because OS/2 does it, too!)

1:35 p.m. **Spacing** Enables you to condense or expand the letters in your text as necessary.

2:15 p.m. **Position** Your text may ^rise^ above the crowds or ~sink~ to new depths. Sounds pretty much like superscripting and subscripting your text, huh? But it's not. It's brand-new technology thought up by those genius developers over at Microsoft. Brand-new. Really!

3:10 p.m. **Kerning** *Kerning* is the process of making juice drinks. In Word, it refers to how snugly letters hug each other — really advanced typesetter stuff, but WHOOMP! —there it is. If you're willing, you can make the kerning for fonts above the indicated Points and Above size automatic. Big deal. Leave this one alone is my advice.

You can make all sorts of text settings in the Font dialog box and then click OK to apply them to your text. That's any new text you type or text already in a block you highlight on-screen.

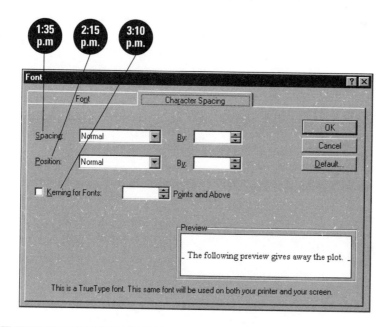

Chapter 10

Formatting Sentences and Paragraphs

Characters are the most basic thing you can format. After that comes sentences and paragraphs, which can be centered, shoved to the left or right, riddled with tab stops, and spaced far enough apart so as not to offend anything. This stuff can be done on the fly, but I recommend doing it just before printing (along with page formatting — see Chapter 11) or by including the formatting in a style sheet (see Chapter 14). That way, you can pull out half your hair while you struggle with spelling and grammar and getting your ideas on paper. Then, when that's perfect and your blood pressure has dropped, you can pull out the rest of your hair while you struggle anew with line and paragraph formatting. Ugh. Will it never end?

If you want to learn to access everything in this chapter through menus, see the last section in this chapter, "Doing it the hard way."

Centering Text

Word lets you *center* a single line of text or an entire block of text. Your text is miraculously centered down the middle of the page on-screen and when it's printed. This is yet another miracle of modern computing.

If you want to center just a single line, follow these steps:

1. Start on a new line, the line you want to be centered.

If the line is already on-screen, skip to the second set of instructions after this set.

2. Use the Center command, Ctrl+E.

I know that E doesn't mean *center* in your brain. But the word *center* does have two *E*s in it. How about E means *equator?* Nah, that goes side-to-side. I give up.

You also can center text by clicking the Center tool on the ribbon. It looks like the thing you yell into when you order burgers at a drive-thru.

3. The cursor zips over to the center of the screen (or thereabouts).

4. Type your title or heading.

5. Press Enter when you're done.

If you want to center more than a line (a paragraph or more, for example), keep typing away. When you tire of seeing your text centered, press Ctrl+L to return to left justification or press the Left Align tool. (Left justification is the way text normally appears in Word; everything is even on the left side of the page on the left margin.)

Follow these steps to center text that's already in your document:

1. Mark as a block the text you want to center.

Refer to Chapter 6 for the best block-marking directions you'll ever read in a computer book.

2. Use the Center command, Ctrl+E.

You see the blocked text along with any paragraph it is in, promptly displayed as center-justified. (You also can click the Center tool.)

The Center command, Ctrl+E, centers only paragraphs. If you want to center just one line at a time, you must end each line by pressing the Enter key — which makes that single line a paragraph.

The easiest way to accomplish quick paragraph formatting, such as centering, is to use the tool buttons on the formatting ribbon. Just click one of them instead of pressing Ctrl+E, Ctrl+L, or whatever, and your text will be formatted accordingly.

To *justify* text — that's when the left *and* right margins align — click the Justify tool or press Ctrl+J.

Flushing Text Right

"Flush right" describes the way text aligns on-screen. (You'll soon discover that a lot of flushing occurs in paragraph formatting.) Text is usually *flush left*, with everything lining up at the left margin. *Flush-right* text aligns at the right margin. In other words, all the text is slammed against the right side of the page — like picking up the paper and jerking it wildly until the text slides over.

You can right-align a single paragraph of text or mark any size of text as a block and flush it right. If you want to flush just a single paragraph, follow these steps:

1. **Position the toothpick cursor where you want to type a line flush right.**

   The cursor is on the left side of the screen; this is okay. Don't press the spacebar or Tab key to move the cursor; the Flush Right command does so in just a second.

   If the text you want to flush right is already on-screen, skip to the second set of instructions following this set.

2. **Press Ctrl+R, the Flush Right command.**

   Golly, R equals *right*. This is amazing. The cursor skips on over to the right margin, on the right side of the screen. (You also can click the Right Align button on the Formatting toolbar.)

3. **Type your line.**

   The characters push right, always staying flush with the right side of the document. It's like writing in Hebrew!

4. **Press Ctrl+L to return to left-justified text when you're done.**

   Again, put the cursor on a new line; otherwise, the Ctrl+L command undoes all your right-justified text. (Or press the Left Align tool.)

For flushing right more than a single paragraph of text that you already have in your document, you have to mark it all as a block. Follow these steps:

1. **Mark as a block the text you want to flush right.**

   Chapter 6 has block-marking details to soothe your furrowed brow.

2. **Press Ctrl+R, the Flush Right command.**

   You see the text zip over to the right margin. Og say block flush right. Block good. (You also can click the Right Align tool.)

   ✔ Be careful not to flush large objects, cardboard, or other foreign objects when you're adjusting your text. Do not flush while the train is parked at the station.

   ✔ *Flush right* is a design term that means the same thing as *right align* or *right justification*.

   ✔ Typographers use words other than *justification.* They occasionally use the word *ragged* to describe how the text fits. For example, left justification is *ragged right;* right justification is *ragged left.* A "rag top" is a convertible with a soft top, and a "rag bottom" is any child still in diapers.

Flushing your dates right

A good thing to flush right at the top of the document is the date. Most people start their letters this way. To flush right the date at the top of a document, follow these handy steps:

1. **Move to the top of the document to the line where you want to put the date. It must be a blank line.**

2. **Press Ctrl+R, the Flush Right command. The toothpick cursor zooms over to the right side of the page.**

3. **Press Alt+Shift+D. This step inserts the current date into your document. (No need to memorize this command; just flag this page.)**

4. **Press Enter.**

5. **Press Ctrl+L to go back to left justification.**

You can continue editing with the current date proudly flushed right at the top of the page.

Changing Line Spacing

On a typewriter, you change the line spacing with a double or triple whack of the carriage return. Sadly, although whacking your computer twice or thrice helps your attitude, it doesn't do diddly for your document's line spacing. Instead, you have to use Word's Line Spacing command.

To change the line spacing for new text, you have three options:

1. **Press Ctrl+1 for single-spaced lines.**

   Hold down the Ctrl key and press 1. (That's Ctrl and the one key, not the L key.) Release both keys, and Word single-spaces your text. Any text you type or a highlighted block on-screen is affected after you press Ctrl+1.

$1^1/_2$. Press Ctrl+5 for $1^1/_2$-spaced lines.

   The $1^1/_2$ spacing means that your lines are between single and double spacing — which gives editors (and teachers) less room to mark up your stuff but still lets in all that "air" that makes the text readable. You press Ctrl+5 to get $1^1/_2$ line spacing in your document or to change the spacing for a highlighted block.

2. **Press Ctrl+2 for double-spaced lines.**

   Double spacing is often required by fussy editors who, without enough room in their precious 1-inch margins, want to write under, over, and between what you write. Press Ctrl+2 to make your text double spaced.

You can quickly change the spacing of a paragraph that is already in your text by placing the toothpick cursor anywhere in the paragraph and pressing the magical key commands!

✔ Ctrl+5 means $1^1/_2$ line spacing, not 5 line spacing.

✔ Refer to Chapter 6 for information on marking a block. The Ctrl+1, Ctrl+2, and Ctrl+5 shortcuts affect any block marked on-screen.

✔ For your Ctrl+5 key press don't use the 5 key on the numeric keypad; that's the command to select all the text in your document. Instead, use the 5 key hovering over the R and T keys on your keyboard.

Unnecessary, more specific spacing stuff

If you want line spacing other than single, double, or 1½, you can choose the Format⇨Paragraph command. The Paragraph dialog box opens, which is covered at the end of this chapter. Make sure that the Indents and Spacing panel is in front. Choose Exactly in the Line Spacing box and the measurement you want in the At box. To triple-space lines, for example, you choose Exactly under Line Spacing and type **3 li** in the At box. This step sets the spacing to 3 lines ('cause in Word a li is the same as a line). If you don't type **li**, Word may use **pt**, which stands for *points* or maybe even some other aggravating typesetting measurement. My advice is to keep it in your brain to type **li** for line and leave the points for the seller to worry about.

Adding Breathing Room between Paragraphs

Some people, myself included, are in the double-Enter habit. That is, you press Enter Enter to end a paragraph, when all Word really needs is a single Enter. It's a similar disorder to pressing Space Space after a period — an utterly useless affliction in the age of modern word processing.

If you want your paragraphs to automatically have some "air" around them, then — just like an insecure guy at the beach — you need only to tell Word to stick some padding down there. Here's how:

1. **Position the toothpick cursor in the paragraph you want more air around.**

   The air can be either above or below the paragraph.

2. **Choose Format⇨Paragraph.**

   The Paragraph dialog box appears, as shown in Figure 10-1.

3. **Bring the Indents and Spacing panel forward.**

   Click on that panel's tab, or press Alt+I, if it isn't forward already. You'll want to concentrate on the area that says Spacing.

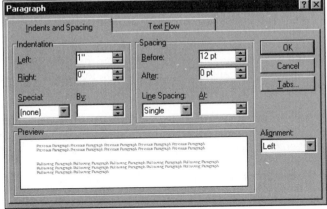

Figure 10-1:
The
Paragraph
dialog box.

4. Type in a value for spacing Before or After.

Personally I use the up or down arrows here. For example, to add space after every paragraph, I click twice on the down arrow by that box. The value **12 pt** means there will be just about one blank line after that paragraph.

A good way to remember the pt nonsense is that Word adds one half line of blank space before or after a paragraph for each time you click one of the little arrows. (**6 pt** equals half a line of text.)

5. Click OK.

Your paragraph has been modified. After you press the Enter key, you'll see the new "air" after your paragraph (or before the next one).

✓ Changing a paragraph this way affects the current paragraph (the one the toothpick cursor is in), as well as any new paragraphs you type.

✓ To make a blank line between your paragraphs, follow the above steps and put **12 pt** into the After box. (My advice is always to add the padding at the end of the paragraph.)

✓ You can always check the Preview window in the Paragraph dialog box to see how your paragraph stacks up with its new before or after spacing.

✓ Adding space before or after a paragraph isn't the same as double spacing the text inside the paragraph. In fact, adding space around a paragraph does not change the paragraph's line spacing one iota.

Indenting a Paragraph

To make a paragraph of text feel good about itself, you can indent it. That makes it stand out on the page. It says: "Hey, notice me! Can I talk here? Please stop interrupting, Mr. Limbaugh." You do this by indenting that paragraph, which is something they all clamor for but you have to be selective about.

Indenting a paragraph doesn't mean just indenting its first line, which you can do with the Tab key. Instead, you can indent, or *nest,* the entire paragraph by aligning its left edge against a tab stop. Here's how you do it:

1. **Move the toothpick cursor anywhere in the paragraph.**

   The paragraph can already be on-screen or you can be poised to type a new paragraph.

2. **Press Ctrl+M, the Indent shortcut.**

   Ummm — indent! Ummm — indent! Say it over and over. It kinda works. (You also can click the Indent button on the Formatting toolbar.)

3. **Type your paragraph if you haven't already.**

   If the paragraph is blocked, it is indented to the next tab stop.

Keep these tips in mind when you're indenting paragraphs:

- ✔ To return the original margin, Press Ctrl+Shift+M or, heck, Ctrl+Z, the Undo command (which is why it's there). You also can click the Unindent tool.

- ✔ To indent the paragraph to the next tab stop, press Ctrl+M again.

- ✔ Although the Ctrl+M and Ctrl+Shift+M shortcuts aren't mnemonic, their only difference is a Shift key. So when you get used to using them (hopefully before the afterlife), they're easy to remember.

- ✔ To indent both the right and left sides of a paragraph, see the following section, "Double Indenting a Paragraph." Also check out "Making a Hanging Indent," later in this chapter.

If you're in a fair mood, refer to "The Tab Stops Here," later in this chapter, for information on setting tab stops.

Double Indenting a Paragraph

Sometimes an indent on the left just isn't enough. There are those days when you need to suck a paragraph in twice: once on the left and once on the right (for example, when you lift a quote from another paper but don't want to be accused of plagiarism). I do this to Abe Lincoln all the time. When I quote his stuff, I follow these steps:

1. **Move the toothpick cursor to the beginning of the paragraph.**

   If the paragraph hasn't been written yet, move the cursor to where you want to write the new text.

2. **Choose the Format⇨Paragraph command.**

   The Paragraph dialog box appears. Make sure that the Indents and Spacing panel is in front. In the upper-left region, you see the Indentation area. It contains three items: Left, Right, and Special.

3. **Enter the amount of left and right indentation.**

   Click in the Left box. Type a value, such as **.5** to indent the paragraph a half-inch. Then click in the Right box (or press the Tab key once) and type **.5** again. This step indents your paragraph half an inch from the left and right.

   You can also press the up and down arrows that cling to the right side of the box to spin numbers up and down with the mouse. Whee!

4. **Click OK or press Enter.**

5. **Type your paragraph if you haven't already.**

The Paragraph dialog box is given a shave and a haircut at the end of this chapter (in a Technical Stuff sidebar).

Obviously, a double-indented paragraph should be inhaled equally from the left and right sides of the page; the numbers in the Left and Right boxes should be the same.

When you modify a paragraph in the Paragraph dialog box, notice the Preview box at the bottom of the card. Your paragraph's format is shown in dark ink on the sample page.

To indent only the left side of a paragraph, refer to the preceding section, "Indenting a Paragraph."

Making a Hanging Indent

A hanging indent has committed no felonious crime. Instead, it's a paragraph in which the first line sticks out to the left and the rest of the paragraph is indented — like the paragraph has its tongue sticking out or it's a side view of a high diving board. To create such a beast, follow these steps:

1. **Move the toothpick cursor into the paragraph you want to hang and indent.**

   Or you can position the cursor to where you want to type a new, hanging-indent paragraph.

2. **Press Ctrl+T, the Hanging Indent shortcut.**

   Ta-da! You have a hanging indented paragraph.

   You can remember Ctrl+T because the English always hang felons just before Tea Time.

   The Ctrl+T in Word moves the paragraph over to the first tab stop but keeps the first line in place.

If you want to indent the paragraph even more, press the Ctrl+T key more than once.

See "Indenting a Paragraph," earlier in this chapter, for more information on indenting paragraphs.

To undo a hanging indent, press Ctrl+Shift+T. That's the unhang key combination, and your paragraph's neck will be put back in shape.

Paragraph-formatting survival guide

This table contains all the paragraph-formatting commands you can summon by holding down the Ctrl key and pressing a letter or number. By no means should you memorize this list.

Key combo	Does this
Ctrl+E	Centers paragraphs
Ctrl+J	Fully justifies paragraphs
Ctrl+L	Left aligns (flush left)
Ctrl+R	Right aligns (flush right)
Ctrl+M	Indents text
Ctrl+Shift+M	Unindents text
Ctrl+T	Makes a hanging indent
Ctrl+Shift+T	Unhangs the indent
Ctrl+1	Single-spaces lines
Ctrl+2	Double-spaces lines
Ctrl+5	Makes 1½-space lines

Hanging indents depend on the placement of tab stops. See "The Tab Stops Here," next, for help with tabs.

The Tab Stops Here

When you press the Tab key, indent a paragraph, or make a hanging indent, Word moves the cursor or text over to the next *tab stop*. Normally, the tab stops are set every half inch. You can change this setting to any interval or customize the tab stops if you want. Follow these steps:

1. **Position the toothpick cursor to a place in the document before the position where you want to change the tabs.**

   If you want to change the tab stops in more than one paragraph, mark the paragraphs you want to change. Refer to Chapter 6 for block-marking instructions.

2. **Click the mouse on the ruler where you want a new tab stop.**

   The mouse pointer changes into an arrow shape when it's not hovering over text. Point that pointer at the spot on the ruler where you want your new tab stop to appear.

   After clicking the mouse button, a little, bold corner — a plump L — appears and marks the tab-stop location.

3. **Modify or fine-tune the tab position by dragging the tab indicator to the left or right with the mouse.**

If you don't see the ruler on-screen, choose the <u>R</u>uler command from the <u>V</u>iew menu.

If you decide that you don't want the tab after all, you can drag it off the ruler altogether; grab it with the mouse and drag it up or down. Thwoop! It's gone.

When I'm working with a lot of tabs, I usually press the Tab key only once between each column of information. Then I select all the paragraphs and drag the tab indicators around so that each of my columns aligns. Using one tab instead of two or three is much easier to edit. And it lets me do fancy stuff, like sorting and math. You learn about this neat-o stuff in Chapter 12.

Meddlesome nonsense about tab types

Word uses four different types of tabs, as depicted by four different icons that can appear on the far left side of the ruler. Whichever one you see determines which types of tabs are set. This list shows what each type does:

The most common tab is the left tab, the plump L. This tab works like the Tab key on a typewriter: Press the Tab key and the new text appears at the next tab stop. No mental hang-ups here.

The right tab causes text to line up right-justified at that tab stop. This tab gives you leeway to do some fancy paragraph justification on a single line, which you can read about in Chapter 26, on fancy document titles.

The center tab stop centers text on the tab stop. Good for one-word columns.

The decimal tab aligns numbers by their decimals. The number is right-justified before you press the period key and then left-justified on the decimal.

The Fearless Leader Tabs

The leader tab is interesting but not required for most writing. It produces a row of dots when you press Tab. You see this all the time in indexes or a table of contents. Word gives you the choice of three different leaders:

Fearless dot leader tabs 109

Zipper line leader tabs - - - - - - - - - - - - - - - - - - 109

U-boat underline leader tabs _____ 109

To choose from among the different types of tabs, follow these steps:

1. **Position the toothpick cursor on the line where you want to have your leader tabs.**

   For example, you're just starting your table of contents for this year's family-reunion newsletter.

2. **Set a tab stop.**

   This step is important. Follow the steps outlined in "The Tab Stops Here," earlier in this chapter. Stick the tab where you want it. For example, put a tab under the 3 on the ruler, which sticks a tab in just about the middle of the page: Click under the 3 with the mouse. This step puts a left tab stop in that position on the ruler.

3. Choose the Format⇨Tabs command.

You see the Tabs dialog box, as shown in Figure 10-2. Door number 3, Leader, is the one you need to focus on.

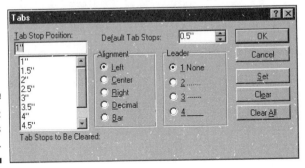

Figure 10-2:
The Tabs
dialog box.

4. Choose the style of fearless leader tab you want.

Click on the appropriate style, as presented at the beginning of this section, or press Alt+1 through Alt+4 to choose a style by using the keyboard.

5. Click the OK button or press Enter.

6. Type the text to appear before the tab stop:

Ugly baby pics from the '50s

7. Press the Tab key.

Zwoop! The toothpick cursor jumps to your tab stop and leaves a trail of, well, "stuff" in its wake. That's your dot leader (or dash leader or underline leader).

8. Type the reference, page number, or whatever.

9. Press Enter to end that line.

Setting the dot leader tabs doesn't work unless you manually stick in your own tab stops, as discussed in "The Tab Stops Here," earlier in this chapter.

You can adjust the tab stops after setting them if some of the text doesn't line up.

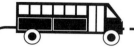

Doing it the hard way — Taking a Yellow Line Bus tour of the Paragraph dialog box

It's possible to get all your paragraph formatting done in one place, just as I'm sure that the Lord Almighty has this one control panel from which He directs the universe. And like that control panel, the Paragraph dialog box is a complex and dangerous place in which to loiter. This figure shows you what it (probably) looks like.

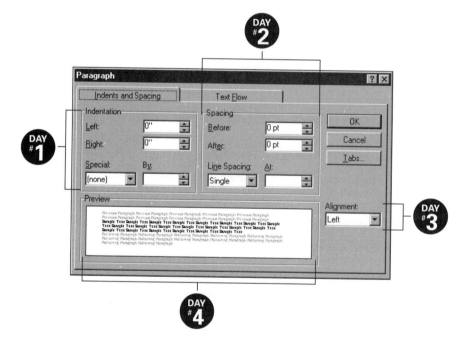

To summon the Paragraph dialog box, choose Format⇨Paragraph. It should open up with the Indents and Spacing panel on top. Another panel for the mysteries of Text Flow is underneath it. To flip back and forth between them, click on the name tab that peeks out from behind.

Most of the stuff that happens in the Paragraph dialog box is detailed earlier in this chapter, along with some quick shortcut keys that make avoiding this dialog box a must. Still, I'd be sent to Word prison and laughed at during the next Word Book Authors' Convention if I didn't take you on the whirlwind bus tour of this dialog box. We begin with the Indents and Spacing card:

Day 1 — Indentation: Where you can enter the formatting for nested paragraphs and hanging indents. Left indicates how far from the left margin your paragraph will be in inches. Right is the same thing, but from the right margin. You can choose Special to either indent or hang the first line of your paragraph. You can type values in the boxes or use the tiny up or down triangles to "spin the wheels."

Day 2 — Spacing: Hmmm, you hum. "Okay, I press Enter at the end of a *paragraph.* But how can I put extra space between paragraphs?" This is the place. Before and After allow you to stick extra lines before or after your paragraphs. If you type **.5 li** in the Before box, Word puts an extra half line before each paragraph — and the same thing for After. The Line Spacing box controls the line spacing for a paragraph; type the proper spacing value in the box or use the up or down triangles to wheel through the values.

Day 3 — Alignment: You can apply any of the following alignments to selected text or to the paragraph where the cursor is currently located: Left; Center; Right; or Justified. Each of these alignments is discussed earlier in this chapter.

Day 4 — Preview: The Preview window shows you how your paragraph will look when you click the OK button; your text changes are shown as black lines, and current text is shown in gray.

Optional walking tour (hiking boots recommended):

Click on the tab Text Flow peeping out from behind Indents and Spacing. A Text Flow panel appears, looking like the following figure. During this part of the trip, keep within sight of your trail guide (he was once named Outback Hunk of Montana, and rumor has it that he's part Sasquatch):

Trail 1 — Pagination: These pretty sophisticated commands tell Word where it is allowed to start a new paragraph. Page Break Before tells Word to start a new page before this paragraph. Keep With Next tells Word that it can't start a new page just yet. Keep Lines Together tells Word not to start a new page in the middle of the paragraph. Widow/Orphan Control keeps the last line from being stranded alone on the preceding or next page.

Trail 2 — Misfits: Suppress Line Numbers prevents Word from numbering the lines in a given paragraph, if you've ordered the rest of a document to have numbered lines. Don't Hyphenate tells Word not to hyphenate that particular paragraph when you've directed Word to hyphenate the rest of your document.

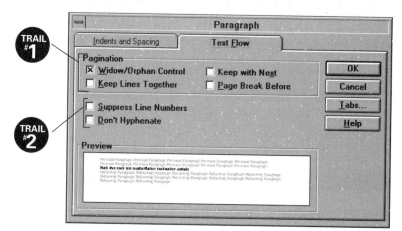

Chapter 11

Formatting Pages and Documents

- -

In This Chapter

▶ Starting a new page with a hard page break

▶ Taking a break — a section break

▶ Adjusting the margins

▶ Setting the page size

▶ Centering a page, top to bottom

▶ Choosing where to stick the page number

▶ Adding a header or footer

▶ Editing a header or footer

▶ Using footnotes

- -

At last, the formatting three-ring circus has come to this. Formatting pages and documents isn't as common as formatting characters or even formatting paragraphs. This major-league stuff affects your entire document, and it can be really handy: headers and footers, page numbers — even footnotes. This is the stuff of which professional-looking documents are made. This chapter explains it all so carefully that even we amateurs fool them.

Starting a New Page — a Hard Page Break

There are two ways to start a new page in Word:

1. **Keep pressing the Enter key until you see the row o' dots that denotes the start of a new page.**

   Needless to say, this method is tacky and wrong.

2. **Press Ctrl+Enter, the hard page break key combination.**

Ctrl+Enter inserts a tighter row of dots that also denotes the beginning of a new page, but with the added notation Page Break to remind you that it's artificial. This method is the preferred way to start a new page.

This line shows a Word hard page break:

··· Page Break···

Keep these things in mind when you're dealing with hard page breaks:

✔ The hard page break works just like a regular page break does, although you control where it lives in your document: Move the toothpick cursor to where you want the hard page and press Ctrl+Enter.

✔ Pressing Ctrl+Enter inserts a hard page-break *character* in your document. That character stays there, always creating a hard page break no matter how much you edit the text on previous pages. The first approach doesn't take into account any editing you may do on the text.

✔ You can delete a hard page break by pressing the Backspace or Delete keys. If you do this accidentally, just press Ctrl+Enter again, or you can press Ctrl+Z keys to undelete.

✔ Don't fall into the trap of using hard page breaks to adjust your page numbering. You can use *the power of the computer* to alter your page numbers without having to mess with page formatting. See "Where to Stick the Page Number," later in this chapter.

Taking a Break — a Section Break

Books have chapters and parts to break up major plot lines. Formatting has something called a *section break* that serves the same function. Word uses all kinds of different breaks: page breaks, column breaks, and section breaks, but not lunch breaks.

You can use a section break when you want to apply different types of formatting to several different parts of a document. You might want different margins to appear in different places, a banner headline, different numbers of columns, or whatever. You can accomplish these tasks by inserting a section break. It's kinda like building an island: All types of weird formatting can live on it, isolated from the rest of the document.

No, this isn't a common, everyday thing, but if you get heavily into formatting pages, you'll be thankful for it.

To insert a section break, do this:

1. **Position the toothpick cursor where you want the break to occur.**

2. **Choose the Insert⇨Break command.**

   The Break dialog box opens, as shown in Figure 11-1.

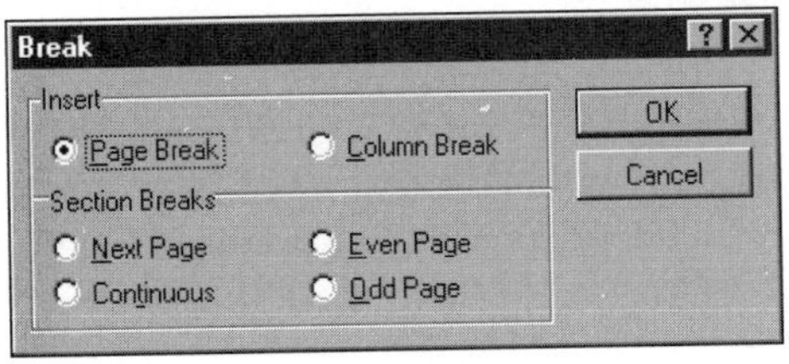

Figure 11-1:
The Break
dialog box.

> **Break** `? X`
> ┌─Insert──────────────────────────┐   ┌────────┐
> │ ⊙ Page Break   ○ Column Break │   │   OK   │
> │ ┌─Section Breaks──────────────┐ │   ├────────┤
> │ │ ○ Next Page   ○ Even Page │ │   │ Cancel │
> │ │ ○ Continuous   ○ Odd Page   │ │   └────────┘
> │ └─────────────────────────────┘ │
> └──────────────────────────────────┘

3. **Choose your break.**

   Click on Next Page if you want the new section to start on a fresh page. Choose Continuous if you want the break to happen wherever you happen to be. You use Next Page, for example, to center text on a title page (see the section "Centering a page, top to bottom" later in this chapter). Continuous is used for all other circumstances.

4. **Choose OK.**

   A double line of dots appears on-screen with the notation `End of Section` in the middle. Lo, you have your section break, and new formatting can begin.

This is a Word section break:

::End of Section::

Section breaks also provide a great way to divide a multipart document. For example, the title page can be a section; the introduction, Chapter 1, and Appendix A all can be made into sections. You can then use Word's Go To command to zoom to each section. Refer to Chapter 2 for more information on the Go To command.

Here are some tips for dealing with section breaks:

✔ You can delete a section break with the Backspace or Delete keys. If you do this accidentally, you lose any special formatting that you applied to the section. Press the Undo command, Ctrl+Z, before you do anything else.

✔ You can also use the Break dialog box to insert a Page Break, but Ctrl+Enter is much quicker; refer to the preceding section.

Adjusting the Margins

Every page has margins. This is the "air" around your document — that inch of breathing space that sets off the text from the rest of the page. Word automatically sets your margins at one inch from the right, left, top, and bottom of the page. Most English teachers and book editors want things like this because they love to scribble in margins (they even write that way on blank sheets of paper). In Word, you can adjust the margins to suit any fussy professional.

You have two basic choices when you're setting margins: from here on and change it all (from the beginning to the end).

If your document is split into two or more sections, a third choice (This Section) is available in step 5.

To change the margins, follow these steps:

1. **If you want to change "from here on," move the toothpick cursor to the place in your text where you want the new margins to start.**

   It's best to set the new margins at the top of the document, top of a page, or beginning of a paragraph (or the beginning of a new "section"). If, on the other hand, you want to change it all, it doesn't matter where you place the cursor.

2. **Choose the File⇨Page Setup command.**

   The Page Setup dialog box appears, as shown in Figure 11-2.

3. **Click on the Margins panel tab if it's not up front.**

4. **Enter the new measurements for the margins by typing new values in the appropriate boxes.**

   For example, a value of 1" in all boxes sets all margins to one inch. A value of 2.5" sets a 2 1/2-inch margin. There's no need to type the inch symbol (").

5. **Choose Whole Document or This Point Forward from the Apply To drop-down list.**

   Whole Document applies the new margins to your document. This Point Forward applies new margins from the toothpick cursor's position to the last jot or title you typed. (Or you can choose This Secton.)

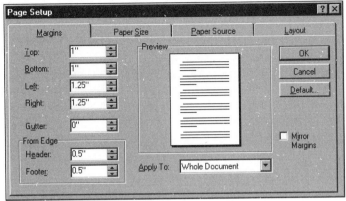

Figure 11-2:
The Page
Setup dialog
box with the
Margins
panel up
front.

6. **Choose OK.**

Your new margins appear.

Yo! Check it out! You have visual feedback on-screen regarding your new margin settings. The Preview window gives you a view of what the document will look like when the changes are finally made.

You don't have to change all the margins every time. If you want to adjust only one or a few values, leave the other items alone. Word remembers the old values and keeps using them until they're changed.

What's in the gutter? The Gutter box applies more to documents printed on two pages and intended to be bound in a book-like format. It's a *bonus margin* that appears on the left side of right-facing pages and vice versa. No need to put your mind in the gutter.

Here are some tips to keep in mind when you're setting margins:

- If you want to change the margins to a different value later and leave the current settings in place for the first part of your document, move to the place where you want new margins in your document. Start at step 1 in the preceding steps and choose This Point Forward from the Apply To drop-down list. A single document can have several margin changes, just as a single driver on the freeway will have several lane changes.

- Laser printers cannot print on the outside half inch of a piece of paper — top, bottom, left, and right. This is an absolute margin; although you can tell Word to set a margin of 0 inches right and 0 inches left, text still does not print there. Instead, choose .5 inches minimum for the left and right margins.

✔ If you want to print on three-hole paper, set the left margin to 2 or 2.5 inches. This setting allows enough room for the little holes, and it offsets the text nicely when you open up something in a three-ring notebook or binder.

✔ If your homework comes out to three pages and the teacher wants four, bring in the margins. Set the left and right margins to 1.5 inches each. Then change the line spacing to 1.5. Refer to "Changing Line Spacing" in Chapter 10. (You also can choose a larger font; check out the section on text size effects in Chapter 9.)

Setting the Page Size

Most printing takes place on a standard, 8 ½ by 11-inch sheet of paper. But Word lets you change the paper size to anything you want — from an envelope to some weird-size sheet of paper. The following steps describe how you change the paper size to the legal 8 ½ by 14-inch sheet of paper:

1. **Position the toothpick cursor at the top of your document or at the top of a page on which you want to start using the new paper size.**

2. **Choose the File⇨Page Setup command.**

   The Page Setup dialog box appears.

3. **Choose the Paper Size panel.**

   The panel is one of the little name tags peeping out on top of the dialog box. Click on it to flip the file open to its card o' controls if you don't see it. Figure 11-3 shows what it looks like.

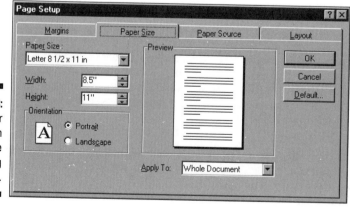

Figure 11-3:
The Paper Size panel in the Page Setup dialog box.

4. Click the Paper Size drop-down list.

It drops down.

5. Choose Legal.

It's legal.

6. Choose Whole Document or This Point Forward from the Apply To drop-down list.

Well, which do you want?

7. Choose OK.

Okay. Type away on the new size of paper.

When your document is split into two or more sections you'll see a third choice (This Section) in the preceding step 6.

Your drop-down list may not already contain the measurements for legal size — or any size paper. In that case, the drop-down list only says Customize and you have to get out the trusty old ruler and type the proper measurements in the Width and Height boxes.

This setup is also how you set up to print on that pretty, perfumed, albeit odd-sized, new stationary that you want to do your mass-mailing love letters on.

Keep an eye on the Preview window in the Page Setup dialog box. It changes to reflect the new paper size. See Chapter 23 for info on Word's Mail Merge command.

The following section tells you how to print sideways on a sheet of paper. This technique really fools the relatives into thinking that you're a word-processing genius.

If you're printing an odd-sized piece of paper, remember to load it into your printer before you start printing.

Refer to Chapter 8 for information on printing envelopes. (There's a special command for doing that; no sense in finagling a new paper size here.)

Landscape and Portrait

Word usually prints up and down on a piece of paper — which is how we're all used to reading a page. However, Word can print sideways also. In this case, the page's *orientation* is changed; rather than up-down, the paper is printed sideways. The technical "I'm an important word-processing expert" terms for the two orientations are *Portrait mode* for the up-down paper and *Landscape mode* for sideways. A portrait picture is usually taller than it is long to accommodate our faces — my immediate family excepted. Landscape is for those lovely oil paintings of seascapes or lakes and trees that are wider than they are tall — the kind Bob Ross used to paint (may he rest in peace; sniff, sniff).

To make Word print the long way on a sheet of paper — the Landscape mode — do the following:

1. **Choose File⇨Page Setup.**

   The Page Setup dialog box appears.

2. **Click on the Paper Size tab.**

   This step brings up the Paper Size panel, if it's not up there already. In the lower-left corner, you see the Orientation area (see Figure 11-3).

3. **Choose Portrait or Landscape.**

   The Sample document and the tiny icon in the Orientation area change to reflect your perspective.

4. **Click OK.**

Avoid printing standard documents in Landscape mode. Scientists and other people in white lab coats who study such things have determined that human reading speed slows drastically when people must scan a long line of text. Reserve Landscape mode for printing lists, tables, and items for which normal paper is too narrow.

Centering a page, top to bottom

Nothing makes a title nice and crisp like having it sit squat in the middle of a page. That's top-to-bottom middle as opposed to left-right middle. To achieve this feat, follow these steps:

1. **Move the toothpick cursor to the top of the page that contains the text that you want centered between the bottom and the top of the page.**

   The text should be on a page by itself — actually a section by itself. If the page that you want centered isn't the first page of the document, press Alt,I,B,N,Enter. This keystroke combination inserts the section or page break, and you see a double line on-screen (the section separator). That line marks a new page, the page that you want to center.

2. **Type the text that you want centered from top to bottom.**

   Refer to Chapter 9 for more information on formatting characters, making text big and fancy, or whatnot for your title or whatever text you want centered. If you also want the lines centered from left to right, refer to Chapter 10 for information on centering a line.

3. **Create a new section break.**

You have to mark the end of the page you want centered with a section break. Press Alt,I,B,N,Enter. This step inserts a *next page* section break: a double line of dots that marks a new page and a new section.

Press the ↑ arrow key to move back up into the section you just created.

4. Choose the File⇨Page Setup command.

The Page Setup dialog box appears.

5. Click on the tab that says Layout.

This step brings forward the Layout panel if it's not up front to begin with (see Figure 11-4). You should focus your laser beams on the lower-left corner, in the area roped in and named Vertical Alignment.

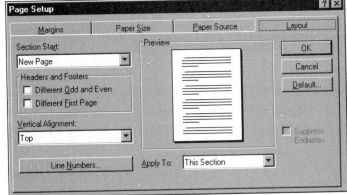

Figure 11-4:
The Layout
panel in the
Page Setup
dialog box.

6. Click the Vertical Alignment drop-down list.

7. Choose Center.

8. Click OK.

In Normal View, you get no visual feedback that you've centered a page on-screen. Choose the View⇨Page Layout command to get a sneak peak at the centered page. (You may have to Zoom out to the *whole page* to see the title centered; see Chapter 27 to learn about the Zoom command.) Choose View⇨Normal to return to Normal View.

All text on the page is centered from top to bottom with the Center Page command. It's a good idea to keep as little text on the page as possible — a title, description, and so forth.

Refer to "Taking a Break — a Section Break," earlier in this chapter, for more information on section breaks.

Where to Stick the Page Number

If your document is more than a page long, you should put page numbers on it. Word can do this for you automatically, so stop putting those forced page numbers in your document and follow these steps:

1. Choose the Insert⇨Page Numbers command.

The Page Numbers dialog box, shown in Figure 11-5, appears.

Figure 11-5:
The Page
Numbers
dialog box.

2. Where dost thou wantest thine page numbers?

From the Position drop-down list, choose Top of Page (Header) or Bottom of Page (Footer). From the Alignment drop-down list, choose Left, Center, Right, Inside, or Outside. There are different possible placements for your page numbering. Ponder this situation carefully and keep an eye on the Preview box — a slight change can alter drastically the power of your document.

3. Choose OK.

The page numbers are inserted.

You also can create page numbering by sticking the page number command in a header or footer. See "Adding a header or footer," coming up soon in this chapter. If you do end up putting the page number in a header or footer, you don't have to use the Page Numbers command.

If you want to get fancier page numbers, click the Format button in the Page Numbers dialog box. This step opens the Page Number Format dialog box. From there, you can select various ways to display the page numbers from the Number Format drop-down list — even those cute little *ii*s and *xx*s.

Starting Off with a Different Page Number

To start numbering your pages with a new page number, heed the instructions in the previous section to conjure up the Page Numbers dialog box. Then follow these steps:

1. **Click the Format button in the Page Numbers dialog box.**

   This opens the Page Number Format dialog box, shown in Figure 11-6.

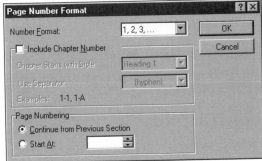

Figure 11-6:
The Page
Number
Format
dialog box.

2. **Click the Start At radio button.**

   Type the page number you want to begin with into the box. You can also press the arrows to wheel up and down. Whee!

3. **Click OK to close the Page Number Format dialog box.**

4. **Click OK to close the Page Numbers dialog box.**

You'll see the new page numbers reflected on the Status Bar's little nonsense line. Cool.

This procedure is something that you may want to do for the second, third, or later chapters in a book. By setting a new page number, the page numbers in all chapters are continuous.

The Joys of Headers and Footers

A header is not a quickly poured beer. Instead, it's text that runs along the top of every page in your document. For example, the top of each page in this book has the section name and chapter name. Those are *headers*. You can stick headers on your work, complete with a title, your name, date, page number, dirty limericks — you name it.

The *footer* is text that appears on the bottom of every page. A great footer is "Turn the page, Shirley," although better uses of footers include page numbers, a chapter or document title, and what have you. The footer is created by using exactly the same steps used to create a header.

Adding a header or footer

Headers and footers can make any document shine. You don't need to use them both; you can use just one or the other. Either way, the same command is used to add or play with them.

To add a header or footer, follow these steps:

1. Choose the View⇨Header and Footer command.

The document window changes, and you're given a sneak peek at your document's header (or footer), roped off with the title Header or Footer up there in the left corner. Also visible is the floating Header and Footer toolbar. Witness Figure 11-7 for an example.

Figure 11-7:
A sample header with the Header and Footer toolbar.

2. Click the Switch Between Header/Footer icon to choose either the Header or Footer for editing.

Click the button once to switch back and forth.

3. Enter your header or footer text.

The text can also be formatted just as though it were a separate document by using most of the tools in the Standard and Formatting toolbars as well as instructions lovingly described in Chapters 9 and 10.

4. Use the buttons in the Header and Footer toolbar for special items.

Hover the mouse pointer over each one to see a brief explanation of its function (just like in the big toolbars!). These buttons are described in detail in the sidebar "The Header and Footer Toolbar unbuttoned."

5. Click the Close button when you are done.

You're back in your document. The header and/or footer is/are there, but you can't see it/them until you print or choose the Print Preview command from the File menu (or use the Preview button on the Standard toolbar) or if you view your document in Page Layout mode.

You can put anything in a header or footer that you can put in a document, including graphics (see Figure 11-7). This capability is especially useful if you want a logo to appear on each page. See Chapter 24 for a discussion of inserting graphics.

Here are some tips for adding headers or footers:

- If you want to insert the page number in the header or footer, put the toothpick cursor where you want it to appear and press the Page Numbers button on the Header and Footer toolbar. The number *1* appears in the header text, but it is replaced by the current page number when the document is printed.

- You probably will want to put some text in front of the page number because a number sitting all by itself tends to get lonely. You can get real creative and type the word **Page** and a space before you click the # button or you can come up with some interesting text on your own.

- To insert the current date or time into the header or footer, click the Date or Time buttons on the Header and Footer toolbar.

- To see your header or footer displayed on-screen, choose View⇨Page Layout. In Page Layout mode, you can see your header or footer, but they appear "washed out" — in gray text and not very appealing. Choose View⇨Normal to return to the normal way you look at Word.

You can have two headers, odd and even, running on different pages — and the same thing with footers. From the Header and Footer toolbar, click the Page Setup button. The Page Setup dialog box opens. On the Layout panel, look in the Headers and Footers area and check Different Odd and Even. Click OK. Create an odd and an even header (or footer) in turn, according to the preceding steps, and they print differently on odd and even pages. Neat-o.

To prevent the header or footer from appearing on the first page of text, which usually is the title page, click the Page Setup button on the Header and Footer toolbar. Then check Different First Page and click OK. In your document, move to the first page header (it says "First Page Header") and leave it blank. This procedure places an empty header on the first page; the header appears on all the other pages as ordered. You also can use this option to place a different header on the first page — a graphic, for example. See Chapter 24 to learn about placing graphics in a document.

A header is a section-long thing. You can change parts of a header, such as a chapter name or number, from section to section, without changing other parts of the header, like the page number. Refer to the section "Taking a Break — a Section Break," earlier in this chapter, for more information on sections.

I've always hated all that fuzz on top of a stein of beer. But recently I was in Germany and had a beer connoisseur tell me that it is an imperative part of a good beer. Hmm. Of course, this from a nation where they drink their beer *warm.* Yech.

Editing a header or footer

To edit a header or footer you have already created, follow these steps:

1. **Go to the page that has the header or footer you want to edit.**

   If you want to change the odd-page header, go to an odd page; if you want to edit the first-page footer, go to the first page.

2. **Choose View⇨Header and Footer.**

   Or press the Alt,V,H key combination. The Header and Footer screen appears.

3. **If necessary, click the Switch Between Header/Footer button to move to the header or footer you want to edit.**

4. **Make any changes or corrections.**

   Do this as you would edit any text on-screen.

5. **Choose Close when you're done.**

Editing a header or footer changes how it looks for your entire document. You don't have to move the cursor to the tippy-top of your document before editing.

You also can edit a header or footer from Page Layout view: Choose View⇨Page Layout or click the Page Layout button. This command adjusts the way Word displays your document and exposes the thinly veiled text sequestered in your headers or footers. If you double-click the mouse pointer on the grayed header or footer text, the magical window of header and footer editing opportunity reopens.

The Header and Footer Toolbar unbuttoned

One little, two little, ten little buttons on the Header and Footer floating palette of button joy. This table shows the official picture, title, and function for each of them:

Button	Official name	Purpose in life
	Switch Between Header/Footer	Like the name says
	Show Previous	View previous header or footer
	Show Next	View next header or footer
	Same as Previous	Copy previous header or footer to this header
	Page Number	Insert page number into the header or footer
	Date	Insert current date into header or footer
	Time	Insert current time into header or footer
	Page Setup	Grant you access to Word's Page Layout dialog box
	Show/Hide Document Text	Allow you to view the main document's text along with the header or footer
Close	Close	Return you to your document and close the Header and Footer screen

The View Next, View Previous, and Same as Previous buttons are necessary because Word allows you to have several different headers and footers in the same document. Want a new header on page 17? Create it. Actually, you can have dozens of different headers and footers (though that's kind of impractical). The View Next, View Previous, and Same as Previous buttons are what let you switch between them.

Using Footnotes

Some folks seem to think that footnotes are pretty advanced stuff. Pooh! A lot of people need them in their documents. I mean, academics use them all the time and look how many people consider them "experts."

Rather than create footnotes obtusely, follow these handy steps:

1. Position the toothpick cursor in your document where you want the footnote to be referenced.

The tiny number that refers to the footnote goes here. For example[1].

2. Choose the Insert➪Footnote command.

You see the Footnote and Endnote dialog box. It's kind of boring, so I'm not putting a figure of it in this book.

If this is the first footnote for a document, you have to decide where you want your footnotes placed. Choose Options from the Footnote dialog box, and you see the Footnote Options dialog box (and I'm not showing it either). Choose where you want the footnotes to appear: on the bottom of the page where the footnote is referenced or beneath the text that contains the reference. (Endnotes — the other panel — can be placed at the end of the current section or at the end of the document.) After this selection is made, you don't have to open this dialog box again, unless you change your mind. Click OK.

3. If you want Word to number footnotes for you (and who wouldn't?), leave AutoNumber selected and then click OK.

The toothpick cursor magically appears in the subbottom of your page.

4. Type your footnote.

You can place in a footnote anything you can place in a document — charts, graphs, pictures, even text.

5. Choose Close, and you have done it.

Figure 11-8 shows what a footnote might look like. Keep in mind that no one reads footnotes, so you can usually stick anything down there you want.

This list gives you some footnoting tips:

✔ To delete a footnote, highlight the footnote's number in your document and press the Delete key. Word magically renumbers any remaining footnotes for you.

---

[1]Made you look!

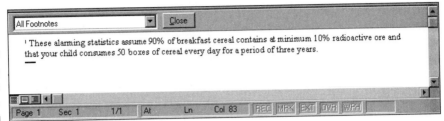

Figure 11-8:
A sample
footnote.

All Footnotes   Close

¹ These alarming statistics assume 90% of breakfast cereal contains at minimum 10% radioactive ore and that your child consumes 50 boxes of cereal every day for a period of three years.

Page 1   Sec 1   1/1   At   Ln   Col 83   REC   MRK   EXT   OVR   WPH

✔ To view or edit footnotes, choose View➪Footnotes.

✔ To quick-edit a footnote, double-click on the footnote number on the page. The footnote text edit area opens.

✔ You can actually insert graphics into a footnote, just as you can a header or footer. Think how embarrassed those academics will be, seething with jealousy at your wondrously creative, graphical footnotes! Such information on inserting graphics into your document can be found in Chapter 24, which tells you almost all you care to know about graphics.

If you decide that some little fact would be better footnoted from another place in the text, you can cut (Ctrl+X), copy (Ctrl+C), and paste (Ctrl+V) footnotes easier even than normal text! Just block the number that denotes the footnote, move it to its new home, and — voilà — Word moves the rest. Better than U-Haul! (For step-by-step instructions on using Cut, Copy, and Paste, refer to "The Kindergarten Keys: Cut, Copy, and Paste" in Chapter 2.)

Chapter 12

Tables and Basic DTP Stuff

*Y*ou can spice up your text with bold and italics and maybe even some large characters when your document doesn't run as long as you like. Paragraph formatting and page formatting add garlic to your document salad (just a touch — not enough to open your mouth, say "Hi," and watch flowers wilt, grown men cry, and women faint). What more can you do? Well, if you're really the daring type, you can pump up your document with fancy tables and formatting that's just one Cicero beneath the official realm of Desktop Publishing. Oh, we've come a long way from the days of word processing with moveable type.

Cobbling Tables Together

A table is this thing with four legs on which you set things — but not your elbows when Grandma is watching. In Word, a *table* is a list of items with several rows all lined up in neat little columns. In the primitive days, you made tables happen by using the Tab key and your handy frustration tool. Face it: Making things align can be maddening. Even in a word processor. Even if you think that you know what you're doing.

Coming to your rescue, of course, is Word. "It's Table Man, Ma, and he's here to rescue us!" Word has an able Table command. It lets you create this prisonlike grid of rows and columns. Into each cubbyhole, or *cell,* you can type information or store society's miscreants, and everything is aligned nice and neat and suitable for framing. The printed result looks very impressive, and if you do things right, your table is even sturdy enough to eat off.

Creating a table (the traditional, boring way)

To create a table in your document, follow these steps:

1. **Place the toothpick cursor on the spot in the text where you want the table.**

   The table is created and inserted into your text (like pasting in a block — a *cell block*). You fill in the table *after* you create it.

2. **Choose the Table➪Insert Table command.**

   Yes, Word has its own Table menu. How handy. Choosing the Insert Table command from that menu opens the Insert Table dialog box, as shown in Figure 12-1.

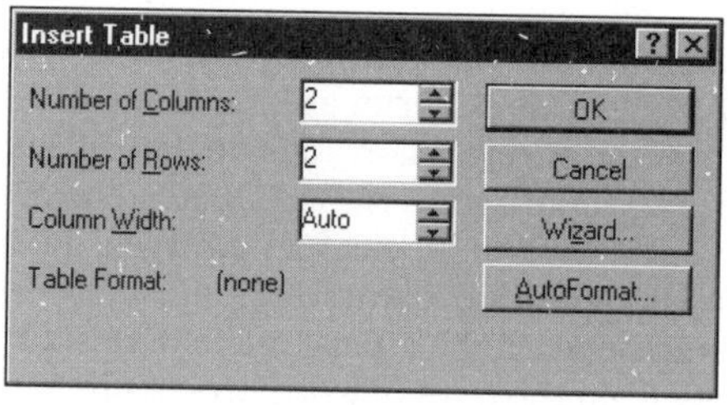

Figure 12-1: The Insert Table dialog box.

3. **Enter the number of columns into the first box.**

   For example, enter **3**. You have three columns going across.

4. **Press the Tab key.**

   The cursor moves to the next box.

5. **Enter the number of rows into the second box.**

   For example, enter **5**. You have five rows, marching down.

   Three columns? Five rows? Who knows? Accuracy isn't a big issue at this stage; you can change your table after it's created if you goof up. (I do this all the time.)

6. **Click OK to leave the Insert Table mini-dialog boxlet.**

   Welcome to prison! After you tell Word how many rows and columns to make, it builds you a table and shows it to you on-screen (something like Figure 12-2, but not filled in).

   Tables look like spreadsheets and smell like spreadsheets, and if I weren't afraid of electrocuting myself, I'd tell you whether they taste like spreadsheets. You're still in Word, however.

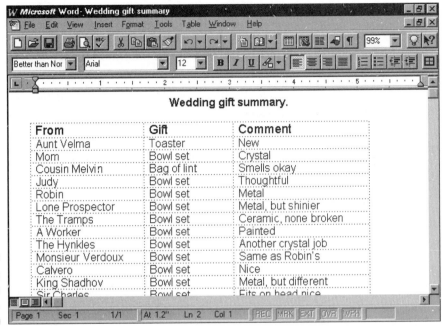

Figure 12-2:
A table is
born.

7. Fill in the table.

Use crayons on your screen or, better still, see the next section.

If you can't see your table, choose Table⇨Gridlines to display the cell borders.

Incidentally, the grid you see around your table doesn't print. If you want to have lines in your table, see Chapter 26 for information on adding borders to your text.

You also can build a table from the toolbar. See the very next section (though I advise doing it as described here until you feel comfortable with your table-creation skills).

Use a table in your document whenever you have information that has to be organized in rows and columns. This feature works much better than using the Tab key because adjusting the table's rows and columns is easier than fussing with tab stops.

Be sure that at least one line of text, or a blank line if the table starts off a new section, is in front of any table. This technique gives you a place to put the cursor if you ever want to put stuff before the table in your document.

You can always add or delete columns and rows to your table after you create it. See "Changing a Table," later in this chapter.

The table may have an ugly lined border around it and between the cells. You can change this feature, as covered in "Changing a Table."

For some Cheater McGee tips on making tables, see Chapter 15, "Templates and Wizards."

Alas, Word does not have a handy Chair command. (Although rumor has it that they are working on barstools.)

Creating a table (the unconventional way)

Here's an easier way to create a table in your document, providing you've already suffered through the steps listed in the preceded section and are ready for a more mousy alternative:

1. **Place the toothpick cursor on the spot in the text where you want your table.**

   This step marks the spot where the table's prisonlike skeleton will appear.

2. **Click the Table button on the Standard toolbar.**

   A grid drops down, looking a lot like the maze of questions that daunts *Jeopardy* players but looking a lot more like Figure 12-3. Using this grid is how you can graphically set your table's dimensions with the mouse.

Figure 12-3:
Creating the table is possible with your mouse and this grid.

3 x 4 Table

3. **Use the mouse to set the table's size.**

   Drag down and to the right to create a table with a given number of rows and columns. The precise values appear at the bottom of the grid.

4. **Release the mouse.**

   Your table is inserted into the document, right at the perfect size.

Refer to the previous sections for any tips worth noting.

Putting stuff in a table

An empty table sits in your document. But before you break out the MinWax and clean it up, why not set the table?

The table is divided into rows and columns. Where they meet is called a *cell* — just like they have in prison but without the TV and metal toilet. Your job is to fill in the various cells with text, graphics, or whatever. Here are some pointers:

- ✔ Press the Tab key to move from cell to cell. Pressing the Enter key just puts a new paragraph of text in the same cell. (Each cell is like its own little document.)

- ✔ The Shift+Tab combination moves you backward between the cells.

  If you press the Tab key in the last bottom right cell, a new row of cells is added.

- ✔ If you press Shift+Enter, you can start writing text on a new line without starting a new paragraph. (Shift+Enter is the new line command which, unlike the Enter key alone, doesn't really start a new paragraph. Weird, huh?)

- ✔ You can press the cursor keys to move from cell to cell as well (how swell). But if there is text in the cell, pressing the cursor keys makes the toothpick cursor dawdle through the words. After all, you can still use the cursor keys to edit text in the cells. (It's best to use the Tab key to move from cell to cell.)

- ✔ Text-formatting commands also work in the cells. You can boldface, underline, italicize, center, flush left, and so on. Refer to Chapter 9 and Chapter 10 for the details. The formatting affects the text in only one cell at a time — or in the cells that you collectively mark as a block.

- ✔ You can apply styles to text in a table. See Chapter 14 for the details.

- ✔ To format a row or column all at once, you have to select it first.

- ✔ To utterly remove the table from your document, highlight the whole darn thing as a block and then choose Table⇨Delete Rows. The table is blown to smithereens.

- ✔ To erase a cell's contents in a table, mark it as a block and press the Delete key.

Changing a Table

Suppose that you create a card table but really need a dining room table — or one of those long dual-time-zone tables rich people eat at — or, because you are participating in a back-to-nature movement, no table at all. You have decided to simply squat down on your haunches around the fire when you eat. (A granola friend once told me that this method was really great for your lower back, but after about five minutes, I lost all feeling in my legs.) Anyway, whatever you decide, it can all be changed and adjusted after the table has been created.

Adding and deleting rows and columns

To add rows to your table, follow these steps:

1. Stick the toothpick cursor in the row above the spot where you want your new row.

2. Choose the Table⇨Insert Rows command.

Thud! The government of the People's Democratic Republic of Word is proud to add a brand-new story to existing workers' apartment complex.

3. Repeat steps 1 and 2 to add as many rows as you want.

Rather than use the Insert Rows command, you can also click the Table button on the Standard toolbar to instantly insert a new row of cells into your table. Indeed, while the toothpick cursor is hovering inside a table, that button magically transmogrifies into the Insert Rows button.

To delete rows from your table, follow these steps:

1. Highlight the row that you want to delete.

Move the cursor into the row and choose Table⇨Select Row.

2. Choose the Table⇨Delete Rows command.

3. Repeat steps 1 and 2 to blast away as many rows as you want.

You also can select rows by moving the mouse cursor into the left margin until it changes its shape to a nor'easterly arrow. Point the arrow at the row and click the mouse button. You can select multiple rows by dragging the mouse up or down.

To add columns to your table, follow these steps:

1. **Move the toothpick cursor into the column to the left of the spot where you want the new one to be added.**

2. **Choose Table⇨Select Column.**

3. **Choose the Table⇨Insert Columns command.**

4. **Repeat step 3 to add as many columns as you want.**

Doubtless you need to adjust the width of the table's columns after adding new columns. See the following section, "Adjusting the column width," for the details.

To delete columns from your table, follow these steps:

1. **Highlight the column that you want to delete.**

   Move the toothpick cursor to that column.

2. **Pluck out Table⇨Select Column from the menu.**

3. **Choose the Table⇨Delete Columns command.**

4. **Repeat step 3 to blast away as many columns as you want.**

Here are some things to keep in mind about rows and columns:

✔ You also can select columns by moving the mouse cursor above the column until it changes shape, to a down-pointing arrow. Point the arrow at the row and click the left mouse button. You can select multiple columns by dragging the mouse across them.

✔ New rows are inserted *below* the current row in a table, which is the highlighted row or the one that the toothpick cursor is in.

✔ New columns are inserted *to the right* of the current column in a table.

Adjusting the column width

Columns, like my waistline, tend to get fatter and, unlike my waistline, thinner too. Fortunately, changing the width of a column in Word is a heck of a lot easier than going on a diet.

To adjust the width of a column, follow these steps:

1. **Put the toothpick cursor anywhere in the table that you want to change.**

   Anywhere.

2. **Choose the Table➪Cell Height and Width command.**

   This step opens the cute little Cell Height and Width dialog box, shown in Figure 12-4.

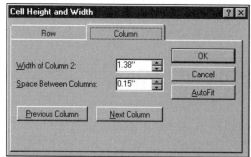

Figure 12-4:
The Cell Height and Width dialog box.

3. **Click on the tab for Column.**

   Or press C. This step brings forth the Column panel (as shown in Figure 12-4).

4. **Enter the new width measurement for the column.**

   The width is measured in inches. So if you want a thinner column, enter a smaller number than the one already in the box. Larger numbers make the columns wider, but keep in mind that a fat table — a gross concept unto itself — will probably not all fit on the page.

5. **If you want to change the following or preceding column as well, press the Next Column or Previous Column button.**

6. **Click OK when you're done.**

If you want to make several, or all, of the columns the same width, select them before you open the Column Width dialog box. Any changes you make apply to all the selected columns.

It's easier to change the width of columns by using the mouse — lots easier because you can see what is going on (like being thin enough to see your feet, I am told). Place the mouse cursor on the border between columns, and it changes its shape into something that looks like a railroad track with arrows pointing east and west. Hold down the left mouse button and drag the column border to a new size.

If you double-click the mouse when it's shaped like the railroad track with arrows, all the columns in your table line up to be exactly the width of the widest item in that column.

If you look up at the ruler when the toothpick cursor is in the table, you see that each column is given its own miniruler. You can adjust the column width by using the mouse and the tiny washboard do-jobbie. When you hover the mouse over the washboard, it changes to a left-right pointing arrow. Drag the washboard left or right to change the size of a column.

Doing the One-, Two-, Three-, Four-Column March

Columns — especially those you can see right on your screen — are one of those features all the magazines, gurus, and other pseudopundits demanded for their word processors. Do we need them? No. Can Word do them? Yes. Do you want to mess with this? Sure, why not? It will give you something to do while the electric chair recharges.

Before I divulge my Word column secrets, here's a healthy bit of advice: The best way to make columns is in a desktop publishing package, such as PageMaker, QuarkXPress, or any of the other fine products geared to such tasks. Those programs are designed for playing with text and making columns much easier to use than Word does (although figuring out the instructions is like playing an eternal chess match with a guy who wears a size 12 hat). In Word, columns remain more of a curiosity than anything you or I want to spend more than 15 minutes of our time on.

To start columns in your document, follow these next steps. If your text has already been written, Word puts it all in column format. Otherwise, any new text you create is placed in columns automagically.

1. **Move the toothpick cursor to where you want the columns to start.**

2. **Choose the Format⇨Columns command.**

   The Columns dialog box opens, as shown in Figure 12-5.

3. **Enter the number of columns that you want.**

   Or click one of the illustrated, ready-to-wear buttons. (Two columns is sufficient enough to impress anyone. More columns make your text skinnier and may be harder to read.)

4. **If you want a pretty line between the columns of text, check the Line Between box.**

   It says Line Between, not Pretty Line Between (though it should).

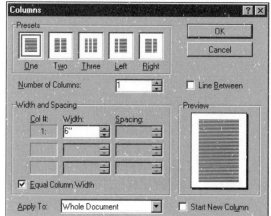

Figure 12-5:
The
Columns
dialog box.

5. **If you want to start a new column right from where you are, check the Start New Column box.**

   This step tells Word to put a column break in the document.

6. **Open the Apply To drop-down list and choose to apply the columns to the whole document or just from now on (This Point Forward).**

7. **Choose OK.**

   Okay!

Word shows you your columns right there on-screen. That's at least $15 of the purchase price right there!

 You also can use the Columns tool. Click the tool, and a baby box of columns appears. Click and drag the mouse to indicate how many text columns you want. When you release the mouse button, the columns appear.

The space between columns is called the *gutter*. Unless you have a bunch of columns or a lot of space to fill, it is best to leave this setting at .5" — half an inch. This amount of white space is pleasing to the eye without being too much of a good thing.

Editing text in columns is a pain. The cursor seems to hop all over the place and take an eternity to move from one column to another. I'm just complaining here because I'm bored and fresh out of rainy-day, popsicle-stick projects.

Using the mouse to poke the cursor to a new spot on a column seems to work nicely.

To get rid of columns, go back and change the number of columns to one. Neat, huh? (Or click the Undo tool or press the Undo shortcut, Ctrl+Z.)

The three-column text format works nicely on landscape paper. This method is how most brochures are created. Refer to Chapter 11 for information on selecting landscape paper.

All the text and paragraph formatting mentioned in this part of the book also apply to text and paragraphs in columns. The difference is that your column margins — not the page margins — now mark the left and right sides of your text for paragraph formatting.

Chapter 13
The Joys of AutoText

Hobart X. Zlotnik loves his name but hates to type it. It's not his fault. Grandma Boswell's maiden name was Xavier. And the guy who laid out the keys on a typewriter, he was mad and typed with only two fingers anyway. So poor Hobart always has to type his name carefully and tends to — no matter how hard he tries — fumble over those frustrating X and Z keys.

How would you like to be Hobart? (It's okay — he's good-looking and makes tons of money.) Worse, how would you like to type that name a gazillion times over your life? Wouldn't it be easier to type, say, **Ho**, and have the rest of that massive moniker magically appear, thanks to your computer? You bet it would! And wouldn't it be nice if you could type **bye**, for example, and have Word automatically zip in your signature block at the end of a letter? Yup. It's all possible in Word, thanks to the miraculous (meaning that it's miraculous they included something to make it easier) *AutoText* command.

The Tao of AutoText (Required Reading If You Haven't a Clue)

AutoText is a shortcut. Word automatically types some text when you give it only a teensy-tiny hint of what you want. It's like expanding a balloon but without the huffing and puffing. You type **balloon**, tap Word's AutoText magic wand, and the word *balloon* is expanded into something like "a bag of stretchy stuff filled with hot air. . . ."

The idea behind AutoText is this: To make the typing job easier, Word lets you type shortcuts that can be expanded into longer text, thanks to AutoText. That's all it is. That, and being incredibly handy when you have the same thing — or something complex — to type again and again.

This list shows you some tips for using AutoText:

- ✔ You must create an AutoText *entry* before you can use the AutoText command. The entry is usually text you've typed in your document. That text is assigned a shortcut by using the Edit⇨AutoText command. The details are outlined in the following section.

- ✔ AutoText entries become a part of the document template. See Chapter 15 for more information on document templates.

- ✔ AutoText can store more than text. You can use AutoText to automatically bring pictures and all sorts of graphical mayhem into a document with a flick of your wrist.

Creating an AutoText Entry

To create an AutoText entry, follow these steps:

1. Type some text you want to use as an AutoText entry.

For example, type your name.

2. Mark the text as a block.

Refer to Chapter 6 for the full details on marking a block of text. Keep in mind that all the text you mark is included in the AutoText entry. This means don't include any extra spaces or periods unless you want them, really want them.

3. Choose <u>E</u>dit⇨AutoTe<u>x</u>t.

The AutoText dialog box opens, as shown in Figure 13-1. You can see the text you selected (at least some of it) in the bottom part of the dialog box.

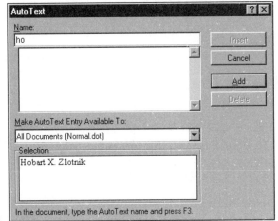

Figure 13-1:
The
AutoText
dialog box.

4. Give the AutoText entry a name.

Type the shortcut name, which can be very short, in the AutoText <u>N</u>ame box. For example, our friend Hobart would have highlighted his full name in the document, so he can type the letters **ho** in the dialog box.

5. Click the <u>A</u>dd button.

You're done. The AutoText entry is now ready to be used, which is covered in the following section.

The shortcut word you type can be in upper- or lowercase. I usually keep everything in lowercase.

When you're done working on your document, Word asks whether you want to save the document and template changes; answer <u>Y</u>es to keep this AutoText entry you just created.

Using AutoText Entries

To put an AutoText entry in a document, follow these steps:

1. **Put the toothpick cursor where you want the AutoText entry to be placed.**

2. **Type the shortcut word.**

   Hobart would type the letters **ho**. That's all — no space or period after it. Suppose that your AutoText entry for your name, address, and city is called *me*. You type **me** and then . . .

3. **Press the F3 key.**

   The AutoText entry is slapped into the document and replaces the shortcut word. So *ho* becomes his full, obnoxious name.

This list shows you some tips for making AutoText entries:

- ✔ You also can choose and insert the AutoText entry by opening the AutoText dialog box (Edit⇨Text), highlighting your bit of text, and clicking the Insert button.

- ✔ If the toothpick cursor is off by a little bit, Word complains that it doesn't recognize the AutoText entry. If you're sure that you've done everything right, choose Edit⇨AutoText and look up your AutoText entry to verify.

Editing AutoText Entries

Changing the contents or appearance of an AutoText entry isn't difficult. You open the AutoText dialog box (Edit⇨AutoText), zero in on the desired entry, change it, and save the changed entry with the same name.

Suppose that you create an AutoText entry (*me*) that has your name and address. And though you hate messing with Word, one day you succumb to the idea of moving. You must update your *me* entry to reflect your new location. Here's how it's done:

1. **Put the toothpick cursor where you want the glossary entry to be placed.**

   You need to "go through the motions" here to make the operation run a bit smoother. Yes, this is a shortcut not sanctioned in the manual. (But then again, that's why you're reading this book.)

2. **Type the shortcut word.**

   Do this just as though you were inserting the entry.

3. Press the F3 key.

The AutoText entry is inserted into the document, at the place where the toothpick cursor is, to replace the shortcut word.

4. Edit.

Make any changes you want to the AutoText entry just pasted into your document (type your new address, for example). When you're done, you resave it by using the same name. The net effect here is that the original entry is changed, but the name is kept the same (to protect the guilty).

5. Mark as a block on-screen the text you want included as the AutoText entry.

6. Choose Edit⇨AutoText.

7. Click the existing AutoText name.

8. Click the Add button.

A dialog box opens and asks whether you want to redefine the AutoText entry.

9. Click Yes.

You're done. The entry has been edited in an underhanded but perfectly legal manner.

Deleting AutoText Entries

Nothing stays the same forever. Hobart flew to Brazil and was captured by a tribe of Amazons. He married their leader, Oota, and was forced to change his last name. And his first name. And he could never use a computer again. Guess it's okay to remove him from AutoText.

To delete an AutoText entry, follow these steps:

1. Choose Edit⇨AutoText.

The AutoText dialog box opens and lists all glossary entries.

2. Click on the name of the entry you want to delete.

Bye ho!

3. Click the Delete button.

The AutoText entry's name is removed from the list.

4. Click Close.

Actually, I hear that Hobart is quite happy now.

Chapter 14

Formatting with Style

. . . .

. . . .

*W*ant to stand out from the crowd? Then do what I do: Eat massive quantities of garlic. Nothing makes you stand alone like that. When you're word processing, however, garlic won't help much (unless you buy garlic paper — refer to a funky former-hippie neighborhood in your town for a shop that carries the stuff). Instead, you can stand out by using Word's Style command.

No matter how pretty your undies are, style — in Word anyway — is not what you wear or even how you wear it. A style is a series of formatting instructions — bold, centered, sideways — that are named and stored for future use. Suppose that you have a series of paragraphs that you want indented in bold tiny type with a box drawn around each paragraph — oh, and an extra line placed at the end of each paragraph. You can create a style that slaps on all of these formats with a single keystroke. Styles may be advanced stuff, but they certainly can save time.

Using the Style Command

Styles bring together character and paragraph formatting under one roof — or in one dialog box, which is the case with Word. That one roof is found in the Format menu: the Style command. When you choose Format⇨Style, you see the Style dialog box, shown in Figure 14-1.

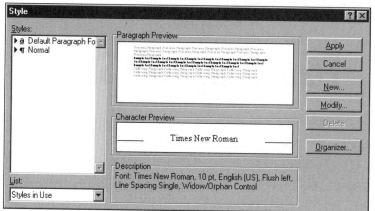

Figure 14-1:
The Style
dialog box.

Three items are worth noting in the Style dialog box: Styles, Description, and the preview windows.

The Styles scrolling list displays easy-to-remember names assigned to each style. Word always starts with the Normal style, which is plain boring text on-screen. You can use the Styles list to select a new style for your document or just to see what's available.

The Description area, near the bottom center of the dialog box, is the technical mumbo jumbo description of the style. For example, the description area may say bold, list tab stops, or mention fonts and such. No need to rest your weary eyes here for long.

There are also two preview windows to show style effects on both paragraph and character formatting.

✔ You can use Word without ever messing with styles. Only if you want to get truly fancy should you ever bother with this stuff. (Refer to Chapter 16 on AutoFormat if you're truly lazy and really don't care.)

✔ Styles are combinations of character and paragraph and other formatting, all saved under an easy-to-remember name.

✔ The idea behind a style is that you don't have to keep selecting font (character) and paragraph formatting while you're working on your document. For example, the style for this bulleted list is saved under the name **Indent**. I formatted the main text preceding this list under the style named **Body**. That way I can write this text without having to constantly mess with the font and character dialog boxes. I just say "Gimme the Body style" and Word willfully obeys.

✔ The Normal style is Word's standard style, the one that always appears when you open a new document. Yeah, it's pretty plain and ugly, but you can add your own styles to make your text fairly fancy if you like.

✔ The Style list actually shows two types of styles. Styles with a paragraph marker (¶) by them control both font and paragraph formatting. Styles with an underlined A (<u>a</u>) affect only font (character) formatting. Refer to "Creating a character-only style" for the details.

✔ Use the <u>L</u>ist drop down box to see some or all of the styles you have available. When Styles in Use is displayed, you'll only see those styles that belong to your current document (as in Figure 14-1). If you choose All Styles from the list, you'll see tons and tons of styles, almost to the point of going mad.

✔ To apply the various styles to your document, select the style name from the Style dialog box.

✔ An easier way to select a style is to grab its name from the first drop-down box on the ribbon — the box that typically says *Normal*. That list contains all the styles associated with your document (those that you create yourself or that come prepackaged with Word).

✔ The new style applies to the paragraph that the toothpick cursor is in or any block you select on-screen.

✔ For more information on font or character formatting, refer to Chapter 9.

✔ Refer to Chapter 10 for the details on paragraph formatting.

✔ The standard styles Word provides for your new documents are Normal and the Default Paragraph Font style. The Normal style is Times New Roman text at 10 points (kinda small), plus no other fancy features.

✔ If you mess with outlines, Word also tosses in the Heading 1, Heading 2, and Heading 3 styles. These are all blocky fonts that exemplify the same lack of imagination as the Normal style. See Chapter 17 for more information on outlines.

Creating a new style

New styles are easy to create. Just follow these loosely outlined steps:

1. Type a paragraph of text.

   It doesn't have to be a whole paragraph; a single line will do. Just remember to press Enter at the end of the line, which makes Word believe you typed an entire paragraph.

2. Mark your paragraph as a block.

3. Select the character formatting that you want for your style.

The character formatting will be applied to the block. Select a font and select a point size to make the text big or little.

Run wildly through Chapter 9 for more information on character formatting, but here's an important word of advice: Stick to fonts and sizes; avoid bold, italics, or underline unless you want them applied to all of your text. (Styles are broad things; only individual words are given bold, underline, and similar character formats.)

4. Select the paragraph formatting for your style.

With the block still highlighted, use the information presented in Chapter 10 to format the paragraph. Indent it, center it, or apply whatever formatting you want to apply to your style.

5. Press Ctrl+Shift+S.

This key combination activates the <u>S</u>tyle command. Actually, it highlights the Style drop-down box on the ribbon — the one that usually says Normal.

6. Type in a name for your style.

A brief, descriptive, one-word title will do nicely. For example, if you create an indented paragraph that you want to use to list things, name the style **List.** Or if you created a special musical style, name it **Liszt.**

7. Press Enter.

The style is added to Word's repertoire of styles for your document.

✔ To use the style — to *apply* it to other paragraphs in your document — refer to "Using a style," later in this chapter.

✔ Give your style a name that is descriptive of the style's function. Names like Indented List or Table Body Text are great because it's easy to remember what they do. Names like Ira or Wangdoodle are somewhat less desirable.

✔ The styles that you create are only available to the document in which they're created.

✔ If you create scads of styles you love and want to use them for several documents, then you need to create what's called a *template*. This procedure is covered in Chapter 15 in "Creating a Document Template to Store Your Styles."

✔ You also can create a style by using the Style dialog box, though this method requires more mental work than doing it the way I've outlined above. Choose Format⇨Style. Click on the New button. The New Style dialog box opens. Click on the Format button to see a menu that allows you to play with the Font, Paragraph, Tabs, and much more. Click OK after setting the Font, Paragraph, or whatever, and then click in the Name box in the New Style dialog box to give your style a name. Click OK and then the Close button to return to your document.

Creating a character-only style

You'll notice that some styles listed in the Style list are marked with an under-lined A, like this: a. That moniker flags character-only styles. What they do is affect only the font and not the paragraph formatting. So if you have a centered block of text and only want to change the font to big, ugly text, you can do so by selecting the Big Ugly character-only style, which leaves the paragraph format-ting alone.

To create a character-only style, follow these steps:

1. Choose Format⇨Style.

The Style dialog box appears (see Figure 14-1).

2. Click on the New... button.

The New Style dialog box appears (see Figure 14-2). This dialog box allows you to create a new style — familiar turf if you've already done it.

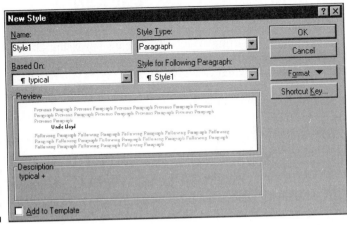

Figure 14-2:
The New
Style dialog
box.

3. In the Name box, type in a name for the style.

Be clever. If, for example, the character style applies small caps in a stocky font, name it **Stubby**.

4. In the Style Type drop-down list, select Character.

This selection gears everything in the New Style dialog box to accept only character and font-related formatting stuff.

5. Use the Format button to select the font formats that you want.

Only two options are available, Font and Language. Forget Language. Font brings up the Font dialog box, where you can set the various character attributes — similar to what I cover in Chapter 9 of this book.

6. Click OK when you're done defining the character style.

7. Click the Close button in the Style dialog box.

And you're done.

✔ Character style names appear with an underlined A (a) by them in the Style list.

✔ The special character styles don't affect any paragraph formatting. Selecting a character style only changes the font, style, size, underlining, bold, and so on.

✔ Also refer to "Stealing Character Formatting," later in this chapter, for a shortcut method of applying font formats.

Giving your style a shortcut key

Styles allow you the advantage of quickly formatting a paragraph of text. Style shortcut keys make formatting even better because pressing Alt+Shift+B to get at the Body style is often faster than messing with the Style drop-down list or dialog box — especially when you have a gob of styles you're messing with.

To give your style a name, follow these steps:

1. Choose Format⇨Style.

Style dialog box, come on down!

2. Select a style for which you want a shortcut key.

Highlight that style in the list by clicking on it once with the mouse.

3. **Click on the <u>M</u>odify button.**

   The Modify Style dialog box appears.

4. **Click on the Shortcut <u>K</u>ey button.**

   A cryptic Customize dialog box appears. Don't waste any time trying to explore here. Just move on to step 5.

5. **Press your Shortcut key combination.**

   It's best to use Ctrl+Shift+letter or Alt+Shift+letter or Ctrl+Alt+letter key combinations, where "letter" is a letter key on the keyboard. For example, press Ctrl+Alt+B for your Body style shortcut key.

   You'll notice that the key combination you press appears in the Press <u>N</u>ew Shortcut Key box (see the middle left side of the dialog box). If you make a mistake, press the Backspace key to erase.

6. **Check to see that the combination isn't already in use.**

   For example, Word uses Ctrl+B as the Bold character formatting shortcut key. This key combination appears under the heading `Currently As-signed To`, which shows up under the Press <u>N</u>ew Shortcut Key box. Keep an eye on that box! If something else uses the shortcut key, press the Backspace key and go back to step 5.

   If the key isn't used by anything, you'll see `[unassigned]` displayed under the `Currently Assigned To` heading.

7. **Click on the <u>A</u>ssign button.**

8. **Click on the Close button.**

   The Customize dialog box sulks away (but remember that there are no losers on *The Price is Right!*).

9. **Click on the OK button.**

   The Modify Style dialog box huffs off.

10. **Click on the Close button in the Style dialog box.**

    Congratulations, you now have a usable shortcut key for your style.

I use the Ctrl+Alt key combinations along with a letter key for my style short-cuts. When I write a magazine article, Ctrl+Alt+B is the Body style; I use Ctrl+Alt+T for "type this in stuff" style and Ctrl+Alt+C for my Caption style. The notion here is to make the shortcut keys kinda match the style name.

Information on using a style — *applying the style*, if you work for Microsoft tech support — is covered in the next section.

Using a style

You don't *use* a style as much as you *apply* it. The character and paragraph formatting carefully stored inside the style is applied to text on-screen, text in a block, or text that you're about to write. Using a style is easy:

1. **Know what you're applying the style to.**

   If it's a paragraph already on-screen, then just stick the toothpick cursor somewhere in that paragraph. Otherwise, the style will be applied to any new text you type.

2. **Select a style from the ribbon.**

   Click on the down-arrow button beside the first drop-down list — the "Normal" list. Select your style from that list. From the keyboard, press Ctrl+Shift+S and then the down-arrow key to see the styles. Highlight a style name and click on it with the mouse or press the Enter key. You also can type the style name directly into the box if you can spell.

✔ Applying a style is a paragraph-level thing. You can't put a style on just a single word in a paragraph; the style will take over the whole paragraph instead.

✔ You can also apply a style by using a shortcut key, provided you've created one for that style. Refer to the long, boring instructions in the preceding section for the details.

✔ To apply a style to your entire document, choose Edit⇨Select All. Then choose the style you want for *everything*.

✔ Herds of styles can be collected in things called *Style Galleries*. Refer to Chapter 15 for more information.

✔ Refer to "Creating a new style," earlier in this chapter, for information on creating your own special styles for a document.

✔ Sometimes you can develop a style so sophisticated that it won't show on your monitor. If you exceed the capabilities of your printer or graphics card, you may see some strange stuff. Don't get excited, it's not the '60s all over again.

Changing the style

Styles change. Bell bottoms were once the rage, but now, well now they mostly define West Greenwich Village from the East. Times New Roman — the bane of the Normal style — is a wonderful font . . . if you're into bow ties and think merengue is a salted tequila drink or an ex-Nazi who lived in Brazil. Still, Times New Roman is a work horse that is used by everyone for almost everything. Maybe you want to put it out to pasture and use a different font in your Normal style. If so, you can change it.

"Uh, what does the Reapply Style dialog box mean?"

As you're goofing with styles, you may stumble upon the Reapply Style dialog box, which tries in its own awkward way to explain the following: "Excuse me, but you selected some text and a style, but they don't match. Should I pretend that the style should match the text from here on, or should I reformat the text to match the style?" An interesting question.

The way Word puts it is `Redefine the style using the selection as an example`. You probably don't want to select this option. Highlighting this option and clicking OK means that the style you already created will match the

selected text. (Of course, if that's what you want, click OK.)

The other option is `Return the formatting of the Style to the selection`. Equally confusing, this option means that Word will format your highlighted text to match the style you selected. You probably want to choose this option; it keeps your style intact.

As a final word, be thankful for Word's Undo command. No matter what you select in the Reapply Style dialog box, the Undo command will return your text to normal (or the way it was before).

Here are the instructions for changing a style — any style, not just the Normal style. (In fact, I don't recommend you mess with the Normal style.)

1. Choose the Format⇨Style command.

Well, Howdy Mr. Style dialog box, how are the wife and kids?

2. Select a style to change from the Styles list.

3. Click on the Modify button.

The Modify Style box erupts on the screen.

4. Click on Format.

A list of formatting options drops down. Font, Paragraph, Tabs, Border, Physique, Rx. It's all there. Figure 14-3 shows what it looks like.

5. Choose the part of the style that you want to change.

For example, select the Font button to open the Font formatting dialog box. There you can change the font, size, or any of the other things controlled in the font box (covered near the end of Chapter 9). Other buttons in the Style dialog box control and allow you to change other formatting aspects.

6. Choose OK.

Choosing OK closes whichever dialog box you opened to modify some aspect of a style. If, for example, you opened the Font dialog box, clicking on its OK button closes that box and returns you to the Style dialog box.

7. Repeat steps 4, 5, and 6 as necessary to change the style.

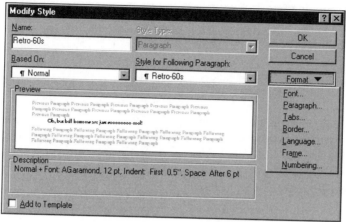

Figure 14-3:
The Modify
Style dialog
box with its
Format
button
hanging
open.

8. **Click OK in the Modify Style box when you're done.**

9. **Oh, and click Close in the Style dialog box to get back at your document.**

✔ Changing styles is advanced stuff — not recommended for the timid. It's entirely possible to use Word without bothering with styles at all, which is the way most people use the program.

✔ Changing a style means that all paragraphs in your document that have that style will be changed, which is a great way to change a font throughout a document without having to select everything and manually pick out a new font.

✔ Don't like it? Click on the Undo button (or press Ctrl+Z) to make it all go away and return to your original headache.

Stealing Character Formatting

To heck with styles! Suppose that you created a neat character formatting and want to copy it to other text in your document. For example:

The format appeals to you and you imagine that it would be effective elsewhere. To copy the character's format only — which sorta fits in with all this style nonsense — heed the following:

1. **Jab the toothpick cursor in the middle of the text that has the character (font) formatting that you want to copy.**

   No need to select anything as a block here.

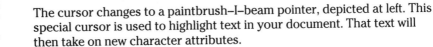

2. **Click on the Format Painter button on the Standard toolbar.**

   The cursor changes to a paintbrush–I–beam pointer, depicted at left. This special cursor is used to highlight text in your document. That text will then take on new character attributes.

3. **Hunt for the text that you want to change.**

   Refer to Chapter 2 for information on Word's navigation keys.

4. **Highlight the text.**

   Drag the mouse over the text that you want to change. You must use the mouse here.

5. **Release the mouse button.**

   Voilà! The text is changed.

✔ Painting the character format in this manner only works once. To repaint with the same format, repeat the preceding steps or refer to the next section. Or...

✔ Double-click on the Format Painter button in step 2. That way, the format painter cursor stays active, ready to paint lots of text. So after step 5, you can continue changing text (repeat steps 3, 4, and 5 as often as you like). Press the Esc key to cancel your Dutch Boy frenzy.

✔ If you tire of the mouse, you can use the Ctrl+Shift+C key command to copy the character format from a highlighted block to another location in your document. Use the Ctrl+Shift+V key combination to paste the character format elsewhere. Just highlight the text in your document and press Ctrl+Shift+V to paste in the font formatting.

U You can sorta kinda remember Ctrl+Shift+C to copy character formatting and Ctrl+Shift+V to paste because Ctrl+C and Ctrl+V are the copy and paste shortcut keys. Sorta kinda.

✔ Don't confuse the format painter with the highlighting tool, which is described in Chapter 17.

Chapter 15

Templates and Wizards

- -

- -

*T*emplates and Wizards both deal with the same thing: creating pretty-looking documents without requiring a third-degree black belt in typesetting. Templates are more of the old-fashioned way of doing things. A template is a collection of styles and other items that make writing certain types of documents easier. For example, the Department of Transportation uses these huge STOP templates that they lay down at intersections. The workers just spray paint over the template and a huge STOP appears on the roadway. Word's templates work sorta like that.

Wizards are more magical — more along the lines of what used to be called *artificial intelligence* in computing circles. Well, it turns out that artificial intelligence is nothing more than the computer doing its job by helping you do your job. In the case of Word, Wizards will help you set up and write sample documents, sometimes even filling in the words for you. Wizards are like magic, and they're ideal for us lazy-minded typists who really want to dazzle with a minimum of effort.

Creating a Document Template to Store Your Styles

Styles are a collection of paragraph and font attributes that you store under one convenient name. Chapter 14 has all the details on how they're created and used.

Oftentimes, you'll want to store a bunch of your styles so that you can use them over and over. For example, you may want to keep all the styles you used in the Dirt Eaters Anonymous Newsletter. To do this task, you create a *document template*, actually a special type of document. In the template, you can store all of your styles, which allows you to use them again and again without the bother of recreating them each time.

You create a document template like you do any new document. Start by creating a new document in Word:

1. **Choose the File⇨New command.**

   You must select the New command from the File menu; clicking on the New button on the Standard toolbar doesn't do the job.

   The New dialog box opens, numbing your brain since it's just way too complex (see Figure 15-1).

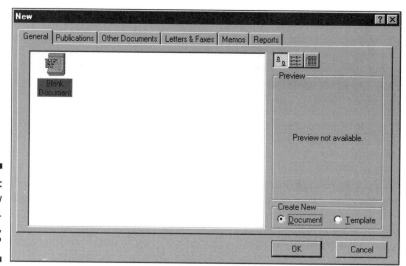

Figure 15-1:
The New
dialog box.
Stunning,
eh?

2. **Scan for the Create New area in the New dialog box.**

   You have two radio buttons: Document and Template.

   I would also refer to the sidebar "Sticking your template into the proper panel," but you don't have to do so right at this very moment.

3. **Choose the Template button.**

4. **Click OK.**

You see what looks like a new document on-screen. Don't be fooled. It's really a document template thing. (The title bar of the new document indicates that you are working on a template.)

5. **Create the styles for your new document template.**

   Follow the instructions for creating styles in Chapter 14, but create a number of styles that you want to save or use for particular documents. For example, this book has a document template that has styles for the main text, numbered lists, figure captions, section headings, and a bunch of other stuff I routinely ignore.

6. **Save the document template to disk.**

   Choose File⇨Save As. The Save As dialog box appears. Type in a name for your template, keeping in mind that you should be descriptive here but that you don't need to use the word "template" since Word keeps track of that for you, and click OK. Then you can close the template document and you're done.

   ✔ Word's document templates are saved in a special template folder on your hard drive. Don't try to save them any place else.

   ✔ To use a document template when you create a new document, refer to "Using a document template," later in this chapter.

   ✔ After creating a new template, you'll see its name appear in the New dialog box's General window (joining the Blank Document shown in Figure 15-1). Choosing that template for a new document is a cinch, but I'll leave the details up to "Using a document template," just a few pages from here.

   ✔ More information on saving stuff to disk, including all-important filename info, can be found in Chapter 20.

   ✔ Be clever with your template names. I send out all my letters by using the LETTER template; faxes start with the FAX template. These filenames are accurate, brief, tasteful, and they describe the types of templates that they represent. Do the same and your Word guru will smile in a delightful manner.

   ✔ Word actually comes with a slew of templates ready for the taking. Refer to "Using a document template," later in this chapter.

Sticking your template into the proper panel

The New dialog box has several panels in it, each of which has its own tab along the top — you know, typical Windows 95 "let's see how much crapola we can stuff into a single dialog box" kind of stuff. Review Figure 15-1 to see what I'm talking about.

Each of those tabs, General, Publications, Other Documents, and so on, contains a different type of document template, a different way to start out something new in Word. For example, the Letters & Faxes panel contains templates the boys and girls at Microsoft have already created for you, templates designed to start off your letters and faxes with the utmost of ease. (You'll even find Wizards in there, which is covered elsewhere in this chapter.)

When you create a new template, you can try to put it where it belongs by choosing the appropriate folder when you save the template to disk. Of course, you don't really have to; feel free to stick all your templates into the General panel, which is what I do (and I'm not that bad of a person).

Creating a template complete with text

There's no rule that says your document templates contain only styles. They also can store text, especially text you may use over and over again in certain types of documents. For example, a common type of Word template may contain letterhead, which allows you to use that template for your correspondence. I have a FAX template that I use to send out faxes; the first part of this template (the To, From, and Re lines) are already typed in, which saves me valuable typing energy that I can use to get down to business.

To create a template complete with text, follow these steps:

1. **Do everything outlined in the preceding section, steps 1 through 5.**

   Gee, a direction like that saves the author a lot of typing.

2. **Before saving your document template to disk, type in some text that you want to be part of the template.**

   Anything you type will be saved to disk along with the template's styles. You can, for example, create your own letterhead, provided you read various other chapters in this book. Or if you're doing up a li'l newsletter, you can create the parts of it that don't change from issue to issue, such as the sample shown in Figure 15-2.

Figure 15-2:
A sample
template
containing
text and
graphics.

3. Save the template to disk, as outlined in the preceding section.

Give it a clever name, something like LETTER or LETTER HEAD or even NEWSLETTER.

You don't have to use the word "template" in the name, since Word keeps document templates separate from normal documents.

✔ You can store lots of text in a document template if you like — anything you normally type into a Word document. However, the idea here is to be brief. A specific template isn't as useful as a general one.

✔ You also can stuff graphics into a document template. Refer to Chapter 24 for information on using graphics in your documents.

✔ Please refer to Chapter 23 for information on Mail Merge — a distant concept from document templates, although the two can be easily confused.

Sticking the current date into a template

Any text that you type into a template becomes a permanent part of that template. This situation isn't good news when you want to add the date to a template, as today's date may differ from the date you put in your letter template. Fortunately, there is a solution. Though the procedure is a bit cumbersome, the following steps will enable you to set an updating date *field* into your template:

1. **Position the toothpick cursor where you want the date.**

2. **Choose Insert➪Field. The Field dialog box appears.**

3. **From the Categories area, select Date and Time.**

4. **From the Field Names area, select Date.**

5. **Click on the Options button.**

   The Field options dialog box appears. (Make sure that the General Switches panel is forward; click on that tab if it's not.)

6. **Select a date format from the Date-Time list.**

   The letters d, M, and y stand for the day, month, and year. The format MMMM d, yyyy prints the month, day, and year in the full (unabbreviated) format.

7. **Click on the Add to Field button.**

8. **Click on the OK button.**

   The Field Options dialog box zooms outta sight.

9. **Click on the OK button in the Field dialog box to make it go away.**

Your template now has a date field in it, which is not the same thing as normal text. Instead, a field is like a mini-block of text that always displays the current date. (You must highlight the block — select it — to delete it; you cannot edit the date field like normal text.)

Using a document template

Oh, this is really dumb. To use a document template, follow these steps:

1. **Choose File➪New.**

   The New dialog box opens. You must use the File➪New command to see the New dialog box; pressing Ctrl+N or clicking the New button on the toolbar just doesn't do the trick.

2. **Under the Template list, select the template that you want.**

   First look for the tab that describes the kind of document you want to create. If you're creating your own templates, however, they should all live in the General tab. Pluck out the proper template for whatever job you're trying to do.

   The Normal template is Word's own boring normal template (which should be renamed *Yawn*).

3. **Click OK.**

Word *attaches* the template to your document, ready for use. You can take advantage of any styles stuffed into the template and view, use, or edit any text saved in the template.

✔ Special templates are given the surname Wizard. Refer to "Chickening Out and Using a Wizard," later in this chapter, for more information on them.

✔ Opening a document with a template does not change the template; your new document is merely "using" the template's styles and any text it already has. To change a template, refer to the next section.

✔ Golly, don't templates make Word kind of easy? Only, of course, if the entire document template and style fiasco hasn't already induced brainlock.

Changing a document template

Changing or editing a document template is identical to changing or editing a normal document. The difference is that a template is opened instead of the document. Yes, Word can deal with this task quite easily.

1. **Open the template.**

Choose File⇨Open. The Open dialog box appears.

2. **In the Open dialog box, select Document Templates from the List Files of Type drop-down box.**

This option directs Word to list only document templates in the Open dialog box file window.

3. **Find your template folder.**

Word ensconces all its templates in a special folder. You'll need to use the Look in drop-down box to help you find this folder. (See Chapter 22 for more information on using this device if you need to, though it's a standard Windows doohickey.)

First, look for the folder named Office 95 on your hard drive. (That should be drive C, unless some fool installed it on another drive.) Open that folder.

Second, look for a folder named Templates in the Office 95 folder. Open that folder.

4. **Open the template that you want to edit.**

Double-click on its filename.

If you stuck your template in a panel other than General (which isn't what I recommended a few pages back), then you'll need to open whichever folder contains your template and *then* repeat this step.

When you open the template, it appears in Word just like any other document — though it's really a template. (Sneaky.)

5. Make your changes.

You edit the template just as you would any other document. Bear in mind that it is a template that you're editing and not a "real" document. Any style changes or text editing affect the template and will be saved to disk as a template again.

6. Save the modified template.

Choose File⇨Save.

Or choose File⇨Save As to assign the modified template a new name and maintain the original template.

7. Close the template document.

Choose File⇨Close.

✔ Any changes that you make to a document template will not affect any documents already created with that template. The changes will, however, affect any new documents that you create.

✔ The Normal template is a special beast. Any change that you make to the Normal template will affect all other templates that you use. The moral of this story is not to mess with the Normal template.

✔ There is a command in the File menu called Templates. Ignore it.

Chickening Out and Using a Wizard

If all this template-style-formatting nonsense has you in a tizzy, sit down and have a cup of tea. And while you're at it, prepare to let Word do all the formatting work. This is all possible, with desirable results, thanks to the wonderful Wizards of Word.

A Wizard enables you to create a near-perfect document automatically. All you need to do is choose various options and make adjustments from a handy and informative dialog box. Word does the rest of the work.

To use a Word Wizard, follow these steps:

1. **Choose File⇨New.**

   This command opens the New dialog box (refer back to Figure 15-1).

2. **Hunt down a Wizard.**

   There are a number of Wizards that come prepackaged with Word. Of course, none of them hides in the General tab. To find a Wizard, you'll have to click on another tab in the New dialog box, for example the Letters & Faxes tab.

   Letter Wizard

   Wizards live along with templates, though the Wizards have their own special icon (pictured at left). Note that, unlike templates, the brainiacs at Microsoft use the word Wizard when naming their wizards. You'll find the Fax Wizard, Letter Wizard, Memo Wizard, Lizard Wizard, and maybe the Wizard of Oz if you look hard enough.

   Whatever Wizard you choose, highlight it in the Template list; click on the Wizard's icon once with your mouse.

3. **Click OK.**

   Word hums and churns for a few minutes. It's thinking — no doubt a painful process. Give it time.

4. **You're enlightened by the Wizard dialog box.**

   A sample of the Wizard dialog box appears in Figure 15-3. Most of them look the same, with three areas to pay attention to: the preview window, which gives you an idea of what your document may look like; the list of options and descriptions; and four buttons: Cancel, <Back, Next> and Finish.

   Generally speaking, you should repeat the following two steps as often as required to create your document:

5. **Choose one of the options on the right side of the Wizard dialog box.**

   Indeed, choose them all, one at a time. See which one you like the best and examine the preview window to see how it affects your document.

   Some options may require you to do a bit of typing, such as entering your name, return address, maybe hat size, and so on.

   Some of the options may have you enter measurements. Don't fuss over this part of the process; just guess! The preview window will show you how your guesses will look on the final document.

   If you're dissatisfied with the choices you're given, click on the <Back button and start again with a new option.

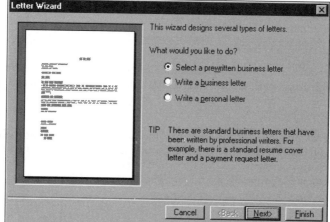

Figure 15-3:
The Letter
Wizard
dialog box
helps you
create the
perfect
epistle.

6. Click on the Next> button.

This button moves you along to the next stage of creating your document, giving you more options to select from. At this point, you continue with step 5 and select more options.

Eventually, you see `Those are all the answers the wizard needs to create your whatever.` A checkered flag on the left of the Wizard dialog box means you're done (or you've just won the Indianapolis 500). You'll also notice that the Next> button is dimmed. Word is ready to slap together your document.

7. Click the Finish button.

The Wizard prepares your document and presents it to you for editing and further primping.

✔ Even though a Wizard created your document, you still must save it to disk when you're done. In fact, most Wizards may just start you on your way. After that point, you work with the document just like any other in Word. Don't forget to save!

✔ Don't forget to look at the preview window! If you don't like what you see, you can either click on the <Back button to rethink your strategy or click on the Cancel button to blow this gig and go back to watching TV and eating salty snack foods.

✔ The preview window shows text in a "greek" manner. (It's actually called *greeked*, which is typesetter talk for tiny text that you can't read.) This window gives you an idea for how your document will be laid out.

✔ Some Wizards even fill in text for you. These are super-cheating Wizards. The Stephen King Wizard, for example, writes his books for him in under a day.

✔ Always read the information on the right side of the Wizard dialog box. I normally wouldn't mark this item with a tip icon, but too many people don't read stuff that the computer tells them, and the text in the Wizard dialog box is actually kinda informative.

✔ There. I've managed to finish this entire section with only one silly reference to the *Wizard of Oz*.

Chapter 16

Some Automatic Formatting Tricks

In This Chapter

▶ Using AutoFormat
▶ Creating automatically formatted headings
▶ Creating automatically formatted boarders
▶ Creating automatically formatted lists

*N*ow that you have a computer, you really need to buy another to help keep you and the first computer organized. It seems that way sometimes. Actually, my biggest beef with computers is that they're just so darn stupid sometimes. For example, some things should be obvious to a computer: The first word of a sentence is capitalized; if you type 1. to start a list, the computer should automatically type 2. for you on the next line; and computers should recognize that the alluring smell of a kraut dog doesn't portend well for the digestive system.

This chapter is about automatic formatting jazz. There's actually an AutoFormat command in Word. Not only that, sometimes Word actually grows brains beneath its skull, figures out what you're doing, and helps you finish the job. That's so amazing it's almost enough to make you forget you're using a computer.

Word will capitalize the first letter of a sentence for you automagically. See Chapter 7 for information on the AutoCorrect command.

Using AutoFormat

Word's AutoFormat command has absolutely nothing to do with formatting in the sense of font or paragraph formatting. No, what it really does is clean up your document, remove excess spaces, add spaces where needed, and other minor housekeeping chores. Yes, it removes the slop most of us add to our documents without thinking about it.

Before AutoFormat can do its job, you need to create the document's text. Write! Write! Write! Write your letter, memo, chapter, poem, whatever. Then follow these steps:

1. Save your document to disk.

This step is most important, and it's something you should be doing all the time. Save your document before you AutoFormat it. Refer to Chapter 1 for the details on saving.

2. Choose Format⇨AutoFormat.

The AutoFormat dialog box appears, as shown in Figure 16-1.

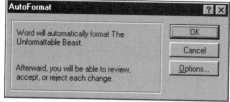

Figure 16-1:
The
AutoFormat
dialog box.

3. Click OK.

Ook! Eep! Ack!

4. Formatting completed.

You'll see the final formatting dialog box displayed, as shown in Figure 16-2. Word has carefully massaged and adjusted your document. You may find new headings, bulleted lists, and other amazing, whiz-bang things automatically done to your text. If you like, you can click on the Review Changes button to see exactly what was done. Otherwise . . .

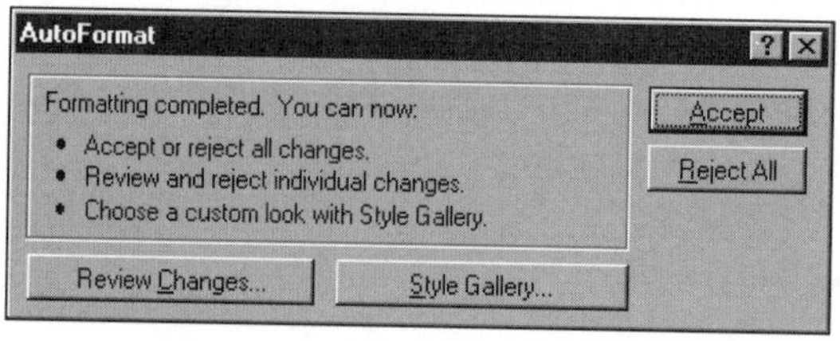

Figure 16-2:
The final
formatting
dialog box.

5. Click the Accept button.

The changes that AutoFormat made to your document are slapped down in place.

✔ If your text is kinda boring, it won't appear as though AutoFormat did anything. Don't despair. AutoFormat is good at creating headings and bulleted lists, but it can't read your mind.

The AutoFormat tool has nothing to do with formatting your document, as in character or paragraph formatting.

✔ If you're interested in formatting your document automatically, refer to the section on Wizards in Chapter 15.

Automatically Formatting (the Strange Way)

Sometimes Word can be so smart it's scary. A long time ago, just having a program remind you to save before you quit was thought to be miraculous. But now . . . why just the other day Word reminded me that I forgot to floss the night before and, boy, though that blackberry cobbler looked tempting, I am several stones over my ideal weight. Scary stuff.

Making the automatic formatting happen

You must direct Word to be smart. It cannot do it on its own. To take advantage of the many automagical things it can do, follow these steps:

1. **Choose Tools⇨Options.**

    The Options dialog box slaps itself down on the screen.

2. **Click on the AutoFormat tab to bring that panel forward.**

    You only need to do this if the AutoFormat panel isn't forward already. But, hey, there are 12 panels there, so you might as well double check. What you see will look something like Figure 16-3.

3. **In the top part of the dialog box, click in the dot by AutoFormat as you Type.**

    This directs Word to wreak havoc with your text as you type it, granting you access to the nifty options listed at the bottom of the dialog box.

4. **Since you don't know what the options do, check them all on.**

    Click by the box in each option to put a check mark in it. This activates all the AutoFormat features, some of which are highlighted in the following sections.

5. Click OK.

You're ready to start playing.

✔ Make sure you switch on the Headings, Borders, Automatic Bulleted Lists, and Automatic Numbered Lists items before you work through the remaining sections in this chapter.

✔ The Straight Quotes with 'Smart Quotes' option tells Word to change the boring " and ' quote marks into the more stylish "double" and 'single' style quote marks. Face it: the " and ' smell of Smith-Corona.

✔ The Ordinals (1st) with Superscript option tells Word to change your text so that when you type **2nd,** it immediately formats it as 2nd — No pencil could ever be that smart.

✔ The Fractions (1/2) with fraction character ($^1/_2$) directs Word to change what you would type as 1/2 with the nifty $^1/_2$ symbol. Again, you lose a degree of dorkiness in your text.

✔ The Symbol Characters with Symbols option is a little less obvious to figure out. Such a symbol would be ™ (TM), for example. There must be a list of them somewhere, but I've yet to find it.

✔ Almost all of these four Replace As You Type options can be emulated using the AutoCorrect feature (see Chapter 7). In fact, quite a few of them are already there.

Automatic headings

This is simple. To stick an automatic heading into your document, type the heading, and then press the Enter key twice. Word instantly converts the line you typed into the Heading 1 format.

- ✔ Word also activates the TipWizard just below the formatting toolbar; click on the TipWizard button after you've been enlightened by its wisdom.

- ✔ See Chapter 14 for more information on the Heading 1 style. You can change this style to be more suitable to your document if you like.

- ✔ Personally, I think this is a silly option. For me, it's easier to format my own headings, primarily because I use A, B, and C level headings, and this trick doesn't apply to those lesser headings.

Automatic borders

In the old Smith-Corona days of yore, we would fancy up our documents by woodpeckering a line of hyphens or underlines or equal signs. It brings back kind of a sentimental tear to the eye, especially for me since I pressed the keys so hard, ripping the paper out of the typewriter often ripped the paper in two. Not with a word processor, though.

If you want a single line border, right margin to left across your page, type three hyphens and press the Enter key:

Then press the Enter key. Word instantly transmutes the three little hyphens into a solid line.

Want a double line? Then use three equal signs:

===

Press the Enter key and Word draws a double line from one edge of the screen to the next.

Again, this is really a cheap-and-dirty trick. If you really want to get fancy with borders, check out Chapter 26.

Automatic numbered lists

The best way to understand this adventure is to *live* it. Heed the following steps:

1. **Start a new document in Word.**

   The simplest way to do that is to press the Ctrl+N key combination. No messing around here.

2. **Type the following:**

   ```
   Things to do today:
   ```

   Press the Enter key to start a new line. Then type:

   ```
   1. Bury the body in the cellar.
   ```

   Now — prepare yourself — press the Enter key to end that line. You'll see the following:

   ```
   2.
   ```

   Not only does Word automatically give you a 2, but it reformats the previous line as indented text. Amazing. Stupendous. Definitely worth $25 of the purchase price.

3. **Keep typing your list.**

   Continue typing your list. Word adds a new number every time you press the Enter key to start a new paragraph.

4. **Press the Backspace key once when you're done.**

   Just backspace over the last number. Word instantly forgets that it was helping you out and returns to its original, rude mode.

This trick also works for letters (and Roman numerals, too). Just start something with a letter and a period and Word picks up at the next line with the next letter in the alphabet and another period.

Part III
Strange Things Living under the Hood

...and so, with a multifunction system like this, whenever you press the DELETE key, you....

OK- this seems like a good time to move on to the UNDO function.

In this part...

Since about 1986 or so, computer word processors have always done more than just process words. It was part of the great Feature Wars, in which rival word processors battled for the hearts and minds of computer magazine reviewers who said, "Oh, but DoodleWriter 4.0 is much better than TurboPencil 3.7 because it has the all important Translate to Latin feature." And so word processing developers kept trying to outdo each other until we find ourselves with the feature rich, nay, feature burdened word processors of the twenty-first century.

The chapters nestled in this part of the book couldn't have been written a mere five years ago. Only with this advancing featuritis does this information even remotely apply to word processing. Skip it if you want to, otherwise sit back and savor some of the truly wacky things Word can do.

Chapter 17

Let's Work This Out Together

For me, writing is a solitary art. Sure, I've collaborated with others over the years, but it wasn't like both of us were sitting at the same computer, fighting over whose thumb got to whack the spacebar. In those instances, my fellow authors and I usually rely upon some of Word's cooperative tools to help us communicate. These are sneaky things authors can do to the text that the reader never sees. Without them you'd often find things like the following in your reading materials:

```
Steve: this entire book reads like your last horror novel. Do
something unique, will ya?
```

But — aha! — with Word's Let's-work-this-out-together commands, you and all of China could write something, and no reader would be the wiser.

Sharing Work with Revision Marks

Rumor has it Abe Lincoln really struggled over that Gettysburg address. Draft after draft. Mary Todd would hear him utter, "Stupid pen," time and time again. Then brilliance hit him, and he composed the speech most of us memorized in grade school. Ever wonder how he did it? Well, had he written in Word, Abe could have use the Revisions command to check out how his initial drafts compared with the final one. He would see what words were changed and what phrases were added. You, too could see them. Right there on the screen, plain as the thing on your chin, would be the various *revisions* old Abe had made.

Less noble documents can suffer the same fate. Want to see what changes your ~~malevolent~~ smart editor made to your masterpiece? Run Word's Revisions command and you'll find out.

The Revisions command requires that you compare one document with another. For example, suppose you're Abe and your Secretary of State is going over your work. When he returns the document, you want to see exactly what was done to it. Suppose you have both versions, GETTY1 (your original) and GETTY2 (the one your Secretary of State messed with). Here's how you'd proceed:

1. **Make sure you have your original document loaded and on the screen.**

   In Abe's case, that would be the GETTY1 document, the first draft of the Gettysburg Address.

2. **Choose Tools⇨Revisions.**

   A handy shortcut to the Revisions dialog box is to double-click on the three-letter acronym MRK on the Status bar. MRK, aside from being the initials of my Junior High School sweetheart, is the shortcut for revision marks on the status bar.

   However you get there, the Revisions dialog box appears, as shown in Figure 17-1.

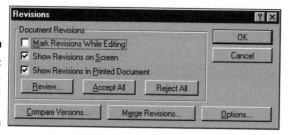

Figure 17-1:
The
Revisions
dialog box.

3. **Click on the Compare Versions button.**

   An Open dialog box appears, though it says Compare Versions on it.

4. **Locate the second, edited copy of your file.**

   In Abe's case, he's looking for the GETTY2 file, the one the Secretary of State brushed up.

   So remember: Your original document is on the screen. The modified version is on disk. Word will compare them.

5. Click Open.

This opens the modified version of your file.

Word thinks long and hard.

Eventually you'll see the revision-marked up result. During the compare process, Word noted changes between the two documents. Blue text indicates changes. New text is underlined. Deleted text is crossed out (the strikethrough-text effect). Unchanged text remains the same. And the areas where text was changed are flagged by a line on the left side of the document. Figure 17-2 shows what Abe may have seen on his screen.

Figure 17-2:
Revision
marks on
the screen.

~~Eight-seven~~ Fourscore and seven years ago, our ~~dads and grandads~~ fathers brought forth upon this ~~land~~ continent a new nation.|

Now you can see exactly what has been changed in your document. For example, you might be able to see where your editor has replaced the word ~~transvestite~~ with IDG's pesky project editors. The replaced text is crossed out; new text is underlined.

- You can continue to edit the document if you like. After all, it's your document.

- Revision marks can get in the way. To remove them, summon the Revisions dialog box again (see step 2 on the preceding page) and remove the check mark by Show Revisions on Screen.

- Don't bother trying to edit away the colored text on your screen: Those are revision marks and not text formatting. From the Revisions dialog box, you can click on the Reject All button to do away with the revisions or click Accept All to keep the changes. Click the Close button to make the Revisions dialog box revise itself outta here.

Annotations, or "Let me just jot this down"

If you're reading someone else's work and you want to make a comment about it but don't want to make any changes, you can include an annotation. These work similarly to footnotes (see Chapter 11), though the annotations never print.

To stick an annotation in a document, follow these steps:

1. Position the toothpick cursor where you want to annotate the text.

For example, if you're commenting on a sentence your co-author wrote, you would position the toothpick cursor at the end of the sentence.

2. Choose Insert⇨Annotation.

The screen instantly splits, as shown in Figure 17-3.

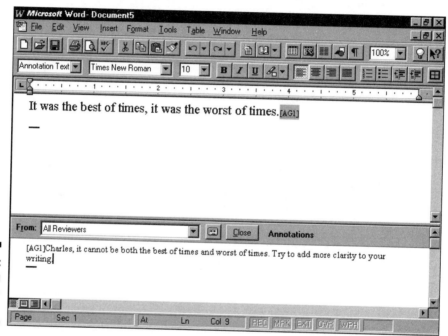

Figure 17-3:
An annoying
annotation
is made.

A hidden code — a field actually — is inserted into the document. The code contains your initials as you entered them when Word (or Microsoft Office) was first installed.

3. Type your comment.

Enter your comment in the lower portion of the screen, in the annotation area. Type away!

4. Click the Close button when you're done.

The annotation area — and your little field flag in the text — disappears.

Repeat these steps to add more annotations to the text.

The beauty of all this is that the annotations remain mute until you want to see them. To view the annotations on your text, choose View⇨Annotations. The annotations area on the screen appears, showing the rude comments made by your reviewers.

✔ Jump around through your text by clicking the mouse on the initials that start each annotation. For example, click on [DG4] to see which part of your text the fourth comment DG made pertains to.

✔ Obviously, if the Annotations command in the View menu is dimmed, there are no comments in your document. Whoopee!

✔ If several people are reviewing your document, each of their comments will appear after their own initials. To see the comments individually, use the From drop-down list.

✔ Yes, they don't print. No way to get them to print, either. Unless, of course, you choose Annotations from the Print What part of the Print dialog box. But don't let me ever catch you doing that in real life.

✔ The little tape cassette button on the annotation area's split bar allows you to actually record comments in your text. I wouldn't bother if I were you.

✔ If you want to change your initials used in Word (and who doesn't), choose Tools⇨Options. The Options dialog box appears. Click on the User Info tab to bring its panel forward. Type your new initials into the Initials box. Click OK.

Whipping out the Yellow Highlighter

The old joke goes that you can always tell when a Canadian uses a word processor because there is White Out on the screen. Well, there's no need to worry about that since Word erases text automatically. But one thing you are likely to goop the screen with would be a yellow marking pen. I've been tempted to do this ever since I used to watch Hobo Kelly on TV and actually drew an umbrella for Mr. Wuzzle so he wouldn't get wet in the rain. With Word, however, there's no need to fear your father beating you because you used an indelible pen on the new color TV.

Yeah, I know it's not a "Canadian" who puts White Out on the screen. But just try getting the original version of that joke past the politically correct editorial staff at IDG.

Using the highlighter

To highlight your text (on-screen, electronically, of course), click on the Highlight button on the formatting toolbar. Click!

Now you've entered highlighting mode. The mouse pointer changes to something I can't describe verbally but can picture in the left margin. When you drag the mouse over your text, that text becomes highlighted — just like you can do with a highlighter on regular paper. Amazing what those whiz kids at Microsoft can come up with. . . .

- ✔ To stop highlighting your text, click on the Highlight button again, or press the Esc key.

- ✔ You can also highlight a block of text by first marking the block and then clicking on the Highlight button. See Chapter 6 for all the proper block-marking instructions.

- ✔ The highlighted text prints, so be careful with it. The highlighted text appears black on gray on your hard copy.

- ✔ See the next section for information on removing the highlight from your text.

- ✔ As with other tools described in this chapter, highlighting is great for sharing your work with others. Personally, I use it to mark text that needs fixing or something that may need my attention later on. Hopefully, the bright yellow text will catch my eye on the screen.

- ✔ If you click on the down arrow by the Highlight button you can choose other colors for your highlighted text. And to think that an office supply store would charge you an extra $1.20 for each color. . . .

Removing highlighter

You tried rubbing, you tried buffing, and still that darn highlighter doesn't come out of your text.

Relax. To un-highlight your text you have two options:

First, choose the None color from the Highlight drop-down list. Click on the down arrow by the Highlight button and then click on the top color, None. Then go around to all your highlighted text and paint over it again with the None color.

Second, mark the highlighted text as a block, then click on the Highlight button. This un-highlights the text automagically. (See Chapter 6 for expert block-marking instructions.)

 If you've highlighted all over your document (like a used book in a college bookstore), then select the entire document using the Edit⊃Select All command (or press Ctrl+A). Then click on the Highlight button on the toolbar. Omigod! All the text is highlighted! Calm down. Repeat those two steps again and your document will be fresh as a daisy (a white one).

Chapter 18
Organizing Your Thots

· ·

In This Chapter

▶ Starting a new outline

▶ Adding topics

▶ Making subtopics

▶ Creating a text topic

▶ Looking at all or some of your outline

▶ Reorganizing your outline

▶ Printing the outline

· ·

All my high school teachers used to urge me to create outlines for my papers. I thought this was silly, and I was correct: If you're writing a three-page paper on why Winnie the Pooh loves honey, you don't really need an outline. But if you're working on something long and involved, you probably need an outline to help you organize your thoughts. In fact, I don't write anything any more without some form of outline.

Outlines in a computer are wonderful. They help by allowing you to view your work from far away or close up. For example, you can view only the major topics in your outline and hide all the details, or you can choose to see everything all at once. Either way, starting off something big with an outline helps you keep your thoughts organized and create a more cohesive document. And who doesn't love the word cohesive?

Making Up a New Outline

I was recently hired by the Disney Corporation to write a script for the musical cartoon version of *Planet of the Apes* (to be directed by Oliver Stone). It's loosely based on the original movie, but still I want to shuffle my ideas into an outline to help me understand it.

You start a new outline like any other document in Word. In fact, an outline *is* just another document. The only difference is in how Word displays it on the screen. Follow these steps:

1. Start a new document.

Press Ctrl+N or click on the New button on the toolbar. (Don't bother with File⇨New since that adds another, annoying step you don't really need here.)

The new document stares at you like the blinding white headlights of an oncoming truck with a dozing driver.

2. Switch to the Outline view.

Ah. The secret. Choose View⇨Outline or click on the outline button crowded into the lower-left corner of the window. See Figure 18-1 (though it has a lot of text in it that you won't see on your screen right now).

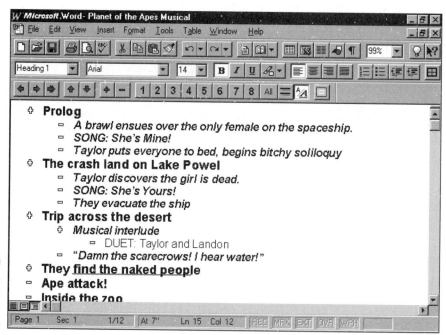

Figure 18-1:
A typical outline.

Two amazing things happen: First, you get to see the Outlining toolbar, which will help you work your outline. Second, a hollow minus sign appears before the toothpick cursor. This means you're typing a *topic* in the outline and the topic has no *subtopics* (which has nothing to do with naval vessels, by the way).

3. **You're ready to start your outline.**

   The details of which are covered in the next few sections.

✔ Word's outlining function is merely a different way to look at a document. It's possible to shift back into Normal view or Page Layout view, but not really necessary when you're working on an outline.

✔ Don't worry about fonts or formatting while you're creating an outline. Word uses preset fonts (the fabulous Heading 1 through Heading 9 series) for your outline. These are more than okay for what you're doing.

✔ All Word's normal commands work in the outline mode. You can use the cursor keys, delete text, spell check, save, insert oddball characters, print, and so on.

✔ The only commands that don't work normally are the block marking commands. In outline mode, Word will only let you mark a paragraph (which is a topic) as a block. You can't mark words or parts of paragraphs. This is only a minor inconvenience and is actually a blessing when you get to shuffling around your topics in the outline.

Adding topics to your outline

An outline is composed of topics and subtopics. The main topics are your main ideas, with the subtopics describing the details. You should start your outline by adding the main topics. To do so, just type them out.

In Figure 18-2 you see several topics typed out, each on a line by itself. Pressing Enter after typing a topic produces a new hollow hyphen at which you can type your next topic.

```
□  Melt 1 stick butter
□  Add one egg
□  1 tsp. Baking Soda
□  1 cup sugar
□  1 cup brown sugar
□  1 cup peanut butter
□  Stir in flour until stiff
□
```

Figure 18-2: Level one topics.

✔ Press Enter at the end of each topic. This tells Word that you're done typing information for that topic and want to move on to the next topic.

✔ Pressing Enter creates another topic at the same *level* as the first topic. To create a subtopic, refer to the next section.

- A topic can be a single word, a few words, a complete sentence, or a big paragraph. However, your main topics should be short and descriptive, like in a book's table of contents.

- You can split a topic by putting the toothpick cursor somewhere in its middle and pressing the Enter key.

- To join up two topics, put the toothpick cursor at the end of the first topic and press the Delete key. (This works just like joining up two paragraphs in a regular document.)

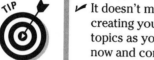

- It doesn't matter if you get the order right at first or not. The beauty of creating your outline with a word processor is that you can rearrange your topics as your ideas solidify. My advice is just to start writing things down now and concentrate on organization later.

- An outline can be the plot to a novel, a speech you're giving, a recipe, an itinerary, a product development cycle— just about anything that requires more than one thought.

- Oliver is such a conspiracy nut. He actually thinks the Statue of Liberty at the end of the original *Planet of the Apes* was put there by the French.

Working with subtopics

The purpose of an outline is to have more than one level of topic. For example, your main topic may be *Things wrapped in aluminum foil in the refrigerator* and the subtopics would be what those things actually are.

To create a subtopic follow these steps:

1. Position the cursor at the end of the main topic.

For example, if your main topic is *Things wrapped in aluminum foil in the refrigerator,* click the mouse on that line to put the toothpick cursor there and then press the End key to move the cursor to the end of the line.

2. Press the Enter key.

This creates another topic, but at the same level! You'll need to move the topic over to the right one notch for it to become a subtopic.

3. Move the subtopic over to the right one notch.

Click on the Demote button or press Alt+Shift+→ to move the topic over.

Instantly the line of text moves over a tab stop and the text style changes. Both of these visually indicate that you're working on a new topic level.

4. Type your subtopic.

For example, type **moldy meatloaf** to continue with the foil in the fridge outline.

Unlike creating main topics, you can get a little wordy with your subtopics. After all, the idea here is to expand upon the main topic. For example, if you're writing a speech, a subtopic would contain a more detailed sketch of your talk. Maybe not the talk itself, just more details.

5. **To create another subtopic, press the Enter key.**

You're presented with another blank, subtopic line on which to jot down your brilliance.

Remember that each topic line should be an individual thought or idea. If your subtopic is:

```
old bologna sandwich and some corn bread
```

you should split it in two:

```
old bologna sandwich
corn bread
```

Each item is a different subtopic in the *Things wrapped in aluminum foil in the refrigerator* main topic.

- ✔ To make a topic into a subtopic you *demote* it. Put the toothpick cursor in the topic and press Alt+Shift+→.

- ✔ To make a subtopic back into a topic you *promote* it. Put the toothpick cursor in the topic and press Alt+Shift+← or click on the Promote button.

- ✔ To create additional subtopics, just keep pressing the Enter key. This continues to create topics at the same level. Only by demoting or promoting topics do they shift to another level.

- ✔ You'll notice that a main topic with a subtopic has a hollow + by it instead of a hollow minus.

- ✔ See "Viewing the Outline" for information on looking at different parts of your outline while hiding other parts.

- ✔ You can create a sub-subtopic simply by repeating the above steps for a subtopic. In fact, Word lets you organize on a number of levels. Most outlines, however, typically have maybe 4 or 5 levels max.

Adding a text topic

If you feel the need to break out and actually write a paragraph in your outline, you can do so. While it's perfectly legit to write the paragraph on the topic level, what you should really do is stick in a text topic using the Demote to Body Text button. Here's how:

1. **Press the Enter key to start a new topic.**

   Do this just as you would create any new topic on a line by itself.

2. **Click the Demote to Body Text button.**

   Or you can press Ctrl+Shift+N. What this does is actually change the style to Normal (which is what the keyboard shortcut key does). In your outline, however, that allows you to write a paragraph of text that isn't a heading. So you can write an actual bit of text for your speech, instructions in a list, or dialog from your novel.

   ✔ The Body Text style appears with a tiny hollow square by it, unlike topics that have hollow plus or minus signs by them.

   ✔ If you change you mind, you can promote or demote your Body Text to a topic or subtopic. Refer to the previous section for which keys to press.

   ✔ Refer to Chapter 14 for more information on the Normal style.

Viewing the Outline

Unless you tell Word otherwise, it displays all the topics in your outline, top to bottom, everything. But this really isn't part of the glory of outlining. What makes outlining on a computer special is that if you want to step back and see the Big Picture, you can do so.

For example, to see all the first-level topics in your outline, click on the Show Heading 1 button. All the subtopics and text topics disappear, and you're left with only the main topics — the overview of your outline, which may sorta look like Figure 18-3.

If a topic has subtopics, not only does it have a hollow plus sign by it, but you'll see a fuzzy line extending out over the last part of the topic name. I haven't met anyone yet who knows exactly what the fuzzy line is supposed to mean.

If you want to see your outline in more detail, click on the Show Heading 2 or 3 button. Each button displays your outline at a different level.

The All button is used to expand your outline out so that *everything* can be seen at once.

> ⊕ **Prolog**
> ⊕ **The crash land on Lake Powel**
> ⊕ **Trip across the desert**
> ⊕ **They find the naked people**
> ⊕ **Ape attack!**
> ⊕ **Inside the zoo**
> ⊕ **Cornelius and Dr. Zaius**
> ⊕ **Taylor speaks**
> ⊕ **The Trial**
> ⊕ **The Forbidden Zone**
> ⊕ **Epilogue**

Figure 18-3:
Only top-level topics are shown here.

> ✔ Word automatically recognizes an outline document and immediately shifts into Outline view when it's loaded. Usually it displays *all* the topics, so if you're used to viewing only at level 1 or level 2, you'll have to click on the appropriate button.

> ✔ You can view an Outline in normal view if you like, but it looks silly. (The outline looks silly, that is. It's not that you look silly looking at the outline in normal view.)

> ✔ You can open or close individual topics by double-clicking on the hollow plus sign with the mouse. Using the keyboard, press Alt+Shift+Plus to open a topic; Alt+Shift+Minus to close it. (The Plus and Minus keys are the gray plus and minus keys on your keyboard's numeric keypad.)

> ✔ As your outline nears perfection you can copy parts of it and paste them into other, new documents. This is the way some writers create their books and novels; the document is merely a longer, more complete version of what starts as an outline.

> ✔ By the way, make sure the Num Lock light is off (press the Num Lock key) before you use the keypad Plus and Minus keys.

Rearranging Topics

Just like shuffling the stack of 3 x 5 cards my high school teachers urged me to use when outlining, it's a cinch to reorganize your topics in a computer outline. And it's more fun, too, since you're using a computer and not something that has your mother's recipes on the backside. (And, boy, was she mad!)

To move any topic in your outline, put the toothpick cursor in that topic and then click on one of the following buttons:

 ✔ Click on the Move Up button (or press Alt+Shift+↑) to move a topic up a line.

 ✔ Click on the Move Down button (or press Alt+Shift+↓) to move a topic down a line.

 ✔ Click on the Promote button (or press Alt+Shift+←) to move a topic left (to subtopic it).

 ✔ Click on the Demote button (or press Alt+Shift+→) to move a topic right.

You can also use the mouse to move topics around: Drag the topic by its plus or minus sign and drop it off at the new location. Personally, I don't use this technique since my outlines are rather complex and moving topics in this manner becomes unwieldy.

If you select a group of topics as a block, you can move them around in your outline as a block. Only a topic and its subtopics can be selected in this manner, and keep in mind you can only select topics in an outline, not individual bits of text.

 It may be a good idea to switch to the All view in your outline before you start rearranging topics. That way you can see where things go and not miss any of the details.

Printing Your Outline

Printing your outline works just like printing any other document in Word. But since it's an outline, there is one difference: Only those visible topics in your outline will print.

 For example, if you only want to print the first two levels of your outline, click on the Show Heading 2 button. This hides all subtopics and when you print your outline, only the first and second topics will be printed.

 If you want your entire outline to print, click on the All button before printing.

TIP

The Outline Shortcut Key summary box

When I'm typing, I like my hands to remain on the keyboard. Because of this, I discovered the following key combinations that work when playing with an outline. Try them if you dare:

Key combo	*Function*
Alt+Shift+→	Demote a topic
Alt+Shift+←	Promote a topic
Alt+Shift+↑	Shift a topic up one line
Alt+Shift+↓	Shift a topic down one line
Ctrl+Shift+N	Insert some body text
Alt+Shift+1	Display only top topics
Alt+Shift+2	Display first- and second-level topics
Alt+Shift+#	Display all topics up to number #
Alt+Shift+A	Display all topics
Alt+Shift+Plus (+)	Display all subtopics in the current topic
Alt+Shift+Minus (−)	Hide all subtopics in the current topic

Chapter 19

A Microscopic Macro Chapter

*G*olly, macros are such an advanced subject that they really have no place in this, a Dummies book. Even so, hordes of readers have written in on the Reader Response cards requesting some form of literature on using macros in Word. Personally, I haven't a clue. I thought Macros was the former dictator in the Philippines. But then I looked up *macro* in the Word help system and found it's really something handy, albeit a wee bit technical to go into in any depth deeper than what's offered in this chapter.

A Brief Description of What a Macro Is

A macro is a secret little program you write to carry out some task in Word. Yes, it's programming. That's one reason why I've never included it in previous editions of this book. You really need to understand programming to get the most from macros. Even so, I'll endeavor to show you some of the ropes in this brief chapter.

There are actually two types of macros: recorded and programmed.

A recorded macro is just like it sounds. As with a tape recorder or VCR (well, let's stick with a tape recorder), you can record something and then play it back. With a word macro, you record your keystrokes, mouse movement, and menu selections for playback later. That's the simplest form of macro.

A programmed macro is a program you write using Word's programming language, WordBasic (or is it Visual Basic now? I forget and it doesn't matter). You write a little program that tells Word to do something, then you "run" the macro and Word goes nuts obeying your instructions. Something like that.

- ✔ Recorded macros are easy to do, which is the main thrust of this chapter.

- ✔ Programmed macros. Oh, I shudder. (Shuddering noise.)

- ✔ Seriously, entire books are written on writing macros in Word. If you're curious, you can check out the help file for WordBasic. It lists all the commands and what they do and even shows you some samples. Choose Help⇨Microsoft Word Help Topics. The Word Help Machine appears. Click on the Contents tab to bring that panel forward, then look at the last "chapter" in the list, WordBasic Reference. (Shuddering noise.)

- ✔ If you somehow turned on the WordPerfect help, the last chapter you'll see on the help contents panel will be "Switching from WordPerfect." It's one of those 12-step things.

- ✔ Almost every computer book I've ever read that goes into a description of macros includes the following line: "Macro is short for macroinstruction." They write that down, expecting us to absorb it somehow and come away with, "Wow. That's *really* interesting. I'm so glad you told me that. I feel completely enlightened now. Thanks a bunch." Honestly, who cares?

Creating a Record-Your-Keystrokes Macro

The simplest form of macro to create is the record-your-keystrokes macro. If you've been paying attention (which means you're not reading this book in bed), you've probably gleaned some information about the AutoText feature (see Chapter 13). That also allows you to record keystrokes and then play them back.

So you're sitting there (or lying in bed) and thinking, "Yeah, so what's the big diff?" The big diff is that a macro not only records your keystrokes, but it also remembers which commands you chose.

Personally, I don't use any macros. However, while I was thinking just a few minutes ago, I thought of one to use as a demonstration. It's the Switch Word macro. What it does is to switch one word with another, so if you have the toothpick cursor on *hardly* in the following sentence:

```
hardly working
```

and you run the Switch Word macro, you'll end up with:

```
working hardly
```

Dumb, but useful as a demonstration.

Follow these instructions to create a record-your-keystrokes macro:

1. **Properly set things up.**

   If your macro requires text to manipulate on the screen, you'll need to type some text. The idea is to set things up the way they would be if you were running the macro; the macro cannot be created unless you first prepare for it.

   In the case of the record-your-keystrokes macro, type the following line of text:

   > Something smells fishy.

   Further, position the toothpick cursor in the word *smells*.

2. **Choose Tools⇨Macro.**

   The Macro dialog box appears. It may contain several macros you've already created, or it may be blank (as in Figure 19-1), or it may have the Macro1 macro already present and ready for you to fiddle with.

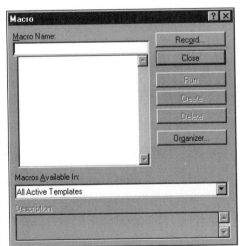

Figure 19-1:
The Macro
dialog box.

3. **Type a name for your macro in the Macro Name box.**

   Be descriptive, but you cannot use any spaces. In fact, just use letters and maybe numbers.

   Call the switch words macro SwitchWord.

4. **Click Record.**

Whoops! Where you think you'd start recording at this stage, you aren't. Instead, you see the Record Macro dialog box, depicted in Figure 19-2.

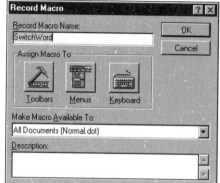

Figure 19-2:
The Record
Macro
dialog box.

The Record Macro dialog box allows you to stick your macro on a toolbar, in a menu, or assign it to a keyboard combination. You choose one of those by clicking on the appropriate button in the Record Macro dialog box. If you just click the OK button, then the macro can only be run from the Macro dialog box after you choose Tools➪Macro. So, for convenience sake, you should assign it someplace else.

5. Click the Keyboard button.

Assign the macro to a key combination.

The Customize dialog box appears, with the Keyboard panel forward. Here you press the key combination you want to assign your macro.

6. Press Alt+Shift+S.

The key combo appears in the Press New Shortcut Key box as Alt+Shift+S. You'll see below that box that this key combo is [unassigned]. That's good. Try to avoid using a key combination that's already used by something else (which rules out all the clever and easy ones).

7. Click Assign.

8. Click Close.

Now, finally, you're back in Word, ready to record your macro.

You'll notice the mouse pointer changes to an arrow with a cassette tape attached. No, you don't click to hear music. That just means you're in macro record mode. And if that weren't enough, there's also the Macro Record floating palette, which is shown in Figure 19-3.

Figure 19-3:
The Macro
Record
floating
palette.

9. **Now you're ready to record your macro.**

   Any keys you type, any commands you choose, everything, will be re-corded as part of your macro.

   To complete the SwitchWord macro, do the following:

   Press the F8 key twice: F8, F8. This selects the word the toothpick cursor is on.

   Press Ctrl+X. This cuts the word.

   Press Ctrl+→. This moves to the next word over.

   Press Ctrl+V. This pastes the word, switching the word order.

   You're done recording.

10. **Click on the Stop recording button on the Macro Record floating palette.**

    Your macro stops recording. You can breathe again. The Macro Record floating thing vanishes and the mouse pointer returns to normal operation.

    Congratulations, your macro has been recorded.

Playing back the macro

To play back the SwitchWord macro you need only press the special key combination: Alt+Shift+S. Position the cursor somewhere in your document and press Alt+Shift+S. Word automatically switches the two words. So where you once had:

```
Something smells fishy.
```

you'll now have:

```
Something fishy smells.
```

Sneaky, huh?

> ✔ If you placed the macro in a menu or on a toolbar, you'll need to access that menu or toolbar to run the macro.
>
> ✔ If the macro doesn't have a menu, toolbar, or keyboard shortcut, then you need to choose Tools⇨Macros to display the Macros dialog box. Locate your macro in the list, click it once to highlight it, and then click the Run button.

Editing the macro

I'm not going to say a word here about editing the macro, which is one big toe in the cesspool of macro programming — a subject way too stinky for this book. Instead, you can take a peek at the SwitchWord macro and see kinda sorta what the WordBasic programming language looks like. Follow these steps:

1. Choose Tools⇨Macro.

The Macro dialog box appears (see Figure 19-1).

2. Highlight your macro in the list.

Locate your macro name in the list and click it once to highlight it.

3. Click Edit.

The Macro dialog box vanishes and you see what looks like a Word document — but it isn't. It's really the Macro as it's written in WordBasic. A special Macro toolbar appears to help those who know how to edit it. Figure 19-4 shows what the SwitchWord macro looks like in this mode.

4. The edit-your-macro step.

If you knew which way was up (or OOP), then you could probably do something here. Otherwise, just gawk.

5. Close the macro document.

Whether you changed it or not, you close a macro in Word just like any other document: Choose File⇨Close. The window closes (you're prompted to save if you haven't already), and you're returned back to regular Word.

If all this has piqued your curiosity, my advice is to check out a more detailed book on Word's macros. They really can be quite powerful and useful. I mean, what you're doing is potentially creating and adding new commands to Word. Fascinating stuff. Wish I had more time to play with it myself.

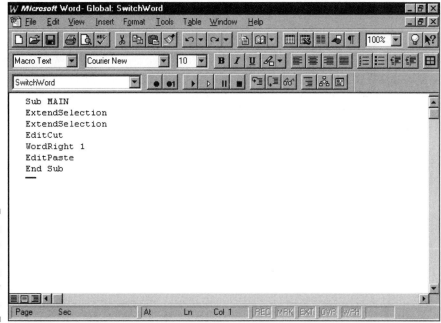

Figure 19-4:
The SwitchWord macro in its ugly, raw form.

Part IV

Working with
Documents

The new extended file name function on Word for Windows 95 became a particularly popular function with the secretary at the AAAAAAAAAA Towing company.

In this part...

"**D**ocument" just sounds so much more important than "that thing I did with my word processor." It implies a crisp, masterful touch. No, this isn't another dreary report; it's a document. This isn't just a letter complaining to the local cable affiliate; it's a document. It isn't a note to Billy's teacher explaining his "rash"; it's a document. It sounds professional, so never mind that you had to tie your fingers in knots and print several hundred copies before you got it just so — it's a document!

This part of the book explores the thing you use Word for, creating documents. This includes printing documents; working with documents and files on disk; and the ugly, sordid story of mail merge, which is right up there next to paying taxes in mental agony and grief.

Chapter 20

More Than a File — a Document

*W*ord lives to serve the document, kind of the way parents (unbeknownst to them) live to serve their children. When a document is up all night, you're there. When a document develops aches and pains, you're there. When your document throws up all over the printer, you're there. But documents aren't there to torture us. They're there for us to love. Oh, I'm getting carried away. . . .

Truly, a *document* is what you see on-screen in Word. It's the text you create and edit, the formatting you apply, and the end result that's printed. But a document also is a file you store on-disk for later retrieval, editing, or printing.

Working on Several Documents Simultaneously

This is handy: Word lets you work on up to a zillion documents at once. Well, actually, you can work on several documents at once, though only nine of them show up in the <u>W</u>indow menu. Still nine is a bunch — a whole Brady Bunch, if you count Alice the indentured servant.

In Word, each document is stored in its own window on-screen. Normally that "window" uses the whole screen, so that document is all you see in Word. To see other documents, you access the <u>W</u>indow menu (Alt,W). From there, choose the number, 1 through 9, corresponding to the document you want to see.

Word politely shows you the document name, right after its number in the menu. Figure 20-1 shows what the <u>W</u>indow menu looks like with a bunch of documents open. If there are more than nine documents open, an extra menu item, <u>M</u>ore Windows, appears. Choose it to see a dialog box from which you can select your documents from a scrolling list.

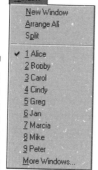

Figure 20-1:
Use the
<u>W</u>indow
menu to
track open
documents.

✔ To switch from one document to another, select its name from the <u>Win</u>dow menu by using the mouse or the keyboard. The names are alphabetized for your convenience.

✔ If you press Ctrl+Shift+F6, you'll be taken to the "next" window; Ctrl+F6 takes you to the "previous" window. If you only have two windows open at a time, then Ctrl+F6 makes for a keen shortcut to skip-to-my-lou between them.

✔ The goings on in one document are independent of any other: Printing, spell checking, and formatting affect only the document you can see on-screen.

✔ You can copy a block from one document to the other. Just mark the block in the first document, copy it (Ctrl+C), open the second document, and paste it in (Ctrl+V). (Don't forget that you can use the Copy and Paste buttons.) Refer to Chapter 6 for detailed block action.

Seeing more than one document

You can arrange all of your documents on-screen by choosing Window⇨Arrange All. This command puts each document into its own "mini-window" — officially known as the Multi-Document Interface by Windows Well-Wishers.

✔ Although you can see more than one document at a time, you can work on only one at a time: the document with the highlighted title bar. You can work on other documents by clicking on them with the mouse or by pressing Ctrl+F6.

✔ After the windows have been arranged, you can manipulate their size with the mouse and change their position.

 ✔ Clicking on a mini-window's Maximize button restores Word to its normal, full-screen view.

✔ The Window⇨Arrange All command works great for two or three documents — when you're comparing text, for example. Arranging more documents than three makes the viewing area so small that it's of little use.

Working on two, or more, parts of the same document

You can look at two or more different parts of the same document — yes, the *same* document — by choosing the Window⇨New Window command. This creates another window on-screen in which you'll find another copy of your document. Unlike having different documents open in separate windows, each copy of this document is "connected" to the other; changes that you make in one of the copies are immediately included in the other.

✔ This feature is useful for cutting and pasting text or graphics between sections of the same document, especially when you have a very long document.

✔ The title bar tells you which copy of your document you're looking at by displaying a colon and a number after the filename. For example, this document is CHAPTER 20:1 in one window and CHAPTER 20:2 in the second window.

✔ You can move back and forth between these windows by using Ctrl+F6.

✔ You cannot use the File➪Close command to close one window. Instead, click on the one window close button (the "X") in the upper-right corner.

 ✔ Another way to view two parts of the same document is by using the old split-screen trick. This feature is discussed . . . why, it's right here.

Using the old split-screen trick

Splitting the screen allows you to view two parts of your document in one window. No need to bother with extra windows here. In fact, I prefer to use Word with as little "junk" on-screen as possible. So when I need to view two parts of the same document, I just split the screen — Solomon-like — and then undo the rift when I'm done. You can accomplish the same splitting-screen feat by following these steps:

1. **Place the mouse cursor on the little gray area located just above the up-arrow button on the vertical scroll bar (on the upper-right side of your document).**

   Oh, bother. Just refer to Figure 20-2 to see what I'm talking about.

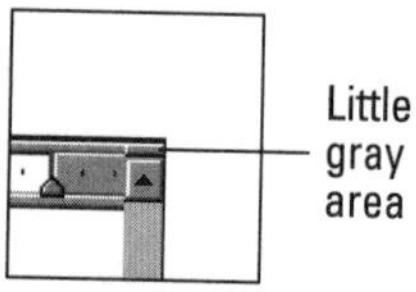

Figure 20-2:
The little gray area you use to split a window.

Little gray area

When you find the sweet spot, the mouse pointer changes shape and looks like a pair of horizontal lines with arrows pointing down and up.

2. **Hold down the left mouse button and drag the pointer down.**

   As you drag, a line drags with you and slices the document window in half. That marks the spot where the screen will split.

3. **Release the mouse button.**

   Your screen looks something like Figure 20-3.

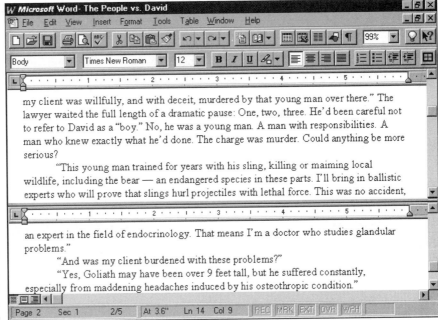

Figure 20-3.
Splitting the
screen.

✔ Each section of the screen can be manipulated separately and scrolled up or down. But the windows still represent the same document; changes that you make in one of the copies are immediately included in the others.

✔ This feature is useful for cutting and pasting text or graphics between parts of the same document.

✔ To undo a split screen, put the cursor on the little gray area and drag it back up to the ruler.

✔ You can also choose Window⇨Split from the menu to split your screen and Window⇨Remove Split to undo it.

✔ The fastest way to split a window is to point the mouse at the little gray area and double-click.

Saving a Document to Disk (the First Time)

There's no need to save your document to disk only when you're done with it. In fact, saving should be done almost immediately — as soon as you have a few sentences or paragraphs. Save! Save! Save!

To save a document that hasn't already been saved to disk, follow the steps listed below. If you've already saved the file, skip up to the next section.

1. Summon the Save command.

Choose File⇨Save; Press Alt, F, S; or press the F12 shortcut key. You see the Save As dialog box shown in Figure 20-4.

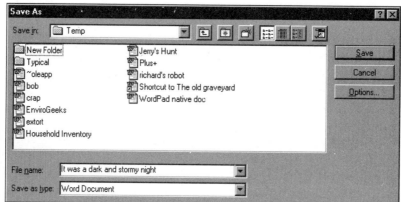

Figure 20-4:
The Save As
dialog box.

2. Type a name for your document.

You can name your document anything, using letters, numbers, a smattering of symbols, spaces, and other whatnot. Though the filename can be tediously long, my advice is to keep it short, simple, and descriptive (which rules out most lawyers from effectively naming files).

You'll notice in the Save As dialog box that Word automatically gives your document a name that equals the first few words of text. Often times this is more than adequate (unless you start everything with "It has come to my attention . . .").

3. Click Save.

If everything goes right, your disk drive churns for a few seconds and eventually your filename appears in the title bar. Your file has been saved.

If there is a problem, you'll likely see one of two error messages:

```
Do you want to replace the existing WHATEVER.DOC?
Yes No Cancel Help
```

There already is a file on disk with that name. Press N, skip back up to step 2, and type in another name. If you press Y, your file will replace the other file on disk, which is probably not what you want.

```
Word cannot give a document the same name as an open
document.
```

This means that you tried to save a file to disk using the name of another document you're working on. Just try again using a different name.

The final problem is the most annoying: Nothing happens. Word refuses to save the file no matter how hard you click the Save button. What Word isn't telling you is that you've used a naughty symbol in the filename. Try again at step 2, and use only letters and numbers in the filename.

- ✔ Always save your document, even after you've typed only a few lines of text.

- ✔ You also should organize your files by storing them in their own special folders on your disk. This subject is covered in Chapter 22 in "Finding a Place for Your Work."

- ✔ Here's the list of offensive characters you cannot use when naming a file:

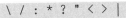

Everything else is fair game (including spaces and periods).

Saving a document to disk (after that)

The instructions in this section assume that you already saved your file to disk once. So why save your file again (and again)? Because it's smart! You should save your file to disk every so often — usually after you write something brilliant or so complex that you don't want to retype it again. (If you haven't yet saved your document to disk, refer to the preceding section.)

Saving your document to disk a second time updates the file on disk. This is painless and quick:

1. **Choose File⇨Save or press the Ctrl+S shortcut.**

   You see the status bar change oh-so quickly as the document is saved. (You can also choose the Save button.)

2. **Continue working.**

   I recommend going back and repeating this step every so often as you continue to toss words down on the page.

   ✔ Save! Save! Save!

   ✔ Save your document to disk every three minutes or so, or any time after you've written something clever.

   ✔ If you are working on a network, you should execute the Save command between each keystroke.

   ✔ If you already saved your file to disk, its name will appear in the title bar. If there is no name there (it says "document" or something equally boring), refer to the preceding section for saving instructions.

Saving a document to disk and quitting

You're done for the day. Your fingers are sore, your eyes glaze over, "I don't want to type no more!" Everywhere you look, you see a mouse pointer. You blink and rub your eyes and stretch out your back. Ah, it's Miller time. But before you slap your buddies on the back and walk into the sunset on a beer commercial, you need to save your document and quit for the day:

1. **Exit.**

   Choose File⇨Exit or press Alt+F4. You see a box that asks

```
Do you want to save changes to whatever?
Yes No Cancel
```

2. **Press Y to save your document.**

   The document is saved and Word closes — quit, kaput.

   ✔ If there is a second document in Word and changes have been made to it since it was last saved, you'll see the same message again. Press Y to save that document.

   ✔ If you haven't yet given your document a name, you can do so after pressing Y to save it. Refer to the instructions for "Saving a Document to Disk (the First Time)," earlier in this chapter.

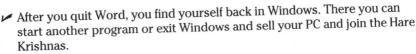

- ✔ After you quit Word, you find yourself back in Windows. There you can start another program or exit Windows and sell your PC and join the Hare Krishnas.

- ✔ Always quit Word and Windows properly. Never turn off your PC or reset when Word or Windows is still on-screen. Only turn off your PC when Windows tells you that it's "safe" to do so.

Saving and starting over with a clean slate

When you want to save a document, remove it from the screen, start over with a clean slate, and choose the File⇨Close command. This keeps you in Word, ready for more word processing action.

- ✔ You also can start afresh in Word and work on a new document by choosing File⇨New or by clicking on the New button on the Standard toolbar or pressing Ctrl+N on the keyboard or waiting for a New moon.

- ✔ If you haven't yet saved your document to disk, refer to "Saving a Document to Disk (the First Time)," earlier in this chapter. Always save your document right after you start writing something (and approximately every 2.3 seconds after that).

- ✔ There is no reason to quit Word and start it again to begin working with a blank slate.

Retrieving a Document from Disk

When you first start Word, or after closing one document and starting again with a clean slate, you have the option of retrieving a previously saved document from disk into Word for editing.

To grab a file from disk — to *retrieve* it — follow these steps:

1. Summon the Open command.

Choose File⇨Open, press Ctrl+O, the Open shortcut, or click on the Open button in the Standard toolbar. You see the Open dialog box, as shown in Figure 20-5.

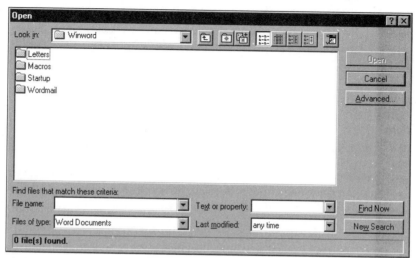

Figure 20-5:
The Open
dialog box.

2. Find your document's folder.

Use the gizmos in the dialog box to browse through various disks and folders on your PC — providing that you're adept at such things or have read through Chapter 22, which touches upon the subject lightly.

3. Click on the document's icon with the mouse pointer.

4. Press Enter.

Word finds the document and loads it on-screen for editing.

5. Go!

✔ If you're not sure of what's in a document, click on the Preview button in the Open dialog box. That adds a window to the dialog box where you can sneak-peek a look at what's in a document before you open it.

✔ If you can't find your document, refer to Chapter 29, the section titled "I Lost My Files!"

✔ If you load a file written by another word processor, you may see a dialog box asking whether it's okay to convert it to Word-speak. Answer Yes. Refer to Chapter 21 for more information on alien word-processor documents.

Loading One Document into Another Document

There are times when you want to load one document into another. Though I can't think of any right now, when you do, follow these steps:

1. **Position the toothpick cursor where you want the other document's text to appear.**

2. **Choose Insert⇨File.**

   Or press Alt, I, L.

3. **Pluck the icon representing the document you want to paste.**

   Click on the document's icon using the mouse.

   You can also use the gadgets and gizmos in the dialog box to locate a file in another folder or on another disk drive or even on someone else's computer on the network. Such power.

4. **Press Enter.**

   The document appears right where the toothpick cursor is.

   ✔ The resulting, combined document still has the same name as the first document.

   ✔ You can retrieve any number of documents into your document. There is no limit, although you should avoid the huge hulking cow document if possible.

   ✔ These steps allow you to grab a block of text saved into one document and stick it into another document. This is often called *boilerplating*, where a commonly used piece of text is slapped into several documents. It's also the way sleazy romance novels are written.

   ✔ Also see Chapter 6 for information on copying scrap icons from Windows desktop into your document.

Doing It All Simultaneously

You Open. You Save. You Close. If you're a busy person (and you wouldn't take time to read this parenthetical clause if you were), it's nice to know that Word can handle these amazing tasks for a bulkload of files all at once.

The subject of opening a group of files all at once is officially covered in Chapter 22. Saving and closing groups of documents is covered next.

Saving a gang of documents simultaneously

Word can work on a multitude of documents all at once. To save them all, you could switch to each window and incant the Save command. Or you could be spiffy and choose the File⇨Save All command, saving all your work in one swift stroke. There is no prompting, no wait and see. Everything is just saved to disk as fast as your PC can handle it.

TIP

✔ If a file has not yet been saved, you'll be prompted to give it a name. Refer to "Saving a Document to Disk (the First Time)," earlier in this chapter, for more information.

✔ I always use the Save All command any time I have to get up and leave my computer — even for a short moment, when the phone rings or when aliens land outside and demand all my corn nuts.

Closing a gang of documents simultaneously

There's a Save All command, but why isn't there a Close All command? The answer is that, lo, a Close All command exists, but it involves some conjuring to get it to appear. When you want to close up all your many documents at once, such as the entire nine-document hoard of the Brady Bunch, heed the following steps:

1. **Press and hold the Shift key. Either one. Doesn't matter.**

2. **Choose File menu.**

3. **Select the Close All item.**

   Normally, it would be the Close item. But because you pressed the Shift key before clicking on the File menu, it magically became the Close All menu item. Nifty.

✔ This trick only works with the mouse, not with the keyboard.

✔ Word still asks whether you want to save any unsaved documents before it closes them.

Chapter 21

Other Documents — Alien and ASCII

*W*ord isn't the only word processor in the world (though Microsoft is trying *very* hard . . .). Other folks use other word processors, and occasionally you may tangle yourself with the files that they create. You may also need to give someone a file in ASCII or plain text format. It's these moments when you must deal with non-Word documents, what I call *alien* file formats.

Loading a Text File

A text file is a special, non-document file that you can load into Word for editing. It's a non-document file because it contains no formatting, no bold or underline, centering, headers, or footers. It's just plain old text.

To open a text file, follow these steps:

1. Do the Open command.

Choose File⇨Open or press Ctrl+O, the Open shortcut. The Open Document dialog box appears.

2. In the Files of type drop-box, choose Text Files.

Click the mouse on the down-arrow by the Files of type drop-box. From the list that drops down, click the mouse once on the Text Files item. This step tells Word to display only text files in the Open dialog box.

3. Hunt down the text file you want to load.

Use the controls in the dialog box to hunt down the file that you want on your hard drive.

Use the Look in drop-box to switch to another folder or hard drive.

Double-click on a folder icon in the Open dialog box's main window to see if your text file is in there.

4. Click on the text file's icon once with the mouse.

5. Choose Open.

Click the Open button or press Enter. The text file appears on-screen, ready for editing just like any Word document — although the formatting will be really cruddy.

✔ Additional information on opening Word document files lurks in Chapter 16.

✔ Check out Chapter 22 for information on using folders and such for storing documents, plus a general review of how the Look in drop-box works in the Open dialog box.

✔ Text files are also called *ASCII* files. ASCII is a technospeak acronym that loosely translates to English as "a text file." You pronounce it *ask-EE*.

✔ Other terms for text files include DOS text file, plain text file, and unformatted file.

✔ The only difficult thing about dealing with a text file is when you're required to save the file back to disk in the *text format — not as a Word document.* These steps are outlined in the following section.

Saving a Text File

Because some applications need to have files in a text format, you need to train Word how to save them that way. Otherwise, Word assumes that you're saving a Word document to disk and junks up the text file with lots of curious Word stuff. Because this procedure is about saving a text file, also known as saving a file in ASCII format, you've got to be more careful.

To save a DOS text file that you just loaded and edited, you need only save it back to disk. Choose the File⇨Save command, press Ctrl+S, or click on the Save button on the Standard toolbar. Word remembers, "Hey, this is a DOS text file," and saves it that way. Miraculous.

To save a new document in the DOS text or ASCII format, follow these steps:

1. **Conjure the Save As command.**

   You must use the Save As command, not the Save command.

2. **The typical Save As dialog box appears.**

   Normally, you enter a filename and Word saves the file as a document on disk. But you want to save the file as a text file, so you must change the *format*, which appears in the Save as type: box.

3. **Click on the down-arrow button beside the Save as type: box.**

   Clicking this button drops down the list of file formats under which Word can save your document.

4. **In the list, look for the Text Only format.**

   Use the up- and down-arrow cursor keys to highlight various formats in the list. When you see Text Only, highlight it by clicking on it once with the mouse.

5. **Select the File Name box again.**

   Click that box with the mouse.

6. **Type in a name for the text file.**

   You can name the file just like any other, but be brief and descriptive.

   If you're from the old school, then *don't* put a .TXT at the end of the filename. This is Windows 95, where all that information is kept track of by Windows, not in a filename. If you're not from the old school, then pretend you didn't read this.

7. **Choose Save.**

   Press Enter or click Save with your mouse to save the file to disk.

   If the file already exists, you'll be asked whether you want to replace it; press Y to replace it. This is one of the rare circumstances when it's okay to press Y to replace the file.

✔ What's the difference between Text Only, Text with Line Breaks, MS-DOS Text, and what else? Gee-whiz, I haven't the foggiest idea. Choose Text Only and you'll lead a happy life.

✔ You can save a document as a text file *and* a Word document file. First, save the file to disk as a Word document by choosing Word Document from the Save as type: box. Then save the file to disk as a text file by choosing Text Only from that list. You'll have a text file, which is what you want, and a Word file, which contains secret codes and prints out really purty.

✔ Fortunately the days of having to save things in a text-only format are waning fast.

Understanding the ASCII thing

Word saves its documents to disk in its own special file format. That format includes your text — the basic characters that you type — plus information about formatting, bold, underline, graphics, and anything else you toss into the document. These elements are all saved to disk so that the next time you use Word, you get your formatting back for editing, printing, or whatever.

Every word processor has its own different document file format. So your Word documents are considered "alien" to other word processors, which use their own non-Word format. It's been this way since the dawn of the PC, so to keep the confusion low, a common text format was developed. It's called the *plain text* or *ASCII* format.

ASCII is an acronym for something I need not mention because there will be no test on this material and you'd probably forget what the acronym stands for two minutes from now. What's more important than knowing what it represents is knowing how to pronounce it: ASK-EE. It's not "ask-two." It's ASK-EE.

An ASCII file contains only text. There are no formatting codes, no bold, underline, graphics, or anything. Just text. It's also called the *plain text* format or sometimes the *DOS text* format. Whatever you call it, an ASCII file contains only text.

Because ASCII files aren't littered with word processing codes, any word processor can read the text. In a way, ASCII files are the Esperanto of document files. Any word processor can read an ASCII file and display its contents. The text will look ugly, but it's better than nothing. Also, to maintain compatibility, Word can save your files in ASCII format, as described in the section "Saving a Text File."

Loading Documents Created by Alien Word Processors

Suppose that crazy Earl gives you a disk full of his favorite limericks. Of course, Earl is crazy, so crazy that he actually uses WordPerfect. Without thinking about it, Earl has handed you a disk full of WordPerfect documents, and it's making you silly.

First, don't press the panic button, and don't worry about the Windows aspect. Although Earl's WordPerfect is one that doesn't use Windows, this fact doesn't affect whether or not you do. A PC disk is a PC disk. No problems there.

Second don't panic button: Word can safely read Earl's limerick files, although he saved them in that whacko WordPerfect file format. To retrieve the files, just follow the steps outlined "Loading a Text File." However, in step 2 choose WordPerfect 5.x (or 6.x) from the Files of type drop-box. That tells Word to only display those types of files in the Open dialog box, which makes it easier for you to pluck out Earl's wacky limericks.

When they're opened, Word recognizes the WordPerfect documents and automatically converts them into Word format. The same holds for any other word processing document; just select its type from the list and you'll be fine.

✔ Not only can Word read WordPerfect documents, it also recognizes several other popular document formats instantly.

✔ If you're unsure as to what format a document is in, then choose All Files from the Files of type drop-box. That displays every file on disk. Word will let you know whether or not it can be opened after you click on the Open button. (No damage can be done.)

✔ Nothing's perfect. The alien document you open into Word may require some fixing up, adjusting fonts, and whatnot. This kind of task is at most a minor bother; at least you don't have to retype anything.

✔ Occasionally, Word finds something so utterly bizarre that it won't recognize it. When this situation occurs, you can try to open the document, but it's probably better to ask the person who created the document to save it in ASCII format.

✔ Another common document format is RTF, the Rich Text Format. This format is better than ASCII because it keeps track of underline, bold, and other formatting. If you'll be sharing files often with other weirdo word processors, try to get everyone to settle on a common format, like RTF. Better still, get everyone to settle on Word.

✔ Word won't recognize anything written in a newer version than itself. Sorta like how professors don't like to call on that smarty-pants who always thinks he has all the answers.

Saving Documents in Alien Formats

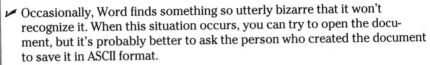

Now comes the time for you to give Earl your collection of leper jokes. Alas, those are all saved to disk in Word format. You could be lax like Earl and just hand him a diskette full of Word documents. But then he'd call you up and complain or ramble on and on about some new word processor conversion program he found. Because you don't have the time for that, just do him a favor and save the file in his own word processor's format.

This task is simple: Follow the steps outlined "Saving a Text File." In step 4, however, select the proper alien word processor format from the list. For Earl, that would be WordPerfect 5.1 for DOS. This process saves the file in the alien format.

✔ Users on Venus prefer Ami Pro for Windows.

✔ Users on Mars prefer WordStar, but hey, they've always been behind the times.

Chapter 22

Managing Files

● ●

In This Chapter

▶ Naming files

▶ Finding a place for your work

▶ Using another folder

▶ Finding files in Word

▶ Finding text in files

▶ Looking at documents on-disk

▶ Working with groups of files

▶ Opening files

▶ Printing files

● ●

*T*he more you work in Word, the more documents you create. And because you always save those documents to disk, the more files you make, which is how a hard drive gets full of stuff: You create it. In a way, your hard drive is like your closet. It's full of stuff. Unless you have a handy closet organizer — like the one I bought on TV for three low, low payments of $29.95 — things are going to get messy. This chapter tackles the subject of files — using and organizing them.

Naming Files

When you save your precious work to disk, which is always a good idea, you need to give your document a specific type of filename. This requirement has nothing to do with Word; point your fingers of blame at Windows.

- A filename can be any length, from one single character to up to 255 characters long. Of course, it would be ridiculous to have a filename that long.

- Shorter, more descriptive filenames are always best.

- You can use any combination of letters or numbers to name your file. Extra points are awarded for being clever. Upper- and lowercase letters look different on the screen but are the same according to Windows.

- A filename can start with a number. In fact, the name of this file, the document that contains this chapter, is 22 (two twos). This name is a perfectly legit filename — and descriptive because it tells me what this file contains. (A better name would be CHAPTER 22, but I personally find the CHAPTER part redundant.)

- Filenames can contain spaces, periods, and all manner of punctuation and symbols, save for the following assortment:

```
\ : * ? " < > | /
```

- If you're from the old school, then forget everything you ever knew about filename extensions. That's all handled internally by Windows now. Ignore extensions. Don't put .DOC at the end of your files! Just, no, never mind.

- A *pathname* is a super-long filename, describing exactly where a file is on a disk drive. The pathname contains a colon, letters, numbers, and backslash characters. For more information, refer to the following section.

- Examples of good and bad filenames are provided in Chapter 1, in the section "Save Your Stuff!"

Finding a Place for Your Work

A hard drive can be a rugged and unforgiving place — like the parking lot at Nordstroms during a shoe sale. Trouble looms like the last pair of off-white pumps at under $10. Unless there is some semblance of organization, chaos rules.

To work your hard drive effectively, you need organization; organization's a big deal. There are special places on your hard drive called *folders*. These things are like holding bins for files. All files of a certain type can be stored — and retrieved — from their own folder.

Your guru or the person responsible for setting up your computer should have built some of these folders and arranged them for your use. If not, you can always create your own, which is shown later in this chapter.

Each of these folders has a specific name. That name is called a *pathname*. The pathname includes the disk drive letter, a colon, a backslash, and a folder name. If you have a folder within another folder (which the geeks call a subfolder), then its name also is included in the pathname along with extra backslash characters to make it all look confusing.

Table 22-1 lists some common pathnames. Please write in additional pathnames that you use, along with their purposes. Or, if this information is making you shake your head, have your guru fill in the pathnames for you.

Table 22-1	Common Pathnames
Pathname	*Contents/Description*
C:	Drive C, main "root" folder
A:	Drive A, main "root" folder
C:\OFFICE95\WINWORD	Word's folder
C:\WINDOWS	Windows' folder
C:\MY DOCUMENTS	Office's main document folder

↳ Directing Word to use a specific folder is covered in the next section.

↳ Creating your own folder is covered in "Creating a New Folder," later on in this chapter.

↳ In prehistoric times, *folders* were known as *directories*, or sometimes the nautical *subdirectory* term was used. There is no difference, other than the guy saying *directory* is a DOS geek.

Using Another Folder

Unless directed otherwise, Word always places its files where it got them. This method is fine if you already saved a file to its proper folder. However, when you open a new file, the new file will go to the folder that was open when you created it. In other words, if I open a new file and I am sitting in the C:\WORD\DUMMIES folder, Word will automatically save the new file in that folder unless I tell Word otherwise. This makes for pretty poor file organization if I'm saving, say, lethal toadstool recipes.

To tell Word to save a file to a specific folder on your hard drive, follow these steps:

1. Summon the File⇨Save As or File⇨Open command.

You can choose a new folder when saving a file to disk or opening a new file. If you choose File⇨Save As, the Save As dialog box opens, as shown in Figure 22-1. If you choose File⇨Open, you see the Open dialog box, shown in Figure 22-2.

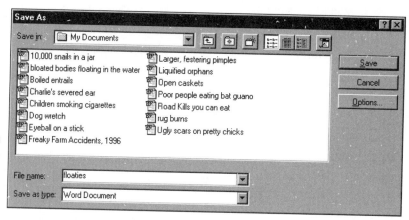

Figure 22-1:
The Save As
dialog box.

2. First, see which folder you're using.

The folder's name appears in the Look in box at the top of the dialog box. In both Figures 22-1 and 22-2 it's the My Documents folder.

If you're already in the folder that you want to be in, skip to step 6 (which means you're more-or-less done).

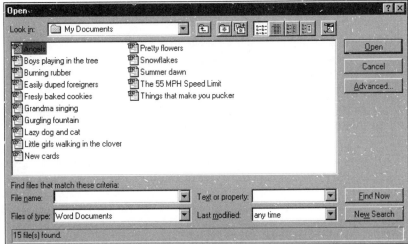

Figure 22-2:
The Open
dialog box.

3. Select the disk drive that you want from the Look in drop-down list.

Click on the down-arrow button or press Alt+I. Select a drive from the list. If it's a floppy drive, ensure that you have a disk in the drive *before* you select it.

If you only have one hard drive, C, then choose it as well. It's best to look for your folder from the "top down."

4. Choose your folder from those listed in the dialog box.

You may have to scroll through the list to find the folder that you want. When you find the folder you want, such as the My Document folder (which should be on drive C), double-click on it with the mouse to open it. All the files in that folder will be listed in the File Name box when you double-click on it. (More instructions on working the folders is offered at the end of this list of steps.)

5. Keep repeating step 4 until you've found the folder you're looking for.

For example, you may have to open My Documents, then Projects, then Memos to finally see the documents stored in the Memos folder.

6a. If you're opening a document, click on its name once.

Refer to Chapter 20 for more information on opening a document from this point on.

6b. If you're saving a document to disk, save it now.

Refer to Chapter 20 for more information on saving your document.

✔ Some folders contain other folders. To see their contents, double-click on the folder's name.

✔ The main folder on every disk is the *root folder*. It's the one with a drive letter followed by a backslash. On drive C, the root folder is named C:\. Other folders on the disk have other names, and sometimes the names will give you a clue as to the folder's contents. Sometimes.

✔ The files in each folder appear in the big window in the middle of both the Open and Save As dialog boxes.

✔ Each disk in your system has its own set of folders. If you can't find the folder that you want on one disk, try another. For example, scope out drive D if drive C turns out to be a dud.

Creating a New Folder

To keep organized, you may need to create new folders for your new projects. For example, suppose you just started your plan to take over the entertainment industry. Heck, you're going to need a new folder to put in all those memos and extortion letters. Here's how you'd do that:

1. Follow the steps in the previous section for saving a document in a specific folder.

Your folder has to go somewhere. You'll need to create it inside another folder. For example, you would first mosey over to the My Documents folder if you were going to create your new folder there.

If you had an Extortion folder under My Documents, you'd want to open that folder up to place your newer folder there as well. (It works that way, not that you'd have an Extortion folder or anything.)

2. Click on the Create New Folder button.

This happy guy lives in the top row of the Save As dialog box. Click him once to see the New Folder dialog box.

3. Type in a name for your new folder.

Be descriptive. Be creative. Short and sweet. To the point. (Try real hard to achieve this goal if you're a politician.)

Word automatically suggests the name New Folder for your new folder. What a joke! Anyone who has a folder named New Folder on their hard drive should be taken out and forced to use DOS on an 8088 for the rest of their corporeal existence.

4. Click OK.

Through the magic of the computer, your new folder is created, sitting right there on the screen for you to marvel at.

5. Marvel at it.

6. Double-click the folder to open it.

After all, this is a file-saving exercise here. You open your folder by double-clicking on it. Its contents (nothing) will then be displayed in the Save As dialog box.

7. Continue saving your document.

And use the techniques in the previous section when you need to reuse this folder for saving stuff in the future.

✔ New folders can only be created in the Save As dialog box. I mean, like *duh*. If you created a new folder in the Open dialog box, there wouldn't be anything in it for you to open. Some people . . .

✔ You can also create new folders using Windows' Explorer or the My Computer thing. Refer to your favorite book on Windows for more information on that.

✔ Folders are named just like files. Same rules. See the first section of this chapter for the nitty-gritties.

Finding Files in Word

It's really hard to lose a file so thoroughly that Word can't find it, even if you have an absolutely horrid memory. I often find it difficult to remember which documents contain the information that I want and also where the heck I put that file anyway. Of course, I often find all sorts of things next to the milk in the refrigerator. Cereal Fairies is what I think. In any case, it's possible to tweak the Open dialog box so that you can easily find any old file, no matter where you stuffed it. To do so, follow these steps:

1. Summon the Open dialog box.

Press Ctrl+O.

2. Choose a disk drive from the Look in drop-down list.

Pluck out any old drive. For most of us, that's just drive C. However, on an older computer I was fond of putting all my word processing stuff on drive D.

3. Click on the Commands and Settings button.

This little guy is located at the top of the Open dialog box. Clicking on him once with the mouse displays a heretofore hidden menu (not that the icon on the button offered any hints or anything).

4. Choose Searc_h_ Subfolders.

Click on that menu item once with the mouse.

Word churns and hums.

Eventually you'll see a cascading list of folders and Word documents — every document that lives on your disk drive. Figure 22-3 shows what it may look like.

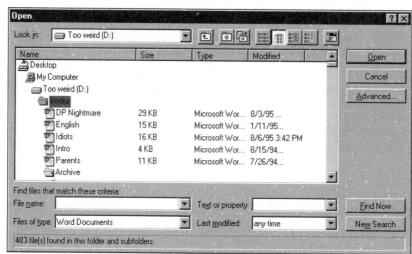

Figure 22-3:
The Open dialog box displays all the Word documents on your hard drive.

5. Find your document.

Use the scrollbar to scan through the list, or obey some of the hints offered in the following bullets.

- Displaying files this way makes the Open dialog box work a bit like the Explorer. You can even open and close folders and disk drives by double-clicking on them. This makes the list a bit more manageable.

- To look for a file containing a specific bit of text, type that text into the Te_x_t or property box, then click the _F_ind Now button. Word will take a while to locate the specific document(s), but this can be a godsend if you forget what a document is called but remember some bit of text inside.

▶ If Word finds no matching files, the list will be empty. The dreadful text `0 file (s) found in this folder and subfolders` will appear. Weep bitterly and curse the computer. Or maybe try again with another word that you're *certain* is in your file.

▶ When you find the file that you want, highlight it and click on the <u>O</u>pen button to open it into Word.

▶ Don't forget that you can search other drives for your files as well. Just choose that other disk drive in step 2.

▶ The Open dialog box stays in the "find all files" mode until you turn it off. Click on the Commands and Settings button again and choose Searc<u>h</u> Subfolders. This returns the Open dialog box's operation back to normal (more-or-less).

Looking at documents on disk

Wouldn't it be nice if you could look into a document before you loaded it, like getting a sneak preview? This task is entirely possible using the Preview button in the Open dialog box.

Follow the steps for peering into a file's contents before opening it:

1. Choose <u>F</u>ile⇨<u>O</u>pen.

Or use your favorite alternative to get at the Open dialog box.

2. Click on the Preview button.

Pictured at left, click once with your mouse.

3. A special preview window opens in the Open dialog box.

Figure 22-4 shows you what it sort of looks like. Now you can see the contents of any file you click on in the left side of the dialog box. Use the scrollbar to peruse before you open.

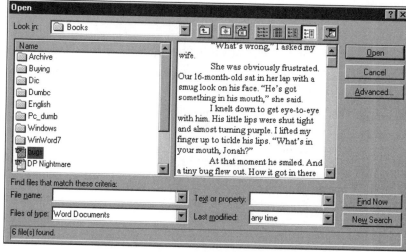

Figure 22-4:
The Open
dialog box
with its
preview
window
hanging out.

4. **Open the file.**

Click the Open button when you like what you see.

Working with groups of files

The Open dialog box enables you to work with files individually or in groups. To work with a group of files, you must select them with the mouse, which follows the typical Windows metaphor for selecting several items in a group:

1. **Press the Ctrl key and click on each document that you want.**

The item becomes highlighted and selected.

2. **Repeat step 1 for each additional item that you want in your group.**

Et cetera and so on.

✔ When you have the preview window active, it displays only the contents of the last file in the group. See the previous section, "Looking at documents on disk," for information on the preview mode.

✔ You can only select a group of files in one folder. However, if you follow the instructions in "Finding Files in Word," earlier in this chapter, you can select files from all over your hard drive.

✔ The commands detailed in the following sections apply to files selected in a group. Actually there are only two of them: Open and Print. Still, these are great commands to use on a group of files, solving lots of problems miscellany and niggling.

Opening files

Here's how you would open more than one file at a time using the Open dialog box:

1. **Select the file or group of files that you want to open from those shown in the Open dialog box's window.**

   Refer to "Finding Files in Word" and "Working with groups of files" for the details.

2. **Click on the <u>O</u>pen button.**

   They open, and Word places each into its own document window.

3. **Work away!**

   ✔ There is a limit on the number of files Word can work with at once. No, I don't know what it is — but you will! You'll see some odd error message about not enough memory or "heap" space or something bizarre. Don't panic. Close a few windows — maybe even quit Word — and start over.

   ✔ Refer to Chapter 20 for information on saving all of your files at once, as well as information on closing them all at once. Wow. Doing it all at once. I'm sure that such a concept was promised in a computer brochure somewhere.

Printing files

You can print one or several documents without opening them in the Open dialog box. To do so, obey the following steps:

1. **Select the file or group of files that you want to print from the Open dialog box.**

   Instructions in "Finding Files in Word" and "Working with groups of files" will tell you how to locate the files and highlight them.

2. **Click on the Commands and Settings button.**

   A drop-down menu appears.

3. **Select the <u>P</u>rint command.**

   The Print dialog box appears.

4. **Click OK to print your document(s).**

   ✔ Make sure that your printer is on and ready to print before you click the OK button in the Print dialog box.

   ✔ Chapter 8 has more information on printing. Chapter 8's information on the Print dialog box applies here as well.

Chapter 23

Mail Merge for the Mental

· ·

In This Chapter

▶ Understanding mail merge

▶ Using the Mail Merge command

▶ Preparing the main document

▶ Preparing the data file

▶ Adding data to the data file

▶ Inserting the fields

▶ Merge mania!

· ·

*M*ail merge. Ugh. What it is: a method of producing several customized documents without individually editing each one. We're talking form letters here — but sneaky form letters that you can't really tell are form letters.

Let's face it, mail merge is not fun. For some reason, with every incarnation of Word, it gets more difficult and baffling. The boys and girls at Microsoft have always cheerfully "improved" mail merge, primarily by adding a hoary hoard of new ugly terms to describe it. I would normally pass on this topic, but in an effort to do my civic duty — and in an attempt to hold down the massive chiropractic bills that result from your picking up and tossing the computer through the window — this chapter contains only the basic, need-to-know steps for mail merging.

Understanding Mail Merge

There are three ways to handle Word's (or anybody's) mail merge:

1. **Read this chapter and then go out and have a drink.**

2. **Skip this chapter and go straight to the booze.**

3. **Hire a professional to do it for you while you are in detox.**

I'll outline the first part of the first approach here. The second approach you can attempt on your own. The third approach shouldn't be necessary. (If you've been through mail merge before, skip to "Using the Mail Merge Command.")

Mail merge is the process of taking a single form letter, stirring in a list of names and other information, and then merging both to create several documents. Each of the documents is customized by using the list of names and information that you provide.

The file that contains the names and other information is called the *data source*. The file that contains the form letter is referred to as the *main document*. No, I didn't make this up. These are the terms Word uses. Get used to 'em.

You start by typing the main document, creating it as you would any other document, complete with formatting and other mumbo-jumbo. But leave blank those spots where you would put the address, "Dear Mr. Zipplebip," or anything else that will change from letter to letter. You will put some fill-in-the-blanks special codes here in a bit. These special codes are called *fields* (another term that I didn't make up).

The data source is a file (kind of) that contains the names, addresses, and other information that you want. Unlike the main document, however, this document is created by using a special format. It's almost like filling in names in a database program. (In fact, that's exactly what it is.)

Each of the names, addresses, and other information in the data file composes what's called a *record*. Word creates a custom letter by using the main file as a skeleton and filling in the meat with the record in the secondary file. I know — totally gross. But nothing else I can think of now describes it as well.

Because no one commits this routine to memory (and for good reason), the following sections provide outlines to follow so that you can create a mail merge document by using main and data files. Cross your fingers, count the rosary, and check the kids. We're goin'-a mail-mergin'.

Please don't feel that my emphasis on intoxication in this section's first three steps is to be taken lightly. In fact, I take all my drinking seriously.

Using the Mail Merge Command

Start your mail merging mania by choosing Tools⇨Mail Merge. This command opens the Mail Merge Helper dialog box, depicted in Figure 23-1. Don't let the title fool you.

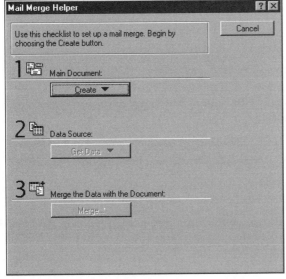

Figure 23-1:
The
misnamed
Mail Merge
Helper
dialog box.

You will be mail merging in three steps, as shown in the Mail Merge Helper dialog box. First comes the Main Document, then the Data Source, and finally the actual merging.

- ✔ Don't let the Spartan nature of the Mail Merge Helper dialog box fool you. Other buttons and gadgets appear as you get into it. Truly, it's frightening.

- ✔ The Data Source (the second step in the dialog box) is really the second document: the names, lists, and other information. I know, it's a horrid name, but it's supposed to make you feel more comfortable.

- ✔ Yeah, there are really more than three steps to this whole operation. Lots more.

- ✔ Please continue reading with the next section.

Preparing the main document

The main document is the fill-in-the-blanks document. To create it, follow these steps:

1. **Click on the Create button in the Mail Merge Helper dialog box.**

   A drop-down list drops down.

2. Select Form Letters from the list.

Another, annoying dialog box appears. Ignore it and . . .

3. Click on the New Main Document button.

This option lets you create a new document in which to write your form letter.

4. Click on the new Edit button, which just appeared out of thin air next to the Create button.

See? I told you the dialog box would get crowded. It gets worse.

The Edit button contains a drop-down list with one item, Form Letter: Document#.

5. Select the Form Letter: Document# item.

You're now allowed to edit your form letter document. The Mail Merge Help dialog box disappears, and you're presented with a new document window in which to work.

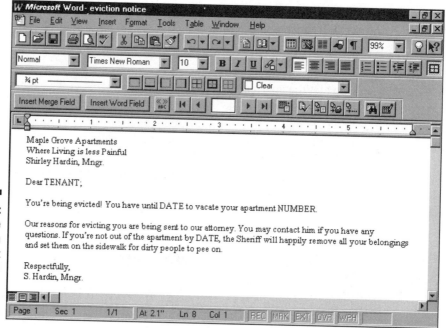

Figure 23-2: A sample main document and the Mail Merge toolbar.

✔ The main document contains all the fill-in-the-blanks stuff. Don't bother putting them in just now; you'll be doing this task in a later step. However, keep in mind what you want to go where.

✔ In my main documents, I usually stick the replaceable, fill-in-the-blanks stuff with ALL CAPS so that I can find the items more easily later (see Figure 23-2).

✔ The new toolbar you see on your screen (see Figure 23-2) is the Mail Merge toolbar. Don't bother messing with it; none of its buttons work at this point. (It's an exercise in frustration if you try, which makes you wonder why it's there in the first place.)

Preparing the data source

A data source is not a traditional Word document. It is a database table of sorts, which includes information stored in *fields* and *records*. Each field contains a tidbit of text that will fill in a blank in the main document. A collection of fields — one form letter — is what makes up a record. Don't sweat the details or the jargon. Word handles the details. I'll ease you through the jargon.

To start a data source, follow these steps:

1. **Choose Tools⇨Mail Merge.**

   The Mail Merge Help dialog box appears again. Don't bother checking with Figure 23-1 — the thing has transformed again. Mostly in step 2, you'll see a new button plus some new information. As usual, ignore the details and keep reading with the next step.

2. **Click on the Get Data button.**

   A drop-down list appears.

3. **Choose Create Data Source from the list.**

   The Create Data Source dialog box appears, full of mirth and merriment (see Figure 23-3). This is the place where you create the fields — the fill-in-the-blank items.

   To be helpful, Word has already dreamt up a whole parade of field names. Your first duty is to erase them all.

4. **Keep clicking on the Remove Field Name button until all the names Word concocted in the Field Names in Header Row list are gone, gone, gone.**

   TIP

   I had to do it 13 times. You may have to click more if you click too fast.

   You are disposing of the preset names so that you can dream up your own.

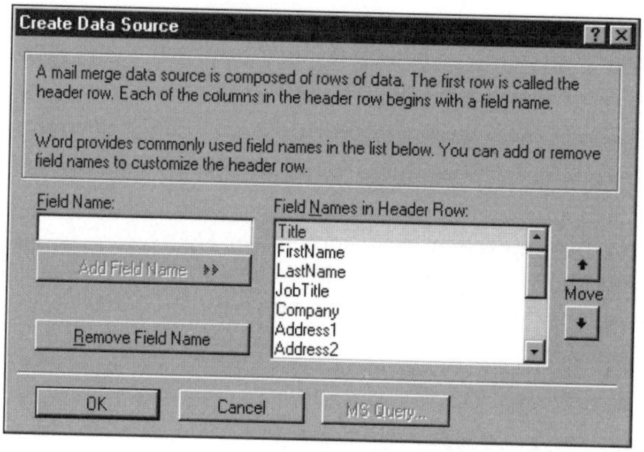

Figure 23-3:
The Create
Data Source
dialog box.

5. **Type a field name into the Field Name box.**

   Here are some suggestions for making this step make sense:

   The field should be named to reflect the kind of information that it will contain. For example, a field named *firstname* would contain first names.

   No two fields can have the same name.

   A field name must begin with a letter.

   A field name can contain up to 20 letters, numbers, and underscored characters.

   You cannot use spaces or punctuation marks in field names.

   When entering addresses, always make separate fields for the city, state, and ZIP codes.

6. **Click on the Add Field Name button after typing your field name.**

   This command inserts the field that you created into the list shown in the Field Names in Header Row box.

7. **Repeat Steps 5 and 6 for each field that you want to include in your data file.**

   In my example (see Figure 23-2), I have a TENANT, a DATE, and a NUMBER. I had to go through steps 5 and 6 three times. For more-detailed form letters, you may be stuck here for an eternity.

8. **Click the OK button when you're done creating field names.**

   The Save As Data Source dialog box appears. This dialog box works just like the Save As dialog box to save a document. In fact, that's what you're doing: saving your data source document to disk.

9. **Give your data source document a name.**

   Be clever. I called my eviction document EVICTION NOTICE. I call the data source document, which contains names, addresses, and other stuff, LOSERS.

10. **Click the Save button.**

    Another annoying dialog box appears after your data source has been saved to disk. Ignore everything — you're almost done with this stage — and . . .

11. **Click on the Edit Data Source button.**

    The Data Form dialog box appears and . . . you're ready to continue reading with the next section.

Adding data to the data source

Because you're obeying step-by-step instructions here, editing the fill-in-the-blanks information — which is technically called "adding data to the data source" — is done via the handy Data Form dialog box, shown in Figure 23-4. The following steps tell you how to fill in the blanks.

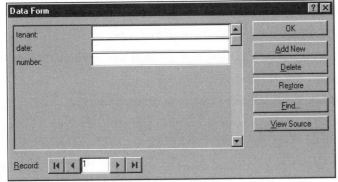

Figure 23-4:
The Data
Form dialog
box.

1. **Fill in the blanks!**

   Each field in your document needs information. For a NAME field, type in a name. Then type in other necessary information as displayed in the Data Form dialog box: street, ZIP code, phone number, hat size, and so on. Use the Tab key to move from box to box.

2. **When you've filled in all the blanks, click on the Add New button.**

   You don't have to click the Add New button after typing the last record. Instead, go right on up to step 4.

3. Repeat steps 1 and 2 for every person to whom you want to mail your form letter.

4. When you're done, click the OK button.

Clicking OK sends the Data Form dialog box away, saving all the information to disk.

✔ Data is pronounced *DAY-ta*.

✔ The names for the boxes in the Data Form dialog box are the field names that you created in the previous section.

✔ Move from box to box by pressing the Tab key.

✔ You can use the Record buttons to scan and modify information that you've already entered.

✔ If you need to reexamine or edit the data source file, refer to the very next section.

Editing the data source file

If you need to look at your data source information, for recreational examination or editing, you can follow these steps:

1. Choose Tools⇨Mail Merge.

The Mail Merge dialog box from Hell appears.

2. Under step 2, Data Source, in the dialog box, click on the Edit button.

A list with one item should drop down.

3. Click on the highlighted Data item or press Enter.

You'll see the Data Form dialog box displayed. There you can peruse or edit your information as you see fit.

Use the Record buttons to scan the various records. You can use the Delete button to remove a record. Edit the text in the fields and click on the OK button when you're done.

Clicking on the View Data Source button also presents the Data Source dialog box. (If it doesn't, and I've seen it work about half the time, then follow the preceding steps to see the Data Source dialog box for sure.)

Inserting the fields

You need to place the fields — the blanks — into your main document. That's done by following these steps:

1. Position the toothpick cursor where you want the field to be placed.

For example, you want a name field after the *Dear* in your letter's greeting, so position the cursor between the *Dear* and the colon.

 The fields created in the data document do not have any punctuation in them. If you want a space or a comma, or anything else, you need to insert it in the main document.

2. Click on the huge Insert Merge Field button in the Mail Merge toolbar.

A list of your fields drops down.

3. Select the field that you want to place in the document.

For example, placing the cursor between *Dear* and the colon, select the firstname field with the mouse. This selection inserts the cryptic code `<<firstname>>` into the main document, which is what Word thinks of as a "blank" for fill-in-the-blanks stuff.

You can have more than one field on a line.

A tad bit of editing may be required after the field. I typically have to add a space, comma, colon, or whatever after fields as Word inserts them.

If you used your own place holders or ALL CAPS thingies, now is the time to delete them.

4. Continue adding fields until the document is complete.

Repeat steps 1, 2, and 3 as necessary to create all the blank spots in your document.

✔ Don't worry if the formatting looks too funny with the `<<Fields>>` in your document. Things get formatted nicely when Word fills in the blanks — *after* merging.

✔ To delete an unwanted field, select it with the mouse and press the Delete key. You can't use the Delete or Backspace keys by themselves! You must highlight a field marker and then delete it.

Merge mania!

After creating the main and data files, you're ready to merge away! Ensure that both main and data files have been saved to disk:

Save!

Save!

This part of the process is very important! When you want to do the merge, follow these steps, which are, you will be glad to learn, a whole bunch simpler than anything else connected with merging:

1. **Choose <u>T</u>ools⇨Mail Me<u>r</u>ge.**

   Golly that dialog box has gotten busy. Fortunately, this is the last time it will offend you.

2. **Click on the <u>M</u>erge button, near the bottom of the dialog box by the third step.**

   The Merge dialog box appears, which you can dally in later after you have the whole process down pat.

3. **Click on the Merge button.**

   As if by magic, Word creates several documents merging your main document with the information that you put into your data source. All of the new documents appear, one after the other, on the screen in front of you in Word.

   Congratulations, you've just merged.

✔ Word merges the names and other information from the data file into the main document and creates lots of little, customized documents in one great big document file. That's what you see on-screen right now. Your options at this point are to review all the documents, save them, or print them. You made it!

✔ Viewing several merges before printing is a good idea. Check for punctuation and spacing.

✔ The main file appears several times on-screen, with information from the data file plugged into each copy. All files are separated by section breaks or hard page breaks.

✔ If your merge isn't humongous, you should save your mail merge in this on-screen format.

✔ You can print right from the screen view of the merged files by selecting File➪Print.

✔ Now you know how to get those custom, uniquely crafted documents out to the foolhardy who actually think that you took the time to compose a personal letter. Ha! Isn't mail merge great?

✔ Always examine the results of the merge. Some things may not fit properly, and some editing will no doubt be required.

Part V
Working with Graphics

"NOPE - I'D BETTER WAIT 'TIL ALL MY FONTS ARE WORKING. A HATE LETTER JUST DOESN'T WORK IN *Filigree Flowerbox Extended.*"

In this part...

Word processing is words, so what's the ugly subject of graphics doing here? After all, you struggle to write; now do they want you to struggle to draw?

Fortunately, using graphics in a word processor isn't that painful, especially thanks to Windows, which lives and breathes graphics, and that's the thrust behind this part of the book. It's more than just cutting and pasting pretty pictures. And, if you're lucky, very little actual drawing is involved. (So dash those images of stick figures lining your literary masterpieces.) You can use many parts of Word to help create graphics — stuff you'd never otherwise know about. It's all covered here in the cheery manner you expect. Be prepared to make your writing not only literary, but flowery as well.

Chapter 24

Making Purty Pictures

· ·

· ·

*I*f a picture were really worth a thousand words, we'd never get some artist types to shut up. And you know how much they love to talk. Go visit a coffee bistro sometime to find out. Makes you wonder if Michelangelo ever said, "How about this, Your Holiness: What if you and I just sit here and sip café mocha wambooli and discuss didacticism and moral fortitude of the first century?" (Julius II would have strewn Mickey's entrails 'round the Sistine Chapel had he dared!)

Graphics can tastefully accent your document. Tastefully. Oh, and they can be obnoxious as well. In Word, you can easily add illustrations, simple drawings called *line art*, and even photos to enhance your creative work. On multimedia-equipped computers — *multimedia* defined as "I paid through the nose for this PC" — you can add movies with sound or animation with your own voice recorded as a soundtrack to your Word document. Cool, but tasteless. Fortunately, Word lets you do it with a minimum of effort, as this chapter shows.

Adding a Graphic Image

You can add a graphic to any Word document in three ways:

1. **Just paste it in wherever the toothpick cursor happens to be.**

2. **Put it in a table.**

3. **Put it in a frame.**

Each method has something going for it; each has something going against it, too:

- ✔ Pasting is the latter half of copy-and-paste. You start by finding or creating an image in another program, one suited to graphics. Then you *copy* the image. Windows remembers it. Then you *paste* it into Word. This procedure works like copying and pasting text, and the same Ctrl+C (Copy) and Ctrl+V (Paste) keys are used in all Windows programs for this purpose.

- ✔ Windows comes with a simple painting program called Paint. (This was after Microsoft fired all the people in the Creative Names Department.) You can use Paint to create interesting, albeit primitive, images for use in Word. The graphics you see in Figure 11-7, as well as other figures in this book, were created in Paint and then pasted into a Word document.

- ✔ Inserting an image into a table works just like pasting text at the toothpick cursor's position. The difference is that the image fits snugly into a cell in a table. Refer to Chapter 12 for more information on tables; your local hardware store has lots of books on making chairs and lawn furniture.

- ✔ Putting an image into a frame is nice because you can write text *around* the image. Otherwise, the image kinda sits by itself, all lonely without text to insulate it.

Whence cometh thy graphical image?

Before you write anything, you should have a good idea in your head what you want to write about. (If you don't, and you just stare at the blank screen, then you have what it takes to be a *real* writer!) The same holds true with graphics. You need to have the graphic image you want to use before you paste it into your text. Word can do a lot of things, but you can't exactly draw with it. Not really.

Graphic images — pictures — come from several places. You can create the image in a graphics program, buy a disk full of images or *clip art*, or you can use a device called a *scanner* to electronically convert pictures and other printed images into graphics files you can store in the computer.

- ✔ Word can deal with many popular graphics file formats, which probably are listed in the manual somewhere, and which appear on the List Files of Type drop-down lists in the various graphics-related dialog boxes. As long as your graphics can be saved in a *compatible* format, Word won't balk.

- ✔ You don't need a graphics file on your disk to use it in a document. You can paste anything you can get onto the Windows Clipboard directly into a Word document as a graphic. This means that you can create a graphic with a drawing program, copy it to the Clipboard, and then paste it into your Word document. This is the "do it on the fly" school of graphics creation.

✔ Table 24-1 discusses various graphics file formats in a brief manner. If you can save your graphics in any of these formats, you're in business, and Word is happily-bappily.

Table 24-1	Common Graphic Formats	
Format	**Pronunciation**	**File type**
BMP	Bee-Em-Pee	Windows bitmap files, used by Windows Paint and other programs
EPS	E-Pee-Ess	Encapsulated PostScript; used by sophisticated drawing programs (mostly from Adobe)
GIF	Jiff (the peanuttier peanut butter)	Graphics Interchange Format, used primarily on CompuServe for "naked lady" images
JPEG	Jay-Peg	Stands for something, currently most popular format for naked lady images on the Internet
PCD	Pee-See-Dee	Kodak Photo CD; pictures from Bill Cosby
PCX	Pee-See-Eks	PC Paintbrush (old Windows Paint)
PICT	Picked	Macintosh graphical format
TIFF	Tiff	Tagged Image File Format, used by some sophisticated drawing programs
WMF	Double-U-Em-Eff	Windows *metafile*, a common graphics file format
WPG	Double-U-Pee-Jee	WordPerfect Graphics files; strange, but true

Slapping a graphic image into a document

To stick a graphic image already created on disk into your text, follow these whimsical steps:

1. **Position the toothpick cursor in the spot where you want your picture.**

   If any text is already there, it will be shoved aside to make room for the graphic.

2. **Choose the Insert➪Picture command.**

   You see the Insert Picture dialog box, as shown in Figure 24-1.

Figure 24-1:
The Insert
Picture
dialog box.

3. **Make sure that the Preview Picture box is visible.**

   Click on the preview button if you don't see the preview window displayed.

4. **Navigate through the drives and folders until you find the graphic image that you want.**

   This step is optional. Word automatically shows you a slew of its own clip-art images right away. Only if you want to find an image saved elsewhere do you need to scour.

5. **Select the image.**

   Select All Graphics Files from the List Files of type list box and highlight the filename.

6. **Choose OK!**

   Splat! The image is pasted into your document, wherever your cursor happened to be.

✔ If you don't see any images on your hard drive, see the sidebar, "Waaa! I don't have any Word clip art images on my computer!"

✔ "Ugh! That wasn't the image I wanted." Hurry and choose the Edit⇨Undo command, or press Ctrl+Z, and try again.

✔ You don't have to use the Insert⇨Picture command if you copy and paste an image. To do that, create the image in another Windows application, select it for copying, and then return to Word and paste.

✔ The image appears right where the toothpick cursor is. In fact, you can almost treat the image as if it were a character in your document, albeit a very huge character.

✔ The section "Adjusting the Graphic Image" offers information on adjusting the image after you place it into your document.

✔ Some images are colorful on-screen. Unless you have a color printer, they'll only print in black, white, and — with a laser printer — shades of gray.

✔ A cool thing to stick at the end of a letter is your signature. Use a painting program like Paintbrush or have it *scanned* by using a desktop scanner to create your John Hancock. Save it as a file on disk and then follow the previous steps to insert it at the proper place in your document.

✔ If you have faithfully followed the preceding steps, and that blasted graphic just won't show up on-screen, it's probably because the paragraph formatting got messed up. Put the cursor in the paragraph that has the graphic, open the Format⇨Paragraph dialog box, and change the Line Spacing to something other than Exactly.

✔ This method of inserting a graphic does not allow you to put multiple lines of text next to the image. See "Slapping it in a table" or "Frame the thing," later in this chapter, to learn how to do this.

✔ Although they're not really "graphic images," Word has an assortment of oddball characters that you can insert into your text, right along with the normal human characters. For example, the ☺ or the ♥ are ever popular with hippie-wanna-bees. Refer to Chapter 9 for more information on Word's oddball characters.

✔ Nothing slows down Word like a few graphical images on-screen. Try pasting them in last.

✔ You can't backspace over a graphic image. To get rid of it, mark it as a block and press Delete.

Slapping it in a table

Tables are wonderful places for a graphic. You can put your image of, say, your favorite politician in a cell and place text in any cell before or after the graphic. This keeps everything neat without interfering much with the text before or after the table. Figure 24-2 shows what I mean.

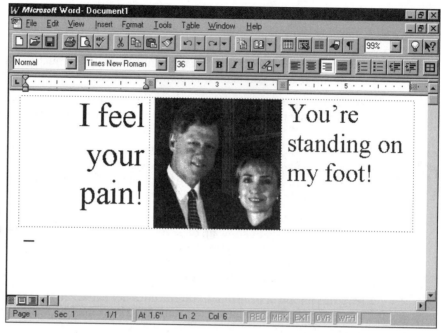

Figure 24-2:
Text and
graphics
mix nicely in
a sneaky
table.

To insert a graphic in a table, follow these steps.

1. Make the table.

Refer to Chapter 12 to learn about tables. Keep in mind that it's okay to make a table with only one row. You can put the image in one column and text in the other.

2. Position the toothpick cursor in the cell where you want your picture.

Point and click with the mouse.

3. Choose the Insert⇨Picture command.

Navigate through the drives and folders until you find the graphic you want.

4. Select the image and choose OK.

Slap! The image is pasted into your table.

✔ If the image has already been saved in the Windows Clipboard (you copied it from another program), then you just need to press Ctrl+V, the Paste command, in step 3 and you're done.

✔ You can "grab" the edges of a cell in a table to change the cell's size or position.

✔ To change the size of your image, see "Adjusting the Graphic Image," later in this chapter.

"Waaa! I don't have any Word clip art images on my computer!"

Installing the clip art images is optional and may not have been done if your PC doesn't have enough disk space. But you can make amends. From the Start thing's menu (which you can get at by pressing Ctrl+Esc), choose Programs➪Microsoft Office➪Setup. This runs the Setup program that came with Microsoft Office and Word. (You'll need to quit Word before running Setup; it will tell you so if you forget.)

In the Setup program, click on the Add/Remove button. Another dialog box appears. Click on

Office Tools in the Options list, and then click Change Option. Yet another dialog box appears! This time, look for Clip Art in the list (it's down toward the bottom so you'll have to scroll to get there). Click on Clip Art to put a check mark in its box. Then click the OK button. That dialog box closes. Then click the Continue button.

Continue to heed the instructions on the screen as the files are copied. You'll be asked to insert your Microsoft Office CD or diskettes so that the files will be copied. Obey your computer!

Frame the thing

The third, and most satisfying, way to put an image into a document is to put it in a frame. A frame is an area in your document where you can stick things — text and graphics, mostly. The frame then becomes a container for the text or graphics, which you can move around in your document. Text in your document will flow around the frame without disturbing the frame's delicate contents.

To put a graphic into a frame, you must first make the frame. Obey these steps:

1. **Switch to Page Layout View.**

   Choose View➪Page Layout. This step is necessary. If you forget it, Word will remind you later. (You can also click on the Page Layout View button, located near the lower-left corner of the screen.)

2. **Choose the Insert➪Frame command.**

   +

   The toothpick cursor changes into a little cross-hair doodad. (Here is where you're reminded to switch into Page Layout view if you haven't already; click the Yes button if you're so reminded.)

3. **Put the little cross-hair doodad where you want the upper-left corner of the frame to be.**

4. **Create the frame by holding down the left mouse button and dragging the little cross-hair doodad down and to the right.**

This creates a rectangle on-screen. Your picture will appear inside that rectangle — okay, *frame*. See Figure 24-3.

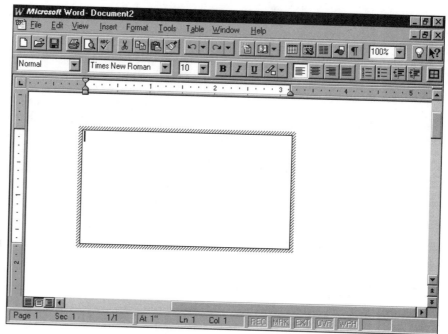

Figure 24-3:
A frame
lurks in your
document.

5. Move the frame to where you want it.

You can move the frame around by pointing the mouse pointer at one edge of the frame. It grows a four-headed arrow kabob. When this occurs, hold down the mouse button and drag the frame to its new location.

After the frame has been constructed, you can plop a graphic into it with these steps:

1. Click anywhere on the frame.

The frame becomes selected and is surrounded by a box with "handles" on it. There are eight handles, one for each of Elizabeth Taylor's husbands.

2. Do Insert⇨Picture.

The Insert Picture dialog box graces your screen. Navigate through the drives and folders until you find the graphic you want.

3. Select the image and choose OK.

Plop! The image is pasted into the frame. Lovely.

✔ More information on the Page Layout view can be uncovered in Chapter 27.

✔ You can also paste an image into a frame, provided that you just copied it from a graphics program.

✔ If something goes wrong, nine times out of ten it is because the frame was not selected before you imported the image.

✔ The following section explains how to change the size of your image after you plop it in.

Adjusting the Graphic Image

To get a graphic image into your text, follow the steps in the preceding section. After the image is there, you can adjust its size — but that's about it. Word won't let you redraw or edit the image. It's a word processor, after all.

Here are the basic "I want to tweak my graphics" steps:

1. Click on the image with the mouse cursor.

The graphic is enveloped in a box with eight tiny *handles* on it. You use the handles to adjust the image's size (see Figure 24-4).

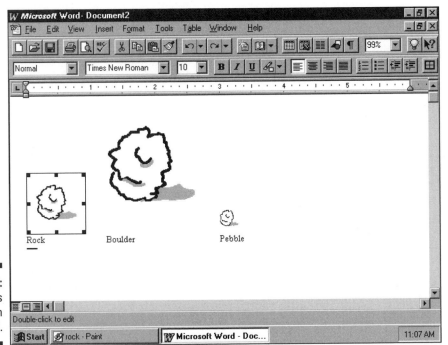

Figure 24-4:
An image is altered in Word.

2. Grab any one of the handles and drag it to change the image's size.

Generally speaking, grab one of the handles and drag toward or away from the image. So, grab the top handle to make the image taller or shorter. Grab the side handle to make the image narrower or fatter. The corner handles move in two directions (diagonally) simultaneously.

3. Release the mouse button when you're done dragging.

Word resizes the image to your specifications.

✔ The graphic can be *scaled* (made larger or smaller without distortion) by while dragging one of the corner handles.

✔ The graphic can be cropped, or chopped off, by holding down the Shift key while dragging a handle.

✔ If you drag it in just one direction or the other without holding down any buttons, the image will stretch or squash in that direction. This is how you can make a graphic fatter and taller or shorter and thinner.

Chapter 25

Word's Amazing Applets: Equation Editor, Graph, WordArt, and Word Picture

. . . .

In This Chapter

▶ The Great Word Applet Hunt

▶ Installing the applets

▶ Employing the Equation Editor (Microsoft Equation)

▶ Grappling with Microsoft Graph

▶ Activating WordArt

▶ Poking around with Microsoft Word Picture

. . . .

*W*ord is not alone. Just as Windows comes with its own "suite" of little programs — mini-applications called *applets* — Word comes with its host of li'l programs as well. With Windows, you get: WordPad word processor; Paint painting program; Terminal communications program; and maybe some games. These give the idly interested Windows users something to play with while they save up enough money to buy real programs.

The programs offered with Word gear themselves toward word processing, so they aren't as broad as the Windows applets (which implies that they actually approach being useful). Bothering with these little gems is optional. However, everyone I've shown them to seems to enjoy them, so maybe you will too. That would be a nice switch, wouldn't it?

The Great Word Applet Hunt

My mom went on one of these a while back. She was hunting for something called Applets and Cotlets, a.k.a. "Turkish Delight." Madly she dashed about, claiming the candies could only be found in my neck of the woods (or Turkey, no doubt). Eventually she found some and hoarded them for the trip back home. I tried some of the candies and found them to be, well, gross. So, fortunately, the Great Word Applet hunt has nothing to do with the Turkish Delight my mother loves so much.

Four programs come with Word (though secretly they really come with Microsoft Office). There may be more, but only four are worth the bother. These applet programs may or may not have been installed at the same time you installed Word:

✔ The Equation Editor, or Microsoft Equation, used to create mathematical-looking equations

✔ Microsoft Graph, a graphical/statistical program

✔ WordArt, a fancy word/letter display program

✔ Microsoft Word Picture, a drawing program, which is more exact than a painting program (this program may only be available if you had an older version of Word installed before you upgraded to Windows 95)

To see whether you have these programs installed, follow these steps:

1. Choose the Insert⇨Object command.

The Object dialog box appears, similar to the one in Figure 25-1. Click on the Create New tab to bring that panel forward if it isn't already, so it looks like the figure. This box contains a list of objects or things you can stick into a Word document.

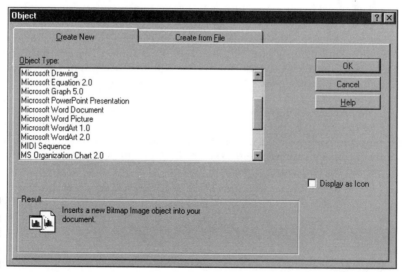

Figure 25-1:
The Object dialog box.

2. Scan the list of items.

You're looking for three of them: Microsoft Equation 2.0, Microsoft Graph 5.0, and Microsoft WordArt 2.0. These are the applets mentioned at the start of this section. If you can't find one or more, then you'll need to install the applets as described in the following section. If they're all there, then you're in business.

Word Picture may only be available on your computer if you installed an older version of Word before upgrading to Windows 95. If it's not there, it's no big deal.

3. Click Cancel to close the Object dialog box.

It's gone.

- ✔ Many other items are listed in the Object dialog box. These represent various things you can paste into a Word document. For example, if you have Excel, you may see an item representing an Excel Worksheet or Chart.

- ✔ The idea behind "objects" is that you don't have to go somewhere else, create something, copy it, and paste it back into Word. The Object dialog box lets you instantly create something and stick it into Word without the excess travel expenses.

- ✔ The Word applets are programs unique to Word, and you can't access them from other programs.

- ✔ Don't despair if the numbers (2.0 and 5.0) don't match up with what you see on your screen. Later versions of Word will probably have higher numbers, but most of this stuff should work the same.

- ✔ Each applet has a specific function and produces a specific graphical object that you can quite handily insert into your Word document.

Installing the applets

The Word applets come with Microsoft Word and should have been installed when you first set up Word or the Microsoft Office. However, they may not be there for a number of reasons: You don't have enough space on your hard drive; you elected not to include them when you installed Word (probably because you didn't know what they were); or someone else set up Word and was a big ninny and wanted to cause you additional pain. We arm-chair psychologists call it *passive-aggression*. Resist the urge to retaliate by putting all of his/her underwear in the freezer. Prove your emotional superiority. The following steps tell you how to install the applets yourself.

1. **Find your original Word or Office CD ROM or diskettes.**

   This is the CD (or floppy disks) that came with Microsoft Word. They might still be in the box, or you might have stored them away in a disk caddy or fire safe somewhere. I keep my disks in the original box, which is buried under a mound of stuff over there in the back corner of my office.

2. **Run the Setup program.**

   Word (or Microsoft Office) installed this program on your computer. It's found on the Start Thing's menu, which you get to by pressing Ctrl+Esc and then choosing Programs⇨Microsoft Office⇨Setup.

   If you're running Word right now, a dialog box appears and asks you to close it. Do so: Click the Exit Setup button, click on it again, and then click OK. Then quit Word. Instructions for quitting Word are offered in Chapter 1 of this book.

3. **Click on the Add/Remove button.**

   A huge and ugly dialog box appears. To the left, you see programs shown in a list box. One of the items with a box by it will read Office Tools.

4. **Click the mouse on the** Office Tools **item.**

   This highlights that item.

5. **Click on the Change Option button.**

   Another dialog box appears, looking remarkably similar to the first dialog box. This time, the scrolling list contains the goodies you want, the applets for Word.

6. **Choose your applets.**

   Press and hold down Ctrl and click on the following items in the list: Equation Editor, Microsoft Graph, WordArt, Word Picture.

7. **Click the OK button.**

   That ugly dialog box disappears and you're back in the original ugly dialog box.

8. **Click on the Continue button.**

9. **Heed the instructions on-screen.**

   Read everything and answer the questions so that the applets are installed on your system. If you're faced with a choice, always press Enter. This selects the item you most likely want.

   You will be asked to insert the original CD (or a floppy diskette). Do as instructed on-screen. This may happen several times for floppy disk installation. Don't try to make sense of why Setup asks for some disks and not others. Heck, it may ask for them all in sequence. Just consider this amusing and laugh every so often during the process.

10. Eventually, the Setup program ends.

Finally. Click OK to return to Windows. The Word applets are now installed, and you can enjoy using them.

✔ If you can't find the original Word distribution diskettes (or a copy you might have made), then you're out of luck. Sorry.

✔ If there wasn't enough room on your hard drive when you first installed Word, there may not be enough room on it now. If so, the Setup program warns you of this problem. There's nothing you can do, aside from freeing up space on your hard drive. That's a technical subject, so you better grab your Windows guru and force him or her to help you.

✔ But, if you do try the underwear-thing, it works best if you lightly mist them with water first. And do their socks, too. And don't say anything. Let them just look in the freezer, like for ice cream or something.

The gestalt of the Word applets

The Word applets are like little programs that produce what are called *objects*. As far as you and I are concerned, the objects are graphics — things you can paste into your documents. But Windows thinks that the graphics are *objects*, or items of extreme importance around which Windows will hop and jump like a little kid high on Cocoa Puffs.

What if, heaven forbid, you want to toss something like this at your readers (see Figure 25-2).

That's a formula that is rumored to appear on this year's tax form. In Word, that item is an *equation object,* created with the Word Equation Editor. It's really nothing at all, as is the following graph (see Figure 25-3):

Figure 25-2:
Sample
Equation
Editor object
thing.

$$S_{xg} = \sqrt{\frac{\sum x_i^2 fi - \frac{(\sum xifi)2}{\sum fi}}{(\sum fi) - 1}}$$

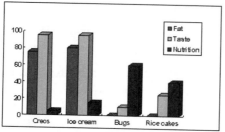

Figure 25-3:
Sample
Graph
object thing.

The preceding, professional-looking and highly impressive graphic was created with the Microsoft Graph applet by the same unskilled laborers who wrote this book .

The steps to get to these impressive doodads are simple:

1. **Position the toothpick cursor where you want the object to appear.**

   The object is a graphic. In some cases, it can appear right in the middle of a sentence or at the start of a line. Other times, it should go on a line by itself or in the midst of a table or frame where it can be dealt with more easily.

2. **Choose the Insert⇨Object command.**

   The Object dialog box opens (refer to Figure 25-1).

3. **Select the object that you want to insert.**

   Suppose that you want to insert a formula for toxic waste in your kid's Sunday School newsletter. You click on the Microsoft Equation 2.0 object in the Object dialog box and highlight it. (Following sections outline how to use the individual applets.)

4. **Choose OK.**

   This zooms you to the applet where you can create the object or graphic for your document.

5. **Toil! Toil! Toil!**

   Create that object or graphic! This can be really easy, so the toil is misleading. (You don't want anyone to assume that you're having fun here, right?) Just last night, I created a simple object for a document by using WordArt. It took maybe five minutes, although it was impressive enough to bill my client for three hours of work.

6. **Quit the applet.**

   This returns you to Word and inserts the graphical object into your document.

- The advantage of inserting an object into a Word document — especially one created by a Word applet — is that the object is "hot-linked" back to the program that created it. To fix up your graphical object, all you need to do is double-click on it with the mouse. Zoom! That takes you back to the applet, where you can edit or tweak the object.

- The Word applets, Graph, Equation Editor, and WordArt, are available only in Word and, well, other Microsoft Office applications as well. You cannot use them in any other, non-Office Windows application, at least nothing I've found yet.

- After the applet places its object into your document, the object functions like a graphic. You can click on the object once, and the telltale dotted graphical outline box appears. You can use the mouse to change the graphic's size by dragging any of the outline's edges or corners. The image resizes itself accordingly.

- To crop the image (literally, to hack off excess white space around the graphic), hold down the Shift key while dragging the handles as you resize the graphical object.

- To edit the applet's graphical object, click it twice with the mouse. The applet that created the object opens, which allows you to make adjustments and tweaks as necessary.

Employing the Equation Editor

Unless you are, like, an algebra instructor, or simply and woefully sadistic (let's be honest here, they are really one in the same), you will probably never have a need for the Equation Editor applet. Yet I suppose there may be some users who want to express mathematical mysticism in its glorious "how'd they do that?" format. This is much better than trying to use the fractured and fragmented symbols on the keyboard to express your Greek math things. Then there also may be the curious users. Nothing can be more fun than *pretending* you know advanced quantum physics and dreaming up some Einstein-level-IQ equation to impress the in-laws in your Christmas letter. Follow these steps:

1. **Move the toothpick cursor where you want your equation to be inserted.**

   It can be anywhere — on a line by itself or in the midst of a sentence.

2. **Choose the Insert⇨Object command.**

   The Object dialog box opens.

3. Click on Microsoft Equation in the list, and then click OK.

If you see more than one Microsoft Equation in the list, click on the one that has the highest number after it.

This activates the Equation Editor applet — a real program. It appears in a window on-screen, right on top of Word and your document (see Figure 25-4). The Equation Editor consists of a toolbar and a boxed-in area in which you'll build your equation.

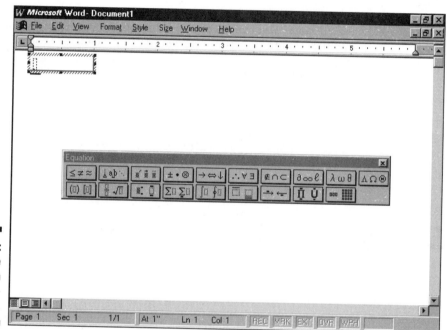

Figure 25-4:
The
Equation
Editor on-
screen.

4. Make up an equation.

Use the Equation toolbar's buttons to get at various palettes of equations, doohickeys, and mathematical thingamabobs. This is how you select various items to go into your equation — to build the equation graphically.

At this point, you're on your own. The Equation Editor can build just about any equation, but it's up to you to know what you want in the equation. You select items from the button-palettes, fill in the dotted rectangles, and poke and change things with the mouse. Have fun!

5. When you're done editing, click the mouse outside the equation box.

That click plops you back into Word and you can see your glorious equation, there to baffle mankind or whomever you send your memos.

✔ The equation you created appears in your document like a graphic.

✔ If you click on the equation, it becomes outlined like a graphic window frame. You can use the mouse to resize the equation by dragging one side of its frame to a new location. The equation changes its shape accordingly.

✔ To edit the equation, click on it twice with the mouse. The Equation Editor opens and allows you to make minor changes.

✔ No, Word will not "solve" your equation. If you're interested in such things, a program called Mathmatica does that job. It's very expensive and well-suited to the pointy-heads among us.

Grappling with Microsoft Graph

Nothing can spin the dust off numbers better than a real cool graph. You don't even need to mess with a spreadsheet or futz with a "chart program." Everything can be done neatly from within Word, thanks to the novel Microsoft Graph applet.

To insert a graph into your document, follow these steps:

1. Move the toothpick cursor to the place you want to insert the upper-left corner of the graph.

Graphs are big square things. Word inserts the big square thing into your document, so move your cursor where you want the graph *before* you start.

2. Choose the Insert⇨Object command.

The Object dialog box appears (refer to Figure 25-1).

3. Choose Microsoft Graph from the list.

The Graph applet opens — a real live program — that appears on top of Word and your document on-screen. Figure 25-5 shows what the Graph applet may look like. There are two windows, one for the graph and another for the data. The Datasheet window looks like a spreadsheet or table. The Graph window looks like a graph. Both windows contain phony data at this point, which you can replace. And you can select another type of graph (pie chart, line chart) if you like.

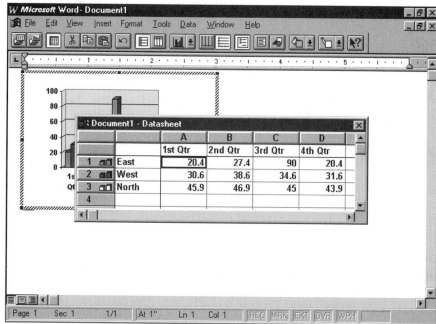

Figure 25-5:
The
Microsoft
Graph
applet.

4. Replace the sample data with the information that you want displayed.

You can add and delete columns and rows the same way that you would do this in any table. See Chapter 12 for info about tables. You need to click on the Datasheet window to activate it before you can input new values. To add new rows and columns, use the last two commands in the Edit menu.

5. Change the graphic, if you like.

The Gallery menu contains all the chart options. If you want a pie chart, for example, you can choose Gallery⇨Pie. You need to follow the instructions on-screen and possibly tweak your data a bit to get the right pie flavor.

6. Fiddle and play!

The information you enter into the table is immediately updated in the chart. This allows you to see your graph evolve. It can really be fun, but please don't let anyone watching believe that you're having fun. That isn't fair.

7. You're done!

Click the mouse outside the graph's area (click on your document). Your document now has a beautiful graph, suitable for framing. (See Chapter 24 for information on framing a graphic.)

✔ You also can make a graphical chart from data already in your document. Suppose that you have numbers sitting in a table. To make it into a Microsoft Graph thing, mark the entire table as a block and then follow all of the preceding steps for creating a new chart. Your data, instead of the "bogus" data, fills in the datasheet for creating the graph. Thoughtful, eh?

✔ If you make a chart from a table already in your document, you can use the first cell for the title of the chart. Any words that you put in this cell (the upper-leftmost) will be centered above the graph as its title.

✔ There are many different flavors of charts available; poke around in the Gallery menu to find the one that perfectly highlights your data.

✔ After the graph appears in your document, it can be treated like a graphic. If you click on the graphic-object, it will be outlined like a graphic window frame. You can use the mouse to resize the equation by dragging one side of its frame to a new location. The graph changes its shape accordingly.

✔ To edit the graph, for modifying or tweaking the graph or changing the type of graph, click on it twice with your mouse. This reactivates the Microsoft Graph program and loads the graphic-object for editing.

Activating Microsoft WordArt

WordArt is sadly neglected by most Word users. This is too bad, because WordArt can add a lot of dazzle quickly to your documents. And it's a fun place to waste time.

Like the other applets (Equation Editor and Graph), WordArt produces a graphical object in your text. It's not text! For formatting text, you really need to use the character formatting rules and regulations outlined in Chapter 9. WordArt is art.

To put WordArt into your document, follow these steps:

1. **Position the toothpick cursor in the spot in your document where you want the WordArt to appear.**

   It can really be anywhere: at the start of a line, in the middle of a para-graph, or on a line by itself. Whatever the case, move the toothpick cursor to that location first.

2. **Choose the Insert⇨Object command.**

   The Object dialog box opens.

3. Select Microsoft WordArt from the list.

You may need to scroll through the list to find Microsoft WordArt. I've installed Excel on my PC, and there are a few dozen Excel-ish "objects" that appear before WordArt. After you select it and click OK, the WordArt applet appears over your document, as shown in Figure 25-6.

4. Type the text you want "artified" into the box.

What you type will replace the Your Text Here in the box in your document. (It won't appear that way until you click on the Update Display button, though.)

5. Mess with it!

The first drop-down list on the WordArt toolbar contains various patterns for your text to flow in or around. Choose one! The second drop-down list contains fonts. Choose one! The next list sets text size. Buttons after that set text attributes. Mess with 'em to find out what they do. I encourage you to play here — especially if you're billing someone by the hour.

6. When you're done, click outside the box in your document.

Click the mouse outside the shaded box your WordArt text appears in. This returns you to your document, and the WordArt object appears like a graphic image in your document.

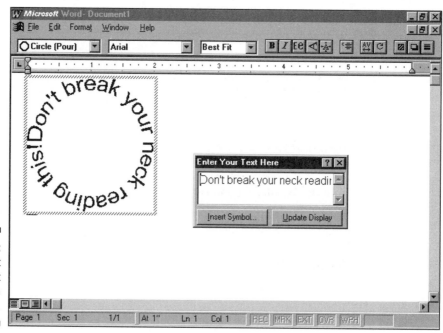

Figure 25-6:
Microsoft
WordArt
looks like
this, sorta.

✔ Like any other applet's graphical-object, click on the WordArt graphic twice with your mouse to edit it.

✔ Refer to "The gestalt of the Word applets," earlier in this chapter, for more information on tweaking your WordArt.

✔ Refer to Chapter 26 for information on creating a drop cap in your document. This is a task that you might assume WordArt could handle, but one that the Drop Cap command does much better.

Poking Around with Microsoft Picture

Microsoft Picture is a neat little applet with a bunch of uses. Sadly, it's not included with the latest edition of Microsoft Office. However, if you're one of the several people who involuntarily upgraded to Windows 95, it may still be lurking around on your hard drive. If so, then you can take advantage of its bountiful graphical features.

A drawing program like Microsoft Picture is different from a painting program like Windows Paint. While you create pictures in a draw program, what you create them with are objects — circles, squares, and lines. Unlike a painting program, you can easily move or manipulate a draw program's objects after they're created. You can line them up, flip them, group them, and so on. This makes Microsoft Picture ideal for technical illustrations, flow charts, and the like.

Obviously, there isn't enough space here to explain the entire Microsoft Picture application. So, instead, I encourage you to explore it on your own — just as you once explored the fun Paint program. Also, refer to the check list at the end of this section for some suggestions on how best to use Picture if your exploration time is hindered by something looming and ominous.

To insert a Microsoft Picture object-graphic thing into your document:

1. Put the toothpick cursor where you want the graphic thing to appear.

2. Choose the Insert⇨Object command.

The Object dialog box opens (refer to Figure 25-1).

3. Choose Microsoft Word Picture from the list.

The Picture applet appears right inside your Word document, as shown in Figure 25-7. There will be a Drawing toolbar at the bottom of the screen and a floating palette, as shown in the figure.

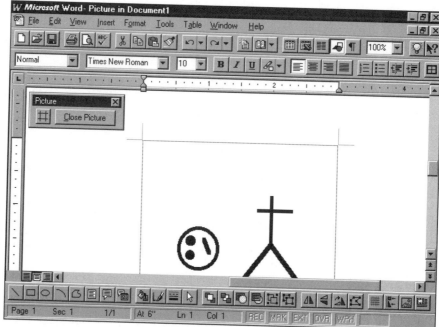

Figure 25-7:
Microsoft
Picture
explodes
onto the
screen.

4. Do something wondrous.

You can create a graphic here, just as you would in any paint program. The image will be created inside the dotted frame you see on your screen.

Drawing programs like this don't paint pixels on-screen — like drawing with an electronic crayon in Windows Paintbrush. Instead, you're working with a graphical object more like an erector set. When you create a box, for example, you can move the box or change its size *after* creating it. The box is an *object* on-screen — not a set of pixels or electronic crayon gunk. (I'm getting too philosophical here.)

5. When you're done, click on the Close Picture button.

You see the graphic right there in your document. Stand back and be amazed.

✓ The buttons on the left end of the Drawing toolbar allow you to draw straight lines, boxes, and circles. The colors along the bottom of the screen allow you to choose the line colors and a fill pattern (the color for the graphic's "middle").

✓ You can put text into your drawing by using the Text Box button. Unlike a paint program, the text you create appears in its own "box." It can be edited later just like you were editing text in Word. Use the Format⇨Font command to change the text style.

✔ By using the Insert⇨Picture command, you can import any graphic that shows up in the Insert Picture dialog box. Refer to Chapter 24 for more information on inserting pictures.

✔ When your drawing is in your document, it behaves like any other graphic. You can click on it once to "outline" it and then use the mouse to change its size if you like. The graphic resizes itself to fit the outline accordingly.

✔ To edit the graphic in Picture again, click on it twice with the mouse.

Chapter 26

Your Basic DTP Stuff

Some graphical things you can do with your document don't involve graphics at all. Instead, these items approach that fuzzy border between word processing and desktop publishing. Indeed, this part of the book would have been considered desktop publishing just a few years ago. So what else is there besides fancy graphics and text? There are boxes. And interesting ways to slap fancy titles and other things into your document. It's not really graphics; it's more along the lines of your basic DTP (desktop publishing) stuff.

Making a Drop Cap

A drop cap is where the first letter of a report, article, chapter, or story appears in a larger and more interesting font than the other characters. Figure 26-1 shows an example. This trick, which requires hours of painstaking work and adjustments in other word processors, is a snap in Word. Just use the handy Drop Cap command, nestled in the Format menu.

Figure 26-1:
A drop cap
starts this
intriguing
novel.

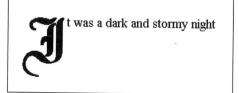

t was a dark and stormy night

Here are some steps you can follow to start your stuff off with a drop cap:

1. **Position the toothpick cursor at the start of your text.**

   Not the title. Not just anywhere. Put the toothpick cursor on the first paragraph of text. It also helps if this paragraph is left-justified and not indented with a Tab or by using any of the tricky formatting discussed in Chapter 10.

   By the way, you *do* have to write something here; the Drop Cap command isn't available until you have some text down on paper. (This is to thwart the efforts of writer's block-plagued authors who'd rather diddle with the Drop Cap feature than start writing anything.)

2. **Select the first character of the first word.**

   For example, the *O* in "Once upon a time."

3. **Choose Format⇨Drop Cap.**

   The Drop Cap dialog box appears, as depicted in Figure 26-2.

Figure 26-2:
The Drop
Cap dialog
box.

4. **Select a drop cap style.**

   There are two because the first one, "None," isn't a drop cap at all. The second style is Dropped and the third is In Margin. I prefer the Dropped style myself. Click on the box you prefer.

5. **Select a Font if you wish.**

6. **Click OK.**

   Word asks you to switch to Page Layout view to see the drop cap in action.

7. **Click Yes.**

   The drop cap appears in your text, looking like you fussed all afternoon to get it right.

  ✔ The drop cap looks best in Page Layout view, where it appears with a little chain link fence around it. Choose View⇨Page Layout.

  ✔ If you switch back to Normal view (View⇨Normal), the drop cap'd letter appears on the line above your text. Funky, but that's the way Word does it. Don't try to "fix" it; instead, return to Page Layout view to see the drop cap more properly.

  ✔ By the way, Chapter 27 goes into detail on the Page Layout and Normal commands.

  ✔ A drop cap is not a graphic or graphical object (see Chapter 24). To fix it, you must follow the above steps again and make adjustments in the Drop Cap dialog box.

  ✔ Flourishy drop caps seem to work the best for pretentious stuff. Otherwise, choose a big, blocky font for your drop caps.

  ✔ You can undo a drop cap by clicking on its box in your text with the mouse and then selecting Format⇨Drop Cap. In the Drop Cap dialog box, double-click on the None position, and the drop cap vanishes.

Creating Cool Document Titles

Nothing dampens the fire of an exciting paper like a dreary, dull heading. Consider the plight of the poor dirt-eating public. Yes, it's true, many people do actually suffer from terraphagia. Think about uncontrollably wanting to wander into the backyard with a spoon, sit down, and feast. I'm serious. Lots of people do it. (So be suspicious when the spouse muses, "Oh, hon, I'm just going out into the garden for a few minutes," but he or she has a hungry look on his or her face.)

In Figure 26-3, I've devised a few sample titles for papers encouraging dirt-eating. Oo, it's enough to make your mouth water! To make your own dirt-eating paper or report stand out, you need more than just a title. You need a *creative* title.

Figure 26-3 shows only a paltry few examples of document titles you can create with Word. It's possible to mix and match the styles to create the ideal title you want. The following sections detail how each element is created: formatting text and paragraphs and creating special effects.

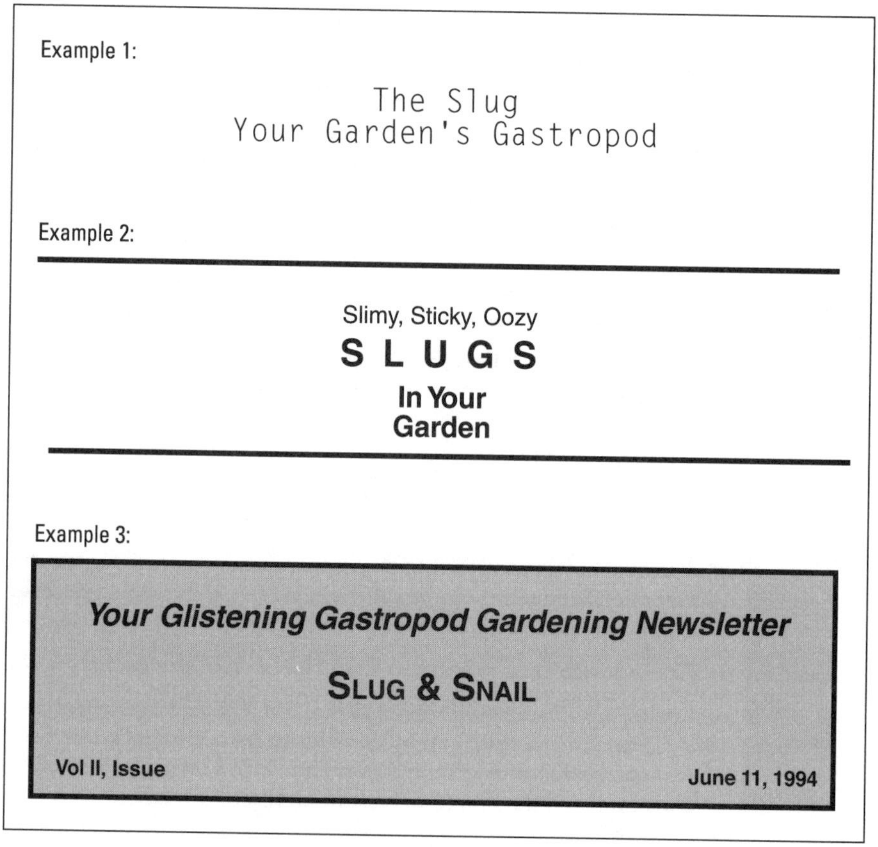

Example 1:

The Slug
Your Garden's Gastropod

Example 2:

Slimy, Sticky, Oozy

S L U G S

**In Your
Garden**

Example 3:

Your Glistening Gastropod Gardening Newsletter

SLUG & SNAIL

Vol II, Issue   **June 11, 1994**

Figure 26-3:
Sample
document
titles.

Formatting the text just so

You use three steps for formatting text for your title:

1. **Select a font.**
2. **Select a type size.**
3. **Select character attributes.**

To select a font, follow these steps:

1. **Choose the Format⇨Font command.**

   The Font formatting dialog box opens.

2. **Scroll through the list of fonts.**

If you know the name of the font you want, you can type it in the <u>F</u>ont box. Otherwise, the list-o-fonts displays all the fonts known to Windows and Word. The best fonts to use for titles are the blocky, no-frills fonts, including Helvetica, Arial, Swiss, Univers, Avant Guard, Optima, and Futura. You're bound to have one of those fonts available in the list. The Preview box on the bottom right helps you shop around, showing you through almost-virtual-reality what the font looks like. Select one.

3. **Enter a size for the font in the <u>S</u>ize box or choose a size from the list of available sizes.**

   To make your title big, select a large font size. This means 14pt or more. I like a 24pt title, which is nice and readable from across the hall (with my glasses on).

4. **Select a style from the F<u>o</u>nt Style menu.**

   A good attribute to give your title is <u>B</u>old.

5. **Choose some effects from the Effects area.**

   To select these attributes, click in the little check boxes by each one. When a check mark appears in the box, that attribute is selected. Notice how the Sample text in the bottom of the dialog box reflects your changes. Try S<u>m</u>all Caps.

6. **Click OK.**

   Click on the OK button or press Enter after you've made your selections.

7. **Type your title.**

✔ Don't worry about centering or shading yet. The character formats come first.

✔ More information on formatting characters is offered in Chapter 9.

✔ If you have a multiline title, you can use different type sizes and styles on each line. Avoid the temptation to change the font, however.

✔ In Figure 26-3, Example 1 uses the Courier font, Bold font style, 14pt size. This is painfully boring, but it's better than nothing.

✔ In Figure 26-3, Example 2 uses the Helvetica font. The first line is Bold, 12pt size. The second line is Bold, 30pt size and typed in uppercase. The third line is Bold and 18pt size.

✔ In Figure 26-3, Example 3 uses the Helvetica font as well. The first line is Bold Italic, 18pt size. The second line is Bold, 24pt size with Small Caps effect. The third line is 12pt size, plain old normal "Regular" text. (Refer to the Tech box "Fancy — and not required — alignment information" on how the date is shoved to the right side of the box.)

✔ To insert the date in your title, use Word's Date and <u>T</u>ime command. Move the toothpick cursor to where you want the date and choose <u>I</u>nsert⇨Date and <u>T</u>ime. Highlight a date format in the list and then click OK.

 ✔ Don't go nuts.

 ✔ Okay, go nuts if you want to.

Centering your title perfectly

After you write text, it's time to align things on-screen. You do this by formatting the paragraphs, which means centering or *justifying* the titles.

The typical title is centered. To center text you already typed on-screen (assuming you've been through the preceding section), follow these steps:

1. Mark the text you want to center as a block.

Refer to Chapter 6 for all the block-marking instructions you'll ever need to know.

2. Choose the Center command.

Click on the Center button on the Formatting toolbar.

You also can choose F<u>o</u>rmat⇨<u>P</u>aragraph, Alignment, Centered, and choose OK.

This centers the block on-screen.

 ✔ No need to mark just one line or paragraph. Just place the toothpick cursor somewhere in that line or paragraph and click the Center tool.

 ✔ To center the page from top to bottom, refer to "Centering a page, top to bottom" in Chapter 11.

 ✔ Additional information on formatting a block of text is found in Chapter 10.

Using the Borders and Shading Command

You can make titles more interesting by putting a box around them — or maybe just some lines along the top and bottom or some fancy shading, as seen in Figure 26-3. You can do this to any text in Word. If you want to set aside a paragraph of text from the rest of the page, for example, you can box it or shade it. Just choose the F<u>o</u>rmat⇨<u>B</u>orders and Shading command.

Fancy — and not required — alignment information

In Figure 26-3, Example 3, at the bottom of the title, you see the volume number on the left side of the page and the date on the right. Both these items of text are on the same line. The trick is to use Word's justification to slam one against the left margin and the other against the right. Blithely follow these forbidden steps:

1. **Press Enter to start writing text on a new line.**

   It's best to start with a blank line, so if you're already on a blank line, there's no need to press Enter. I'm just being safe, that's all. You know, meticulous instructions are my trademark.

2. **Type the text you want aligned along the left side of the page.**

   Type away, la, la, la.

3. **Don't press Enter when you're done!**

4. Instead, click on the Tab button on the ribbon. It's on the far left side of the toolbar, possibly with a little L sitting in it. Click on that button until you see the right-align tab, which looks like an L pointing the other direction. Click on that button with the mouse.

5. **Click the mouse on the ruler, just to the left of the right-margin triangle.**

   The right-margin triangle is on the right side of the ruler, between the white and gray parts. (If you can't see it, click on the left-pointing arrow on the bottom horizontal scroll bar.) Click the mouse about a quarter inch or so to the left of that triangle. This places the right-align tab-thingy right there and erases all the other tab stops on that line.

6. **Press the Tab key.**

   The cursor hops over to the right side of the page.

7. **Type the text you want aligned along the right side of the page.**

   Type away, la, la, la. Or insert the date, as discussed in the previous section.

8. **Press Enter. You're done.**

Putting a box around your text

If you're creating a title, you can draw a nice square box around it. Or you can draw a box around any paragraph or group of paragraphs in any document or even a graphic. To do so, follow these steps:

1. **Mark the paragraph you want to box as a block.**

   Use the handy block-marking instructions in Chapter 6 to carry out this deed. You can mark any text, such as a title you want to snazz up.

2. **Choose the Format➪Borders and Shading command.**

   The Paragraph Borders and Shading dialog box opens, as shown in Figure 26-4.

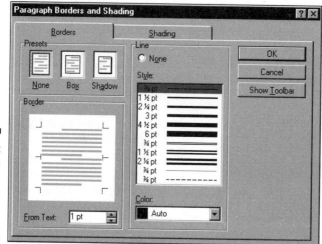

Figure 26-4:
The
Paragraph
Borders and
Shading
dialog box.

3. Make sure the Borders tab is up front.

Click on the Borders tab if it's not.

4. Look for the area labeled Presets at the upper-left corner.

This contains three quick, easy-to-use, pop-n-fresh border styles.

5. Double-click on the icon above Box.

Your title now has a box around it, similar to the one shown in Figure 26-3, Example 3, but without the shading inside the box. To get shading, refer to "Shading your text."

✔ Word draws lines around only full paragraphs of text — not bits and pieces.

✔ To put a border with a shadow around your text, double-click on the Shadow icon.

✔ You can make the border thinner or thicker, or use a double or dashed line if you like. Just select a line style from the Style list in the Paragraph Borders and Shading dialog box. Do this before you double-click on the Box or Shadow icon.

✔ To remove any border from your highlighted text, double-click on the None icon.

✔ You can also place a border around a graphic you've inserted into your document. Refer to Chapter 24 for more information.

Putting less than a box around your text

In Figure 26-3, Example 2, the boxed title has lines only on the top and bottom. To make that happen with your title or any other text, follow steps 1, 2, and 3 as outlined in the preceding section. And then do the following:

1. **Click on the Box icon to put a box around your text.**

   Yeah, this isn't how you want to end up, but it's how you must start. (Just click once — don't double-click here.)

2. **Select a line style from the Style area in the Paragraph Borders and Shading dialog box.**

   You can choose from several thicknesses and double or single line patterns. Click on the line style you want. Notice that the text in the Border preview box changes to match the line style you select.

3. **Now focus on the Border preview box.**

   The box tells Word where to put lines around your text — top, bottom, left, right, middle, and so on.

4. **Click the mouse on the left and right lines in the Border preview box.**

   This eliminates those lines.

5. **Click OK when you finish making your box.**

   Which is now missing two sides, so it's really not much of a box at all and will probably spill all of its contents if you tip it the wrong way, so be careful.

Using the Border toolbar

Word is top-heavy on toolbars. One of them is the Border toolbar, which allows you to create borders in your document — without messing with the Paragraph Borders and Shading dialog box.

 To activate the Border toolbar, click on the Borders button on the Formatting toolbar. A new toolbar appears with drop-down lists and buttons for adding borders to highlighted text.

- ✔ The first drop-down list on the Borders toolbar sets the size of the border's lines.
- ✔ The buttons on the Borders toolbar tell Word where to stick a border around your highlighted text: Top, Bottom, Left, Right, Middle, Around, and None.

✔ The second drop-down list sets the shading for the boxed-in area.

✔ Refer to the very next section for more information on shading text.

✔ To make the Border toolbar go away, click on the Borders button a second time.

Shading your text

The neatest Border dialog box effect of them all is shading your text — or a title, such as the sample shown in Figure 26-3, Example 3. You can shade a title with or without a border around it. Use these steps:

1. Mark your text or entire title as a block.

Refer to Chapter 6 for efficient block-marking instructions. If you want the shaded area to cover more than the title line, highlight the lines before and after the title.

2. Choose Format⇨Borders and Shading.

The Paragraph Borders and Shading dialog box appears (refer to Figure 26-4).

3. Make sure the Shading panel is up front.

Click on the Shading tab with your mouse if it's not. The Shading tab jumps to the front, as shown in Figure 26-5. Lots of interesting things can happen here, but your concentration should focus on the large menu box labeled Shading.

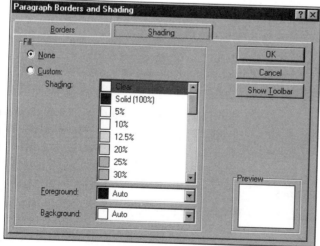

Figure 26-5:
The Shading panel in the Paragraph Borders and Shading dialog box.

4. Scroll through the Shading list to find the degree of shading you desire.

Shading patterns (in percentages of black) vary from 5 percent to 95 percent (including clear and solid). A value of 50 percent is equal parts black and white — solid gray. The 95 percent value is almost solid black. Other patterns appear at the end of the list, but you don't care about them.

The best values to select for shading your text are 10 percent, 20 percent, or 30 percent. I prefer 20 percent because it prints on my laser printer — not too dark to overpower the title text but still dark enough to see that it's the all-important shading that's so hard to do in other word processors.

5. Select your shading from the list.

For example, highlight the 20 percent item from the list.

6. Click OK.

Your text appears shaded on-screen! This is definitely the coolest way to head off your in-depth dirt-eating report.

✔ Nope, just because you visited the Border dialog box doesn't mean you have to put a border around your text.

✔ If the shading stinks (and we're all allowed a little latitude for screwing up here), then you can remove it. Just follow the steps outlined previously, but select None in the Shading panel in step 5.

✔ At the bottom of the list of shades, you'll find some shading patterns as well. Choose something to match the drapes.

✔ Shaded titles look best when they're at the top of your first page — not on a page by themselves.

Printing white on black

After shading, the next most fun thing to do is print white text on a black background. This is a very bold move and stands out prominently in your text —like being hit in the face with a cinder block. So don't use this technique casually.

`Oh, La-de-da`

To produce white-on-black text, you must do two things. First, you must create a black background; and second, you must create white-colored text. Here is how you create a black background:

1. Mark your text as a block.

Chapter 6 has all the details. It's best to start with text you've already written. At some point here, you will have black text on a black background, which you cannot see. If you already have the text written, it will be easier to see when you're done.

2. Choose Format⇨Borders and Shading.

The Paragraph Borders and Shading dialog box appears (refer to Figure 26-5).

3. Making sure the Shading panel is forward.

Click on the Shading tab if it's not. The Shading dialog card reshuffles itself to the top of the pile (refer to Figure 26-5).

4. Click your mouse on the down arrow by the Background drop-down list (near the bottom of the dialog box).

You see a bunch of colors displayed in the drop-down list (which may actually pop up on the screen). The current color will probably be Auto.

5. Select Black from the list.

This sets the background color to black — one half of your white-on-black text.

6. Click OK to exit the Shading dialog box.

Now you don't see anything on-screen because you have black text on a black background. (Actually, with the block highlighted, you will see what looks like a large white block floating over a black block. Don't freak!)

Yes, the text is really black on black, even if you see white on black right now on your screen. You must do these things deliberately in Word. Never make assumptions.

With the block of text still highlighted, you need to change the text color to White. This is done by using the Font dialog box, as follows:

1. Choose Format⇨Font.

The Font dialog box opens.

2. Make sure the Font panel is up front.

Click on the Font tab if it's not.

3. Look for the Color drop-down list in the dialog box, just above dead-center.

4. Click on the down arrow by the Color drop-down list.

You'll see a bunch of colors displayed.

5. Select White from the list.

This is the "color" you want; white text over the black background you already created.

6. Click OK.

You can now unhighlight your block. The text appears on-screen and printed in *inverse* white letters on a black background.

✔ Yes, although I said you can't print in color in Chapter 8, you can print with white text on a black background.

✔ I don't recommend reversing vast stretches of text. White text on a black background prints poorly on most computer printers. This stuff is best used for titles or to highlight smaller blocks of text.

✔ You cannot highlight a word or part of a paragraph with white text on a black background. The black background can be applied only to an entire paragraph.

✔ When you highlight a block of white text on a black background, it appears on-screen "normally." That is, the reversed text will appear inverted — or black on white — when you mark it as a block. This can really goof you up, so just try not to go mental when you highlight reversed text.

✔ You can use the white-on-black text sample you created to make a white-on-black *style* in Word. Highlight that text; then press Ctrl+Shift+S. In the Style box, type **Inverse** or some other appropriate name for the style. Press Enter and you've added that style to your document. Refer to Chapter 14 for more information on styles.

Part VI
Help Me, Mr. Wizard!

"OOO-KAY, LET'S SEE. IF WE CAN ALL REMAIN CALM AND STOP ACTING CRAZY, I'M SURE I'LL EVENTUALLY REMEMBER WHAT NAME I FILED THE ANTIDOTE UNDER."

In this part...

Word is not the sole cause of your woes. When you use a computer, you have several things to contend with: the computer, Windows, your printer, phases of the moon. . . . It's like starring in a bad French farce with too many villains. Fortunately, some humans — yes, humans — really like computers. When you're in dire straits, you can call on their expertise. Call them wizards; call them gurus; call them when you need help. And when you can't call on them, refer to the chapters in this part of the book to help you through your troubles.

Chapter 27

Face to Face with the Interface

. . . .

. . . .

*B*y now you probably have noticed that approaching Word and the strange and unusual ways that it shows stuff on your screen is about as calming as having the waiter personally assure you that the food is supposed to taste that way and nothing is wrong — and meanwhile you hear a siren approaching and the cook rushes to the bathroom holding his mouth with one hand and his stomach with the other. Don't you agree that there are too many buttons, icons, gizmos, and whatzits? Don't answer too quickly because there are even more than that — including some wild things that you've never seen and probably don't want to see. This chapter mulls over the lot, explains just what's what on-screen, and tells you whether it's important and why.

Looking at Your Document

The way you look at your document is controlled by Word's View menu, as shown in Figure 27-1. The View menu contains all sorts of options for controlling the display: the way your document appears, various optional goodies that you may see along with your document, and how big the document looks (set by the Zoom command). These and other items are discussed in the check mark list that follows, as well as in the rest of this chapter.

✔ The Ⅳormal command sets Word to look at your document in the Normal view — what you probably want most of the time while you work in Word. The Normal view icon, at the far-left end of the bottom horizontal scroll bar, also switches you to this view.

✔ The Ⲣage Layout command directs Word to let you see your entire document, including the header and footer plus the graphics and other effects that may not look proper in the Normal view. Clicking on the Page Layout icon on the horizontal scroll bar also activates this view.

✔ In Page Layout view, there is a second, vertical ruler that appears along the left side of your document. You'll also see a misty gray region to the top and bottom of each "page" in your document. That void is made of the same stuff that they find in the Bermuda Triangle.

✔ Several Word commands will automatically shift you into Page Layout view.

✔ The Ⲟutline command shifts Word into the outline mode, which is covered in Chapter 18 (though it's really an advanced topic, many readers insisted). The last of the three view buttons on the horizontal scroll bar switches on Outline view.

✔ I touch upon the Master Document view in Chapter 28.

✔ The interesting Fᵤll Screen command in the Ⅴiew menu lets you look at your document without being encumbered by menus, toolbars, or any other whatnot. This command is well suited for the white-page purists among us. Click on the only remaining button on-screen to return yourself to the safety of the normal mode.

✔ Other commands in the Ⅴiew menu are discussed elsewhere in this chapter.

✔ Yet another check mark item.

✔ Chapter 20 offers information on working with document windows, splitting them, windexing them, and so on.

"My toolbar (or ruler) vanished!"

Missing something? Notice that the sample screens in this book or in the manual don't look a darn thing like your screen? Frustrated? That's because everything on-screen is adjustable. You can change the looks of just about anything by using the Vıew menu shown in Figure 27-1.

- ✔ To get the ruler back, choose View⇨Ruler.

- ✔ To get other toolbars back — or to rid yourself of them — refer to the next section.

- ✔ Oh, other funky things can happen to the display; just keep reading.

- ✔ Word also has the capability to view multiple documents at a time. Refer to Chapter 20 for additional information.

Summoning toolbars

You control toolbars in Word — and there are a lot of them — with the View⇨Toolbars command. Choosing that command displays the infamous Toolbars dialog box, depicted in Figure 27-2.

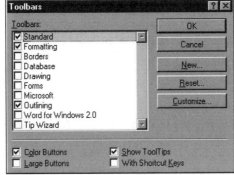

Figure 27-2:
The
infamous
Toolbars
dialog box.

To display a toolbar, click on its name so that a check mark appears in the box. Removing the check mark from the box makes the toolbar go away. Click the OK button to return to Word and enjoy (or be freed from) the toolbars.

- ✔ Some toolbars appear like the Standard and Formatting toolbars — as a strip of buttons across the screen. Other toolbars appear as *floating palettes*, or buttons in their own wee windows. The floating palettes have the advantage of mobility. You can make them vanish by clicking on their minute li'l close button (in the upper-left corner of the window).

✔ Some toolbars appear automatically when you're working on specific things in Word. For example, the Drawing toolbar appears when you're working with Microsoft Picture (see Chapter 25). A special Merge toolbar appears when you're merging documents (see Chapter 23).

✔ You can create your own, custom toolbars by clicking on the New button in the Toolbars dialog box. This topic is way too advanced to be covered in this book. Besides, Word junkies are probably already messing around with custom toolbars even before reading this little note.

✔ Having tons of toolbars sates the button gluttons, but it leaves little room on the screen for your all-important text. Typically, you'll only need the Standard and Formatting toolbars. Everything else is just for show.

Out, Damn Spots!

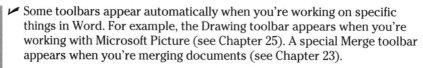
This·can·be·very·annoying.¶

What you see on your screen when your text looks like the preceding line are *nonprinting characters*. These symbols represent spaces (produced by the space bar), end-of-paragraph marks (the Enter key), and tabs. They show up on-screen but — fortunately — not when printed. There are two ways to feel about these characters:

✔ The marks let you see things that would otherwise be invisible, such as rogue tabs and spaces and other stuff that may foul up your document if you don't see them.

✔ The marks look gross on-screen; who wants to edit a document that looks like it has the chicken pox?

You turn off the specks from the Standard toolbar. Click on the Show/Hide button, the *paragraph* symbol. Doing so shuts off the effect.

A good way to clean up rogue spaces and such in a document is to use the AutoFormat command. Refer to Chapter 16.

"There's a Line Down the Left Side of My Screen!"

Ah, that annoying line down the left side of the screen doesn't mean that your monitor is out of whack. Instead, you have discovered the *style area*. That thing shows you what style is applied to what paragraph, and there's really no reason to have it visible.

To turn off the style area, follow these steps:

1. **Choose Tools⇨Options.**

   The Options dialog box appears.

2. **Coax the View panel into coming forth.**

   Click on the View tab with the mouse.

3. **Just about dead-center in the dialog box, you'll find the Style Area Width.**

4. **Type the number 0 (zero) into the box.**

   Or use your mouse and the spinner buttons to reset the value to zero.

   You've just set the width of the style area thing to zero inches, which effectively makes it nonexistent. Yeah!

5. **Click OK.**

   The style area is forever gone.

 Although the style area is annoying, having it visible can really help you edit strange documents. If you're having trouble applying styles to your document, you can switch the style area back on. Just follow the preceding steps again and enter a value of .5 or 1 for a half-inch or inch-wide style area.

"The Mouse Button Produces This Pop-Up Menu Thing!"

There are two mouse buttons: the right one and the wrong one. Normally, you'll use the left mouse button in Word. You use this button to select things, pull down menus, and poke buttons. The right mouse button, on the other hand, will pop up a handy menu in Word, full of shortcuts plus some useful items.

This is a typical Windows 95 thing, the right button popping up various short-cut or "context" menus all over the place.

Figure 27-3 shows the right mouse button's pop-up menu when you position the mouse over your text. The top items in the menu are Cut, Copy, and Paste; the bottom items deal with formatting your text.

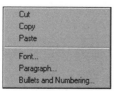

Figure 27-3:
The right
mouse menu
over text.

Figure 27-4 shows which menu the right mouse button produces when you click it over bulleted, numbered or outline text. This is essentially the same menu in Figure 27-3, but on steroids.

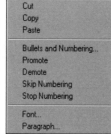

Figure 27-4:
The right
mouse
button over
bulleted or
outline text.

Figure 27-5 shows what the right mouse button produces when you click it over one of the toolbars. This pop-up menu is essentially a mini-toolbar menu from which you can summon various toolbars for use in Word.

Figure 27-5:
The right
mouse menu
over the
toolbars.

✔ After you click the right mouse button, the menu that pops up stays in place. Go ahead — release the button and move the mouse around. The menu doesn't go away until you click the mouse again.

✔ For more information on Cut, Copy, and Paste, refer to Chapter 6.

✔ More information on the Font command can be had in Chapter 9; Chapter 10 covers paragraph formatting.

✔ Information on the various toolbars is covered earlier in this chapter. See "Summoning toolbars."

"The Ruler Changed into a Line of Arrows, Numbers, and Whatnot!"

When the strange things mentioned in the preceding heading happen, you've simply discovered Outline view. This feature is a really neat gizmo designed especially by Microsoft for people who really, really love to outline stuff.

Word's outlining function is covered in this book in Chapter 18. But if you accidentally stumble onto the Outline view and see those weird arrows instead of a ruler, you can choose View⇨Normal to return to Normal view.

Zooming About

The Zoom command at the bottom of the View menu controls how big your document's text looks. No, it doesn't change the text size — that's done in the Font menu. Instead, the Zoom command controls how much of your text you'll see at once. Follow these steps for a quick demonstration:

1. **Choose View⇨Zoom.**

   The Zoom dialog box appears, looking much like the one depicted in Figure 27-6.

2. **Select a Zoom size from the Zoom To area.**

   For example, 200% makes your text look real big — ideal for Grandpa. The Page Width option sets the zoom so that you see your entire document from left to right margins.

   You can set individual percent sizes using the Percent box.

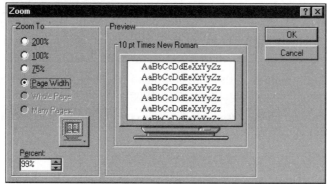

Figure 27-6:
The Zoom
dialog box.

3. Click OK to view your document at a new size on-screen.

✔ You can only choose some of the options in the Zoom dialog box when you're in Page Layout view. Choose <u>V</u>iew⇨<u>P</u>age Layout and then select the <u>Z</u>oom command to play, er, experiment with those options.

✔ When zooming takes you too far out, your text will change to shaded blocks, called "greeking." Although not keen for editing, zooming out that far gives you a good idea of how your document looks on the page before printing.

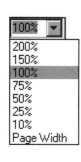

✔ There is a Zoom drop-down list on the Standard toolbar, way over to the right. Click on it to quickly set a Zoom size for your document.

✔ Unless your PC has a sound system, you'll have to make the *zoom* noise yourself when you select the Zoom command.

Chapter 28

The Printer Is Your Friend

*I*s the printer your friend? Perhaps. Unfortunately, friend or foe, the printer is just as stupid as the computer, which means that you must beat it with a stick a few times to get it to behave, or else you wind up hitting yourself in the head with the same stick. But give yourself a second of repose, and consider leafing through this chapter before causing yourself or your printer any physical harm.

Feeding It Paper

The way the paper feeds into your printer depends on which printer you have. Some printers eat paper one page at a time. Other printers may suck up continuous sheets of *fan-fold* paper directly from the box (the "spaghetti approach"). And laser printers delicately lift one sheet of paper at a time from their paper tray and then weld the image to the page by using dusty toner and inferno-like temperatures. Printing can be quite dramatic.

Whichever way your printer eats paper, make sure that you have a lot of it on hand. The end result of a word processor's labors is the printed document. So buy a box or two of paper at a time. I'm serious: You'll save money and trips to the store in the long run. And as a suggestion, look for a huge paper store or supplier and buy your printer paper from them instead of an office supply or computer store. The prices will be better.

✔ Try to get 20 lb. paper. The 18 lb. paper is too thin. I like 25 lb. paper, which is thicker and holds up very well, but it's more expensive. Paper that's too thick, such as "card stock," may not go through your printer.

✔ Colored papers and fancy stuff are okay.

✔ Do not print on erasable bond paper! This paper is awful. After all, the point behind erasable bond is that you can erase it, which doesn't happen much with a computer printer.

✔ Avoid fancy, "dusted" paper in a laser printer. Some expensive papers are coated with a powder. This powder comes off in a laser printer and gums up the works.

✔ Only buy the "two-part" or "three-part" fan-fold papers if you need them. These may contain carbon paper and are commonly used for printing invoices and orders. Also, the old "green bar" paper makes for lousy correspondence. It has "nerd" written all over it.

✔ If you need to print labels in your laser printer, get special laser printer labels. I recommend Avery labels.

✔ Laser printers can print on clear transparencies — but only those specially designed for use in a laser printer. Anything less than this kind will melt inside your printer, and you'll have to clean out the gunk. If you are going to print transparencies, it's cheaper to print on a piece of paper and then have the image photocopied onto transparency film, anyway.

✔ Always buy double-ply toilet tissue. It's comfier.

Unjamming the Printer

Next time you're in San Francisco, there's a little psychic you can visit on the Haight. She'll do a chart for your printer, which will explain why it jams on some days and not on others. This is the best solution I can offer to the question, "Why can't the paper always go through the printer like it's supposed to?"

If you have a dot-matrix printer and the paper jams, cancel printing in Word. (Refer to Chapter 8, the section "Canceling a Print Job.") Then turn the printer off. Rewind the knob to reverse-feed the paper back out of the printer. Don't pull on the paper, or it will tear and you'll have to take the printer apart to get the paper out. (If dismantling the printer becomes necessary, call someone else for help.)

For laser printers, you need to pop open the lid, find the errant piece of paper, remove it, and then slam the lid down shut. Watch out for various hot things inside your printer; be careful of what you touch. There's no need to cancel printing here because laser printers have more brain cells than their dot-matrix cousins. However, you may need to reprint the page that got jammed in the printer. Refer to Chapter 8, the section "Printing a Specific Page."

If the jam was caused by using thick paper, retrying the operation probably won't work. Use thinner paper.

Stopping Incessant Double-Spacing!

Nothing is quite as disenchanting as a printer that constantly produces double-spaced documents, whether you want them or not. This problem is terribly annoying, but it has a handy, one-time solution — if you kept your printer manual when you bought your printer.

Somewhere on your printer is a tiny switch. That switch controls whether your printer double-spaces all the time or only single-spaces. Right now, the switch is set to double-space no matter what. You need to find that switch and turn it off.

- ✔ Sometimes, the little switches are on the back or side of your printer; sometimes they're actually inside your printer.

- ✔ Turn your printer off and unplug it before you flip the switch. Cutting the power is especially important if the switch is inside the printer. It also prevents people from trying to print while your fingers are in the way of the printer's buzzsaw-like gears.

- ✔ The switch may be referred to as "LF after CR" or "Line feed after carriage return" or "Add LF" or "Stop double-spacing!" or something along those lines.

Changing Ribbons and Toner

Always have a good ribbon or toner cartridge in your printer. Always! Most printers use ribbons; laser printers use toner cartridges. This aspect of printing is something that you should never skimp on, lest the Printer Pixies come to you in your dreams and smear ink on your fingers.

- ✔ Keep a supply of two or three extra ribbons or toner cartridges. The extra supplies will hold you in case you need a new one over a working weekend.

- ✔ When the ribbon gets old and faded, replace it. Some places may offer re-inking services for your ribbon. This service works if the ribbon fabric can hold the new ink. If your ribbon is threadbare, you need to buy a new one.

✔ You can revitalize an old ribbon by carefully opening its cartridge and spraying some WD-40 on it. Reassemble the cartridge and put the ribbon on some paper towels. Let it sit for a day before reusing it. This tip should give the ribbon some extra life, but it can only be done once (and only works with ribbons — not toner cartridges!).

✔ Ink printers use ink cartridges. Replace the ink cartridges when they run low on ink, just as you should replace a ribbon or toner cartridge.

✔ When a laser printer's toner cartridge gets low, you see a flashing "toner" light or the message Toner low displayed on the printer's control panel. You can take the toner out and "rock" it a bit, which makes it last about a week longer. When you see the message again, you should replace the toner immediately.

✔ There are services that offer "toner recharging." For a nominal fee, they take your old toner cartridges and refill them with new toner. You can then use the toner cartridge again and squeeze some more money out of it. Nothing is wrong with this service, and I recommend it as a good cost-saving measure. But never recharge a toner cartridge more than once, nor should you do business with anyone who says it's okay.

"Where Did the Weird Characters Come From?"

If strange characters appear on your output — almost like the printer burped — it's a sign that Word may not be set up to use your printer properly. Those stray @ and # characters that appear on paper but not on-screen indicate that your printer may not be properly installed.

Installing your printer is a job best done by your computer guru. You'll need to know the manufacturer, make, and model number of your printer, and then run the special Printer Setup program that came with Windows.

Chapter 29

Help Me! I'm Stuck!

. . . .

In This Chapter

▶ "I can't find Windows!"

▶ "I can't find Word!"

▶ "I lost my files!"

▶ "Where did my document go?"

▶ "Where am I now?"

▶ "It's not printing!"

▶ "Oops! I deleted my document!"

. . . .

"There I was, minding my own business, when all of a sudden — for no apparent reason — Word *fill-in-the-blank*. Where is my baseball bat?"

It happens all too often. And it happens to everyone. "It worked just great when I did this yesterday. Why doesn't it work today?" Who knows? Retrace your steps. Check the grounds for signs of gypsies. But in the end, turn to this chapter for some quick solutions.

"I Can't Find Windows!"

Nothing so induces the sensation that you just accidentally stepped out of the shower to find the crew from *60 Minutes* in your bathroom than returning to your computer and seeing . . . *nothing!* Uh-oh. Looks like Windows saw the Baskin-Robbins a few blocks back and didn't bother to tell you it was on an ice cream hunt. But where did it really go?

First things first. If the screen is blank, try pressing the Enter key. A screen-saver type of program may have taken over your computer's brain and you need to wake it up.

If — peril of perils — you see the DOS prompt on the screen, don't think that your PC has gone retro-1988. Instead, type **EXIT** at the DOS prompt and press Enter. This command may turn the trick for you.

Some joker in the office may have told your computer to start in the "DOS mode" instead of Windows. (Yes, it can happen.) If so, try typing **WIN** at the DOS prompt now.

If this remedy *still* doesn't help, reset your computer. Press and hold the Ctrl and Alt keys and press the Delete key. Release all three keys. Your computer resets. When your computer is done restarting itself, start over yourself.

"I Can't Find Word!"

Sometimes Word takes a vacation. Where did it go? It all depends on how you "lost" it.

If you just started your computer, started Windows, and can't find Word, you have a few options. The first is to press Ctrl+Esc to pop up the Start Thing's menu. Then look for Word, which should be right on the main Programs menu. If not, try looking in a WinWord or Word submenu. Chances are, if it was there yesterday, it should be there today.

If you were just using Word and now . . . it's gone! . . . several things may have happened. Most commonly, you probably "switched away" from Word by pressing Alt+Esc or Alt+Tab. To get back into Word, look for Word's button on the taskbar, as shown in Figure 29-1. When you find the button, click on it to return to Word.

Figure 29-1:
Word lurks
on the
taskbar,
third button
over.

If you still can't find word, or the taskbar has more buttons on it than the clown parade at the circus, take these steps:

1. **Press Alt+Tab.**

   Press and hold the Alt key, and then tap the Tab key. Release both keys. This action switches you to the "next" program running in Windows.

2. **If you found Word, you're done!**

3. **Keep repeating steps 1 and 2.**

   Hopefully, you'll eventually find Word.

✔ If none of these steps works, then you probably accidentally quit Word, which has been known to happen in the "easy-to-use" (and goof-up) Windows environment. Just restart Word as discussed back in Chapter 1.

✔ Word does not self-destruct. If you used your computer and Word yesterday, Word is still on your computer today. It just may be hidden or out of reach. Under no circumstances should you reinstall Word unless your guru directs you to do so.

✔ If all else fails, check your wallet for missing credit cards and then call the airlines. Remember, even in the summer months, Word can find great skiing bargains south of the equator.

"I Lost My Files!"

Sometimes Windows has a hard time bolting files down on a disk. Because the disk is constantly spinning, I assume that centrifugal force flings the files outward, plastering them to the inside walls of your disk drive like gum under a school desk. That's the mental picture I get. Whatever the case, you can find a lost file quite easily. Doing so just takes time — a putty knife is optional.

If you're in Word, finding files can be done with the handy Find File command. This feature is covered in detail in Chapter 22 in the section "Finding Files in Word."

If the Find File command doesn't help you locate your file, you need to use the Windows File Finder program. Follow these steps:

1. **Activate the File Finder.**

   The File Finder is located on the Start Thing's main menu. Click on the Start button or press Ctrl+Esc. Then choose Find⇨Files or Folders. The Find: All Files dialog box appears, looking a lot like Figure 29-2.

2. **Choose My Computer from the Look in drop-down list box.**

   Click on the down arrow by the Look in box and choose My Computer from the list. Doing so directs Windows to look all over your computer, in every disk drive, on every hill, in every mountain and village, for the file in question.

3. **Make sure there's a check mark in the Include subfolders box.**

   Never mind the reason, just do it.

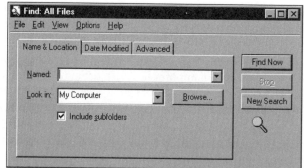

Figure 29-2:
The Find: All
Files dialog
box.

4. Click the mouse in the Named box.

Type in some semblance of the file's name. For example:

> LETTER

Now that's pretty dumb, but typing in **LETTER** will cause Windows to find every file named **LETTER** or containing the word **LETTER** all over your computer.

You can type all or part of a filename; Windows will find the closest matches. For LETTER, Word would find everything from LETTER1 to LETTER TO THE EDITOR to LETTERHEAD.

5. Click Find Now.

Windows busily looks everywhere for your file. An entertaining magnifying glass icon amuses you while you wait.

6. Eventually (and hopefully), files are found.

Windows lists its results in a new hangy-on thing at the bottom of the Find File dialog box (see Figure 29-3). Scroll through the list to hunt down the file you're looking for.

If no matching file can be found, you'll see the message 0 file(s) found appear in the bottom of the Find File dialog box. Try again using another name (or check to see if the file was deleted; see the section "Oops! I Deleted My Document!," later in this chapter).

7. To begin editing the file in Word, double-click on its name.

This "opens" the file, starting Word and loading the document for editing.

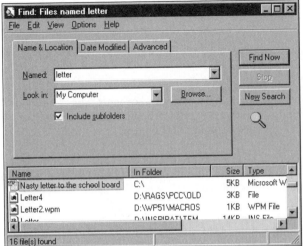

Figure 29-3:
The results
of a
successful
search.

✔ If you aren't sure of the characters in a filename, substitute the
* (asterisk). For example, T*S would locate all files from TIPS to
TABLE OF CONTENTS.

✔ If you double-click on a found file and it doesn't open Word, then what you
found probably wasn't a Word document. Try again.

✔ All Word documents have a word icon by their name.

✔ If the file isn't found, consider that you may have saved the file under a
different name.

✔ To return to your adventures in word processing, click the Microsoft Word
button on the taskbar.

"Where Did My Document Go?"

"Whoa! What's the blank screen doing there? Wasn't I already five pages into
this report on human fungus?"

Never fear, documents slide away. Try moving the cursor up and down a few
pages: Press the PgUp or PgDn keys. What may have happened is that the next
page in your document is blank and you're only seeing the blank part on your
screen. Fiddling with the cursor keys should get you reoriented.

Another trick: Look in the Window menu to see whether you accidentally
switched windows.

Finally, as a last resort, press Ctrl+Z just in case you deleted everything.

"Where Am I Now?"

If the keys appear to be too close together, or your fingers suddenly swell, you may find yourself accidentally pressing the wrong cursor keys and, lo, you're somewhere else in your document. But where?

Rather than use your brain to figure things out, press Shift+F5. Shift+F5 is the Go Back command, and pressing it moves you to the previous cursor position and resets your document as you remember it. (Also refer to Chapter 2.)

"It's Not Printing!"

Golly, the printer can be a dopey device. You tell Word to print, and the printer just sits there — deaf as a post! "Doe, dee, doe," it says. "Aren't you glad you paid twice as much money for a laser printer? Yuk! Yuk! Yuk!"

Believe it or not, the printer is not being stupid. Now stop banging your head on the table — it's not you either. Someone's connections are probably just loose. Check the printer's first. Make sure that the printer is on. Make sure that it is online. You then need to check for paper to print on. Then confirm that the printer cable is still connected. Only after these steps should you phone the local computer store about free pickup of loony bin merchandise. (It does happen.)

- ✔ If a large picture or drawing has been inserted into your document, it will make the computer and printer think harder before it starts to print. Have patience.

- ✔ Do not try printing again; don't try pressing harder on the keys. When the printer doesn't work, it doesn't work. Fixing this problem requires more attention then telepathy.

- ✔ If you keep pressing the Print command, each print order will just keep stacking up one behind the other and when you do finally get the printer to respond, it will spend the next 72 hours printing out your report on the mating habits of Monarch butterflies. You really don't want that, do you?

- ✔ Refer to Chapter 8 for additional information about printing.

- ✔ Make sure that the computer and printer are off — and unplugged — before you plug in a printer cable.

- ✔ The printer probably needs to be connected to the computer before the two are simultaneously turned on so that they can *recognize* each other.

"Oops! I Deleted My Document!"

Deleting files is necessary, just like stepping on cockroaches. But what if you found out a cockroach was really a reincarnation of your Aunt Mildred? Wouldn't you want her back? The same thing holds true with files. Sometimes you may accidentally delete a file. If you do, follow these steps to reincarnate your file:

1. **Minimize everything.**

   You need to shrink down all the windows on the desktop so that you can see the desktop.

   The easiest way to minimize everything is to right-click the mouse on the taskbar, preferably a blank part of the taskbar (and if you can't find a blank part, right-click on the far right side of the taskbar, where the time is displayed). Choose Minimize All Windows from the shortcut menu that pops up.

2. **Open the Recycle Bin icon.**

   The Recycle Bin contains all the files you've recently deleted since, sneaky-sneaky, Windows doesn't delete anything. Just like a cat prowling for a fish bone, you're about to dig through Windows' own dumpster to look for your lunch, er, lost file.

   Open the Recycle Bin by double-clicking on it with the mouse. Doing so displays the Recycle Bin window, which looks like any other old My Computer window.

3. **Click on the Date Deleted heading.**

   Doing so sorts all the files in the order they were deleted, most recently deleted first. (If it doesn't, then click it again).

4. **Look for your file in the list.**

5. **When you find your file, click on it once to highlight it.**

   This selects the file.

6. **Choose File⇨Restore**

   Ahhh! Ahhh! (Song of angels rejoicing.) Your file has been restored, put right back on disk, and in its old, comfy folder, just as it was before you accidentally murdered it.

7. **Close the Recycle Bin window.**

   Click on its X close button.

✔ Some files are gone for good. Oh, well. Be more careful when you delete next time.

✔ You cannot use the Undelete command on a network drive. Contact your network guru and explain the problem. Try not to refer to anything as "dumb" or "asinine."

Part VII
The Part of Tens

In this part...

Don't you just love trivia? (Most intelligent folk do.) And what's the best type of trivia? Lists! For example, "Ten things the baby has tried to eat (at least the ten we've actually found before he swallowed them)" or "Ten things you always pack in your suitcase that you never end up using" or "Ten things you never want to hear your doctor say when he's looking at something you can't see yourself." This book deals with Word, so this part of the book is devoted to interesting lists about Word.

Most of the chapters in this section contain ten items. Some chapters will contain more, some less. After all, if I was as thorough as I could be in Chapter 33, "Ten Features You Don't Use but Paid for Anyway," this book would be as fat as all those other books on Word.

Chapter 30

The Ten Commandments of Word

*J*ust imagine Bill Gates as Moses. His spindly frame is draped magnificently with those ancient Hebrew robes. His towering figure daunts the word processing masses. The tablets . . . okay, so someone else is helping him hold the tablets. But anyway, upon the tablets are written the Ten Commandments of Word. Nay, isn't that the fire of the Lord in his heart — or just indigestion from Burrito Day at the commissary?

And, lo, it came to pass that the tablets were transcribed. And over the course of time, their wisdom found its way into this book. Ahem! It's very hard for me to write stiffly, like the characters in a Cecil B. DeMille movie. Rather than drag this thing out, this chapter contains a bunch of do's and don'ts for working in Word. Most of these items are covered previously in this book, especially way back in Part I (the contents of which have probably spilled out your left ear by now — so listen closely to the recap).

I. Thou shalt not use spaces.

Generally speaking, you should never find more than one space anywhere in a Word document. Yeah, I know, most of us former touch-typists typed two spaces at the end of a sentence. With a word processor, that's unnecessary, so wean yourself from the habit.

Any time you have more than one space in a row in your document, you should probably be using the Tab key instead. Use the spacebar to separate words and to end a sentence. If you align lists of information, use the Tab key. If you want to organize information into rows and columns, use the Table command (see Chapter 12).

II. Thou shalt not press Enter at the end of each line.

Word automatically wraps your text down to the next line as you approach the right margin. You have no need to press Enter, except when want you to start a new paragraph. (Of course, if your paragraph is only a line long, that's okay.)

III. Thou shalt not neglect thy keyboard.

Word is Windows, and Windows is mousy. You can get a lot done with the mouse, but some things are faster with the keyboard. For example, I routinely switch documents with Ctrl+F6. And stabbing the Ctrl+S key to quickly save a document or Ctrl+P to print works better than fumbling for the mouse. You don't have to learn all the keyboard commands, but knowing those few outlined in this book will help a lot.

IV. Thou shalt not reset or turn off thy PC until thou quittest Word and Windows.

Always exit properly from Word and especially from Windows. Only shut off or reset your computer when you see the "It's now okeydokey to turn off this PC" type of prompt on-screen — never when you're running Word or have Windows active. Believeth me, if ye do, ye are asking for mucho trouble, yea, verily, woe.

V. Thou shalt not manually number thy pages.

Word has an automatic page numbering command. Refer to Chapter 11 in the section "Where to Stick the Page Number."

VI. Thou shalt not use the Enter key to start a new page.

Sure, it works: Press the Enter key a couple of dozen times, and you'll be on a new page. But that's not the proper way, and you'll mess up your new page if you go back and re-edit text. Besides, pressing Ctrl+Enter is quicker. Doing so inserts a *hard page break* into your document. Refer to Chapter 11, in the section "Starting a New Page — a Hard Page Break," for the details.

VII. Thou shalt not quit without saving first.

Save your document to disk before you quit. Shift+F12 is the key combo to remember. Or Ctrl+S is the one you don't even have to remember because it's so sensible. If only all of life — no, forget life — if only all of Word were so sensible.

VIII. Thou shalt not press OK too quickly.

Word has many Yes/No/OK-type questions. If you press OK without thinking about it (or press Enter accidentally), you could be deleting text, deleting files, or performing a bad Replace operation without knowing it. Always read your screen before you press OK.

IX. Thou shalt not forget to turn on thy printer.

The biggest printing problem anyone has is telling Word to print something and the printer isn't on. Verify that your printer is on, healthy, and ready to print before you tell Word to print something.

X. Thou shalt not forget to back up thy work.

Keeping emergency copies of your important documents is vital. Computers are shaky houses of cards, which can collapse at any sneeze or hiccup. Always make a safety copy of your files at the end of the day or as you work.

Chapter 31
Ten Cool Tricks

● ●

In This Chapter

▶ Printing labels

▶ Bullets and numbering

▶ Instant floating palettes

▶ Draft view

▶ Select all

▶ Inserting the date

▶ Sorting

▶ Automatic saves

▶ Fast saves

▶ Inserting cool characters

● ●

Determining what's a "cool trick" (and what's not) is purely subjective. I'm sure people who formerly numbered their pages manually think Word's Page Numbers command is a cool trick. I think AutoCorrect is a great trick. And I'm certain some Neanderthal out there thinks the on-the-fly spell checker is "keen." Now if the boys and girls in the Word labs could only come up with a handy tool that lets you take back something you said aloud, we'd all truly be blessed.

This chapter explains some of the neater Word tricks — mostly obscure stuff that I may not have mentioned elsewhere in this book. Some are simple and straightforward; some take a little longer for the human mind to grasp.

Printing Labels

Labels are those gummy things that you can peel and chew just like gum! Seriously, they stick to envelopes. Because my handwriting is so darn lousy, I print labels with my return address on them and stick those on my bills and whatnot I send out. I do it as a favor to the overworked men and women of the U.S. Postal Service.

To print labels, you choose the same command as when you want to print envelopes. Same command, different panel. Before you mess with this, I recommend that you go out and buy some Avery sticky labels for your computer. I use Avery laser labels in my laser printer. Stock number 5160 is ideal for return address and mailing labels. (Avery even has its own cool label printing program — but that's not needed since you have Word.)

Here are the instructions — way too terse for the main part of this book — for printing labels in Word:

1. **Choose Tools⇨Envelopes and Labels.**

2. **Make sure that the Labels panel is in front.**

3. **Click on the Options button.**

4. **Select Avery Standard from the Label Products list.**

5. **Select 5160 (or whatever product number you're using) from the Product Number list.**

6. **Click OK.**

7. **Type what you want printed on the label in the Address box.**

8. **Make sure that the printer is on, ready to print, and loaded with the proper label sheet.**

9. **Click the Print button.**

If you're disgusted with the font the labels print in (and I'm disgusted), click the New Document button instead of Print in step 9. When the labels appear in a document window, you can change their font and so forth by using the Font and Paragraph formatting dialog boxes. Refer to Chapters 9 and 10 for the details. (The New Document button essentially sticks your labels in a giant table; see Chapter 12 for more information on tables.)

Bullets and Numbering

Often, you need to drive home several points, and nothing brings that home like putting bullets in your text. No, these aren't the lead-propelled things used to kill tourists and innocent bystanders. Bullets are typographical dingbats, like this:

- Bang!

- Bang!

- Bang!

To apply bullets to your text, highlight the paragraphs you want to shoot and choose Format⇨Bullets and Numbering. You don't need to dawdle in the dialog box; just click OK and your highlighted text will be all shot up, nice and neat. (You also can click on the Bulleted list button on the Formatting toolbar.)

 You can also apply numbers to your paragraphs. When you see the Bullets and Numbering dialog box, click on the Numbered tab to bring that panel forward and then click OK. (Or click on the Numbered List button on the Formatting toolbar.)

Instant Floating Palettes

This feature may not be so much a cool trick as it's annoying when you're not ready for it. The ugly truth (and there's a lot of ugliness here, gentle reader) is that all those toolbars you see on your screen are potential floating palettes, just waiting for the right opportunity to break away and float free, free, free!

To convert a toolbar into a floating palette, point the mouse at a blank part of the toolbar and drag it down into the editing part of the window. There she floats!

To move the floating palette back into a toolbar, just drag it (by its title bar) back up to the top of the Word screen. Staggijt! It attaches right back.

Actually, you can make any floating palette into a toolbar and vice-versa. Check out Chapter 27 for more information on the View⇨Toolbars command.

 I don't recommend floating your palettes if you like the way your toolbars look, the way Word set them up; you never can quite reposition them back the way they were after they've floated. Something about being formerly free makes the toolbars stubborn.

Draft View

Word demands a lot of its owner. If you have a file that has a lot of graphics or a lot of different fonts, a slower computer can take forever to display a page of text. You can avoid this delay by switching on the ugly Draft view for your document:

1. **Choose Tools⇨Options.**

2. **Locate the View panel and bring it forward.**

3. **Put a check mark in the Draft Font box, in the upper-left corner of the panel.**

4. **Click OK.**

There is a problem here, however. Because no graphics appear and because you can't see the different fonts, you may as well be using WordPerfect 5.1. Yech! Buy more memory; buy a better machine; sell your dog; anything but that!

Repeat the preceding steps to remove the check mark and rid yourself of Draft view. (But keep in mind that Draft view does pep things up on slower computers.)

Draft view works only from Normal view. This option is not available from Page Layout view. Also, you must show proper ID before ordering a Draft view in some parts of Wyoming.

Select All

There are times when you will want to block the whole shooting match; highlight everything from top to bottom, beginning to end; select the entire document. When you want to do so, click the mouse three times in your document's left margin. Click, Click, Zowie! There it is.

Oh, and you can hold down the Ctrl key and press the 5 key on the number keypad. Zap, Zowie! There you go.

Oh, and you also can press F8 (the Extended Text key) five times. Zap, Zap, Zap, Zap, Zowie! There you go again.

Oh, and the Edit⇨Select All command does the same thing. Press Ctrl+A. Zowie!

Inserting the Date

Word's date command is named Date and Time and hangs under the Insert menu. Selecting this option displays a dialog box full of date and time formats, one of which you're bound to favor.

Sorting

Sorting is one of Word's better tricks. Once you learn it, you go looking for places to use it. You can use the Sorting command to arrange text alphabetically or numerically. You can sort paragraphs, table rows, and columns in cell tables and tables created by using tabs.

Always save your document before sorting.

Sorting is not that difficult; all you have to do is save your document before sorting, highlight the stuff you want to sort — after you save your document first — and then select the text you want to sort. Save again. Then choose Table⇨Sort Text. Oh, did I mention that you first should save your file? Then mess around in the dialog box and decide how you want the information in that file you saved to be sorted, though clicking OK usually sorts in alphabetical order.

Why all this concern with safety? Well, sorting takes a bunch of memory, and the machine could hang or crash. Or you may just decide that you don't like the way the sorted document looks a split second after you hit the spacebar or type a letter — no more Undo command. You have to go back to square one.

Automatic Save

When the Auto Save feature is active, your document is periodically saved to disk. This isn't the same as pressing Ctrl+S to save your document. Instead, Word makes a secret backup copy every so often. In the event of a crash, you can recover your work from the backup copy — even if you never saved the document to disk.

To turn on Auto Save, choose Tools⇨Options. Select the Save tab to bring that panel up front. Click on the Automatic Save Every box to put a check mark in that box if one isn't already in place. Then enter the backup interval in the Minutes text box. For example, I type **10** to have Word back up my documents every ten minutes. If the power is unstable at your home or office, enter **5**, **3**, **2**, or even **1** minute as the backup interval. Press Enter to return to your document.

With Automatic Save, you won't recover all your document in case of a mishap, but you will get most of it back.

Fast Saves

Fast Saves is one of those ideas that sounds real good . . . until you use it. The idea is to avoid having to save everything every time. "Why not just save the changes? This will make things go oh so much faster," the folks at Microsoft said. "Because," retorted this Word Dummy, "you can't give a Fast-Saved file to other people and expect them to be able to read it on their computers."

If Word only saves your changes to disk, what's someone else going to make of such a file? What if Tolstoy only changed a character's name in Chapter 43? He would have turned in a disk to his publisher with a Chapter 43 file that contained only the single word *Ludmilla*. That just doesn't work.

My advice is to disable Fast Saves. Choose Tool⇨Options. Then select the Save panel by clicking on its tab. If the Allow Fast Saves box is checked, click on it. Make it empty. Press Enter to return your document.

Cool Characters

You can use the Symbol command in the Insert menu to stick odd and wonderful characters into your document. Quite a few Windows fonts have a few weird and wonderful characters in them. The Symbol font is full of neat stuff; the Wingdings font has all sorts of fun doodads; even the "normal" font, Times New Roman, has several cool characters in it.

You can insert any of these funky characters into your document at your whim. Simply put the toothpick cursor where you want the symbol to appear, choose Insert⇨Symbol, point at the cool character you want inserted, and click your mouse.

Refer to Chapter 9 for more information.

Chapter 32

Ten Weird Things You Probably Don't Know About

*W*elcome to the bizarre. No one could say that better than Rod Serling. If good old Rod were still with us, I'm certain he'd love using Word to help him concoct more wonderful and, yes, bizarre stories. He'd probably enjoy using the strange and macabre features discussed in this chapter. No, none of this is "secret." None of it is cool. It's all weird, strange, not-really-necessary, and somewhat bizarre.

Paste Special

Paste is paste, right? Well, not according to Windows. You can't just paste anything anymore. I mean, it's so, well, *kindergarten*. To help assist you with more-daunting paste tactics, the folks at Microsoft have come up with the Edit⇨Paste Special command. Choosing it brings up a Paste Special dialog box, which enables you to paste something into your document in several ways.

The paste methods all depend on what you just copied. You can paste in text as "Unformatted text," which I do all the time because I don't like copying stinky formatting between documents. You also can experiment with "linking" items, which is the OLE stuff Microsoft is so big on with Windows. Strange stuff. Worthy of playing with, but definitely too weird to go anywhere but in this chapter.

The Style Gallery

The Style Gallery is a fun place to play. Basically, the Style Gallery is a workshop where you can experiment with applying various Word styles to your document. To do so, choose Format⇨Style Gallery. A humongous Style Gallery dialog box appears, with a list of styles on the left and a preview of how they affect your document on the right. It's kind of fun to poke around with different styles and see how they tweak your work.

If the results in the Style Gallery dialog box don't impress you, consider clicking on the Example button. That way you'll see a preview of a sample document rather than your own text.

More style madness can be found lurking in Chapter 14.

The Language Command

The Language command in the Tools menu allows you to mark a block and tag it as being written in another language, say Norwegian Bokmål. There's only one reason to do this: When Word is spell-checking and comes across a foreign word, it uses the appropriate language's dictionary instead of attempting to decipher the word as English.

A better purpose behind the Language command is to format some text as "no proofing." In other words, you tell Word not to spell-check that text. For example, I have a style I use for typing in instructions to my editor or to the production department. That style has the Language set to "no proofing"; otherwise, Word would stop and try to spell-check my rude comments and, really, why would I want to bother myself with that nonsense?

- ✔ Catalan is spoken in Catalonia. I wonder how many Word 6 users live there?

- ✔ No, dude, there is no "Surfer" language. Bummer.

The Customize Command

The Tools⇨Customize command is an odd place to not only waste mountains of time but also feel that you have ultimate control over Word's fate. This command tears at the heart of the very fabric that is Word. By using the various controls in the Customize dialog box, you can actually change the way Word looks — for the better, for good.

The three panels in the Customize dialog box let you change Word's toolbars, menus, and keyboards. Hey, this stuff is real, and it's not for the faint of heart. You can build your own toolbar, add or remove menu items, and assign your own keyboard shortcuts. The whole program is up for grabs! I don't recommend messing with anything here. Wait a few months. Get comfy with Word. Then slash away and make the program your own!

Using the Options Dialog Box

Choosing the Tools⇨Options command accesses the Options dialog box. What you get in this dialog box is 12 — count 'em, 12 — panels of various things Word does. The settings in the panels control how Word behaves.

There are really no hints or secrets in the Options dialog box. In fact, you've probably been here a few times if you chose any Options buttons in the various Word dialog boxes. No big deal. Just weird.

Inserting Fields

A field looks like text in your document. It smells like text. And it prints like text. But it's not text. Instead, it's a special marker — a fill-in-the-blanks thing that Word knows to complete at some later time. For example, typing the date in your document just slaps some words on the page. But sticking a date *field* in your document means that that field always displays the current date, no matter what the current date is.

You insert fields into your document by using the Insert⇨Field command. The Field dialog box displays a list of field categories and then individual types of fields. For example, the Date and Time category lists several types of date fields: the date the document was created, saved to disk, printed, the current date, and so on. An Options button allows you to further customize the field.

When you select them, fields appear like selected text but with a hazy gray background. Unlike real text, you must select and delete the entire field all at once. (Remember, fields are not text.)

WordPerfect Help

I suppose that I could go on and on about how the title of this section wastes a perfectly good word; anyone who uses WordPerfect needs help as a matter of definition. Anyway, the folks at Microsoft seem to think that WordPerfect users can be saved from the multicolored loony bin.

If you are a born-again Word convert from WordPerfect, you will find a special section of Word designed just to unconfuse you and put you back on the path of productive and sane word processing. Choose Help⇨WordPerfect Help to learn how the big boys do it. Doing so lets you grow accustomed to Word's commands as your contorted WordPerfect function key fingers learn to grow straight again.

Mousy Shortcuts

Here are some interesting things you can do with the mouse:

- Double-click on any toolbar to change it into a floating palette of tools. Double-click on the floating palette's title to switch it back into a toolbar.
- Double-click *on* the ruler to see the Page Setup dialog box.
- Double-click *in* the ruler to see the Tabs dialog box.

- Click on the Help button on the Standard toolbar and then point at some text on the screen. A pop-up cartoon bubble appears, describing that text's formatting.
- Click the right mouse button over your document to see a quick pop-up menu with several editing and formatting commands on it.
- Click the right mouse button over a toolbar to display the Toolbars menu.
- Double-click the mouse on the three-letter acronyms in boxes on the Status bar to switch those items on or off.
- Double-click elsewhere on the status bar to bring up the Go To dialog box.

Constructing a Master Document

How big should your document be? Technically speaking, Word can handle a document probably as big as you could write it. Practically speaking, you don't want things to get too big. Word starts acting weirder than normal with big documents.

But how big is big? Here's my advice: Keep your documents at chapter-size.

Each chapter in this book is a document unto itself. This chapter is called CHAPTER 32 on disk. That's the way most writers work — a chapter is a document. The only drawback to this method is that it makes printing everything a pain. And if you dare to take advantage of Word's indexing and table of contents commands (I don't), they just don't work in separate documents.

The solution to the problem is to create what Word calls a Master Document. That's just another Word document, but it contains information about other documents and kind of links them all together. You still work with each chapter as its own document. But the whole shooting match can be printed, indexed, table-of-contents-ed, or otherwise manipulated through the Master Document.

Yes, the concept is novel. Unfortunately, wrestling with it in Word is not fun.

To create a Master Document, start with a new document in Word. Choose File➪New. Then choose View➪Master Document. This changes the display and adds the Outline/Master Document toolbar. The buttons on the far right of the toolbar are used to add documents to the Master Document. (Hover the mouse over a button to see its function "balloon" display.)

Alas, that's all the help I can give you here; working with a Master Document involves a full tutorial.

The Unbreakables

There are two weird keys on your keyboard: the spacebar and the hyphen. Both keys produce characters on the screen, but not "normal" characters. The space. What is that? Space! Outer space? And the hyphen isn't really a character at all. It's used to split text — to hyphenate words — between two lines. Indeed, both the space and the hyphen will *break* your text between two lines. There is no problem with this — unless you don't want them to break the line in two.

There are times when you want to be sure that a space was not interrupted by something as mundane as the end of a line. For example, suppose that you work for the firm of Bandini, Lambert, and Locke and, by golly, Mr. Locke doesn't like to be left on a line by himself. If so, insert a nonbreaking ("hard") space between each name to make sure that they're always together.

To prevent the space character from breaking a line, press Ctrl+Shift+spacebar.

The hyphen key, which also is the minus key, works to hyphenate a long word at the end of a line. But, sometimes, you may not want the hyphen to split a word. For example, you may not want a phone number split between two lines. Inserting a hard hyphen prevents text from splitting between two lines.

To prevent the hyphen character from breaking a line, press Ctrl+Shift+ - (hyphen).

And two weird things you should avoid at all costs

Over the years of using Word, I've discovered two of the most annoying commands in the history of word processing. One is just annoying, but the other is terrifying. Whatever you do, don't tangle with these two weirdos.

The first annoying command is Window⇨New Windows. This command is *not* the same as the New command in the File menu. Instead, what it gives you is another window on the screen with the same document. Okay, that may be fine, but you cannot close that window with the File⇨Close command without closing both it and your original document window. (A better way to accomplish something similar is to use the Window⇨Split command, which is discussed at the end of Chapter 20.)

The second terrifying command is the horrid menu-item-remover, something you may stumble over accidentally someday (hope you don't). If you press Ctrl+Alt+- (hyphen), the mouse pointer changes to a thick, horizontal line. That's the menu item removal cursor. Just choose any menu item and—thwoop!—it's gone, deleted, zapped, dead. And there's no way to get that menu item back, either. Deadly! Scary! Not even Rod Serling could dream up something that bizarre.

If you do accidentally press Ctrl+Alt+-, quickly press the Esc key to cancel that mode. Yikes! What kind of sick mind thought up that trick, huh?

Chapter 33

Ten Features You Don't Use but Paid for Anyway

*W*ord comes with many more features than you'll ever use. There are definitely more than those listed here and probably several dozen that I've never heard of. Some people writing those massive "complete" Word tomes have been known to disappear into a room and not emerge for months — or years! Indeed, I seriously doubt if anyone who knows everything about Word has kept his or her sanity.

This chapter lists ten of the more interesting features that you bought when you paid for Word. (I'm not even bothering to mention some of the things that Windows lets you do with Word, such as embed sounds and other cute, but useless, things.) You probably didn't know that these goodies existed. That's okay — they're a bit technical to work with. This chapter covers each one briefly, but don't expect to learn how to use any of the paid-for-but-forgotten features.

Table of Contents

It used to be that figuring out a table of contents could make a grown human of the masculine persuasion cry. (It has never had the same effect on my wife, but, after childbirth, I guess not much is daunting.) Who, in their right mind, would want to go to the front of a document, type in all of those names, then all of those dots, and then figure out what page what should be on? (And there's not even a coach standing by reminding you to breathe.)

Word, man, that's who! If you have been careful with your styles (see Chapter 14 to learn about styles), inserting a table of contents is a sure bet. Well, almost. Choose Insert⇨Index and Tables and then click on the Table of Contents tab. Word will look through your entire document and take everything that has been tagged with a style of Heading (followed by some number), determine what page it is on, and build the table of contents for you.

Sounds like fun? Yeah, but it's complex to set up. If you didn't follow these steps when you created your document, then you might as well do it the old-fashioned way, weeping bitterly and all that.

Hyphenation

Hyphenation is an automatic feature that splits long words at the end of a line to make the text fit better on the page. Most people leave it off because hyphenation tends to slow down the pace at which people read. However, if you want to hyphenate a document, choose Tools⇨Hyphenation. Continuously jab the F1 key when you need Help.

Index

This feature is interesting but complicated to use. The Index and Tables command in the Insert menu (click on the Index tab) marks a spot in a document to include in an index. For example, you can select that command to mark a word and tag it for inclusion as an index entry. Then, using other commands too complicated to mention here, you can have Word generate an automatic index at the end of the document. This feature is a handy thing to have, but it takes time to learn, and you often don't need a full index for a five-page letter to Mom.

Cross-Reference

The Insert⇨Cross-reference command allows you to insert a "Refer to Chapter 99, Section Z" type of thing into your document. This feature works because you've taken the Krell brain booster and now have an IQ that can only be expressed in scientific notation. Fortunately, you may have also used the Heading style to mark text in your document that you want to cross-reference. Doing that means that the Insert⇨Cross-reference command will work and will stick a "Refer to Chapter 99, Section Z" type of thing in your document — complete with an updating reference to that page should you overhaul your document.

Math

Did it ever dawn upon the Word people that math and English are two separate subjects for a reason? The math and English parts of the SAT scores are separate. Math and English are always taught as separate courses. So who needs a math function in a word processor? I don't know. Even if you did, it's still easier to calculate the numbers by using your desk calculator and typing them in manually.

To use the Math command, you must first have your data in a table. Then highlight the row or column that you want computed. Choose Table⇨Formula. Word will suggest a formula type, or you can tell Word what you want done with the numbers. On second thought, I guess this woulda been kinda handy during algebra class. Anyway, Word will put the answer wherever you left the insertion pointer.

Address Book

 Lurking around various Word dialog boxes, you'll find a cutesy little button with a drop-down arrow by it. Lo, it's the Address Book button, containing a link to your e-mail address book, the one you never bothered setting up when Windows insisted on installing its own mail system.

Mail is a bother. I told Windows not to install it on my PC and it did anyway. So when I press the Address Book button, my computer instantly, and most efficiently, wastes about four minutes of my time (during which I stew and repeatedly press the Cancel button). Don't bother with this button unless you really have an address book and really know how it works.

Various Send Commands

Lurking in the File menu you may find two interesting e-mail commands: Send and Add Routing Slip. The Send button supposedly allows you to use Word as your e-mail editor and then instantly send your document to someone else on your network or on the Internet. Sounds great, works terribly.

Fear has prevented me from ever choosing the Add Routing Slip command. I haven't any idea what it does, nor do I want to know.

Random Statistics

This feature is something that you never use because it is a very unpopular thing. Besides that, it is a royal pain in the digit. Word tracks all sorts of statistics about your document. To see them, choose File⇨Summary Info. Yuck! That wouldn't be bad enough, but then click on the Statistics button. Yoikles! Word tells you all sorts of things about your document, such as how many words it contains. Writers who are paid by the word use this feature to make sure that they get their full load in. It can also give you a good idea of how "big" your document is, although this stuff is really all pretty silly.

Repagination Nonsense

In the beginning, Microsoft Word was a mere DOS application (and a slow one at that.) To make the program faster, Microsoft left out a bunch of features that were standard in most word processors. One of those features was *repagination*, or the capability of the word processor to automatically insert "page breaks" on the screen (those dotted lines of death). In Word, repagination is done automatically. However (to be compatible I suppose), a Repaginate command still exists. From the Tools menu, choose Options; click on the General tab. You can turn off the Background Repagination.

Chapter 34

Ten Shortcut Keys Worth Remembering

This is sacrilege! You are forbidden — *forbidden* — to use the keyboard in Windows! Shame on you! Seriously, you can do lots of interesting things with the keyboard, things that can be done quite rapidly and without breaking off any nails. Although Word has a whole armada of key combinations, only a handful are worth knowing. This chapter contains the best, a shade more than ten, but those I feel you'll grow fond of as time passes.

Besides, the guy who invented the mouse doesn't even profit from it. He's an academic, so it's the intellectual property (or whatever that lame excuse is called) of Stanford University. But now he's on late night TV where he gets to tell people how for 20 years people thought the mouse was an impractical and eccentric tool that would never take off for real computer use. He encourages the ingenious among us to invent and not be discouraged. He says he doesn't even mind not profiting from the mouse because his whole point was to fill a need in the computer industry. Because the creation is the thing. Kinda gives you warm fuzzies, huh?

Strange, WordPerfect-esque Function Keys

Thank goodness this program isn't WordPerfect. Those folks have lots of
function keys, all of them required just to work the program. In Word, using the
function keys is optional . . . so why bother? Actually, there are five function
keys that you may want to become friendly with. No handy mnemonic here.
You'll just have to get used to them; fortunately you only have to remember five
of them.

F1, the Help! key

In any Windows program, pressing F1 displays helpful information. In Word, the
F1 key is geared to whatever you're doing. If you're in the Save dialog box, press
F1 to get help on it. If you see an error message, press F1 for more information
(you hope).

Shift+F3, the Switch Case key

To change the case of your text between all caps, lowercase, and mixed case, mark
the text as a block and then press Shift+F3 until the text looks the way you like.

The F4 Repeat Command key

If you're applying formatting to a number of paragraphs or various text or just
doing the same command over and over, press the F4 key. This key directs
Word to pull a "do-over" and work the same command again. A common use for
this key may be when pasting in symbols. If you're using the Symbol command
in the Insert menu to poof up your document a bit, just press F4 to repeat the
insert.

The Shift+F4 Repeat Find key

Find a bit of text. Great! Want to find it again? Shift+F4 makes Word look without
you having to visit the Find dialog box again.

Shift+F5, the "Take me back to where I was" key

It's easy to get lost in Word. If you just pressed Ctrl+End for no apparent reason and suddenly find yourself at the end of your document, press Shift+F5 to get back to where you once were. This key is a big time-saver.

The Document Keys

There are four things you can do with documents and there are four handy — and mnemonic! — key combinations with which you can do them:

    Ctrl+N, New

    Ctrl+O, Open

    Ctrl+S, Save

    Ctrl+P, Print

The only one missing here is a Close command. Don't bother with Ctrl+C; it's used to Copy text. Drat! We need a larger alphabet.

Save! Save! Save! Always save your document. Get in the habit of reaching up and pressing Ctrl+S often as you work.

The Kindergarten Keys: Cut, Copy, Paste

When you're working with blocks, three shortcut keys will come in most handy:

    Ctrl+X, Cut

    Ctrl+C, Copy

    Ctrl+V, Paste

To use these keys, first highlight a block of text. Then press Ctrl+X to cut the block or Ctrl+C to copy. Move the toothpick cursor to where you want the block pasted and press Ctrl+V. Refer to Chapter 6 for more information on playing with blocks.

The Undo-Redo Keys

The Ctrl+Z key is Word's Undo key. It will undo just about anything Word can do and undo what was done before that, too.

If you need to redo something — that is, un-undo — you can press Ctrl+Y.

Text-Formatting Shortcut Keys

You can use these four shortcut keys — either as you type or on a marked block of text — to affect that text's character formatting:

> Ctrl+B, Bold
>
> Ctrl+I, Italics
>
> Ctrl+U, Underline
>
> Ctrl+spacebar, Normal

Type Ctrl+B when you want unbolded text made bold. Or, if the text is already bold and you mark it as a block, Ctrl+B will unbold the block. The same holds true with Ctrl+I (italics).

The Ctrl+spacebar key returns text to normal. So if you mark a block of text that has all sorts of crazy, mixed-up formatting, press Ctrl+spacebar for an instant sea of sanity. Pressing Ctrl+spacebar as you're entering text can be used to instantly switch off whatever formatting you're currently using.

Font Formatting Keys

Forget the Font dialog box. If you have enough spare memory cells after all that alcohol in college (or from the Mail Merge chapter), you can use these key combinations to ease text formatting:

> Ctrl+Shift+F, Font
>
> Ctrl+Shift+P, Point Size
>
> Ctrl+Shift+S, Style
>
> Ctrl+Shift+>, Make text bigger
>
> Ctrl+Shift+<, Make text smaller

The Ctrl+Shift+F, Ctrl+Shift+P, and Ctrl+Shift+S key combos work to highlight the list boxes on the Formatting toolbar. Type in the font name, point size, or style that you want. This method of selection seems like quite a bit of work, but it can be quick if you get the hang of it.

The Ctrl+Shift+> and Ctrl+Shift+< nonsense makes no sense. But sometimes it's fun to mess with the text size of a selected block by using those key combinations. It's much more graphical than trying to mentally figure numbers in a dialog box.

Paragraph Formatting Keys

Select a paragraph as a block and then use one of the following key combinations to format it:

Ctrl+L, Left-justify

Ctrl+R, Right-justify

Ctrl+E, Center

Ctrl+J, Justify

Ctrl+1, Single-space

Ctrl+2, Double-space

Ctrl+5, 1 $^1/_2$ space

The only oddball here is Ctrl+E to center a paragraph. Ack! Never mind. Just use the buttons on the Formatting toolbar. I actually used Ctrl+2 to double-space a document the other day, which is why I'm listing it here.

Chapter 35

Ten Things Worth Remembering

There's nothing like finishing a book with a few heartening words of good advice. As a Word user, you need this kind of encouragement and motivation. Word can be an unforgiving, but not necessarily evil, place to work. This book shows you that having a lot of fun with Word and still getting your work done is also possible. To help send you on your way, here are a few things worth remembering.

Don't Be Afraid of Your Keyboard

Try to avoid pressing Enter repeatedly to start a new page, using the spacebar when the Tab key will do better, or manually numbering your pages. There's a handy Word command to do just about anything, and you'll never learn the commands if you're afraid to try them.

Have a Supply of Diskettes Ready

You need diskettes to use your computer, even if you have a hard drive! You need diskettes for backup purposes and for exchanging files with other PCs running Word, such as between home and the office.

Keep one or two boxes of diskettes available. Always buy the proper size diskette for your PC, either $5^1/4$- or $3^1/2$-inch disks. Make sure that you buy the proper capacity as well, which is usually the high-capacity or high-density diskettes. And format those diskettes!

Keep Printer Paper, Toner, and Supplies Handy

When you buy paper, buy a box. When you buy a toner cartridge or printer ribbon, buy two or three. Also keep a good stock of pens, paper, staples, paper clips, and all the other office supplies (including diskettes) handy.

Keep References Handy

Word is a writing tool. As such, you need to be familiar with and obey the grammatical rules of your language. If that language just happens to be English, then you have a big job ahead of you. Even though they're an electronic part of Word, I recommend that you keep a dictionary and a thesaurus handy. Strunk and White's *The Elements of Style* is also a great book for finding out where the apostrophes and commas go. If you lack these books, visit the reference section of your local bookstore and plan on paying about $50 to stock up on quality references.

Keep Your Files Organized

Use folders on your hard drive for storing your document files. Keep related documents together in the same subdirectory. You may need someone else's help to set up an organizational system. Refer to Chapters 20 and 22 for additional information.

Remember the Ctrl+Z Key!

The Ctrl+Z key is your undo key. If you're typing away in Word, press it to undelete any text you may have mistakenly deleted. This command works for individual letters, sentences, paragraphs, pages, and large chunks of missing text.

Save Your Document Often!

Save your document to disk as soon as you get a few meaningful words down on the screen. Then save every so often after that. Even if you're using the Auto Save feature (discussed in Chapter 31), continue to manually save your document to disk: Ctrl+S.

Use AutoText for Often-Typed Stuff

To quickly insert things that you type over and over, like your name and address, use an AutoText entry. Type your entry in once and then define it as a glossary entry under the Edit menu. Then use the shortcut key to zap it in whenever you need it. See Chapter 13 for more about AutoText.

Use Clever, Memorable File Names

A file named LETTER is certainly descriptive, but what does it tell you? A file named LETTER TO MOM even more descriptive but still lacking some information. A file LETTER TO MOM, APRIL 23 is even better. Or if you want to be brief, try 4-23 MOM LETTER. You get the idea here: Use creative and informative filenames.

Don't Take It All Too Seriously

Computers are really about having fun. Too many people panic too quickly when they use a computer. Don't let it get to you! And please, please, don't reinstall Word to fix a minor problem. Anything that goes wrong has a solution. If the solution is not in this book, consult with your guru. Someone is bound to help you out.

Index

hyphenation, 360
hyphens, 357–358

• I •

I-beam cursor, 15
icons
  in book, 6
  renaming in Windows, 76
Indent (Ctrl+M) keyboard shortcut, 132
Indent command, 132
Indent tool, 132
indents, hanging, 134–135
index, 360
information, technical, 5–6
Insert (Alt, I, L) menu shortcut, 245
Insert key, 52
Insert mode, 52
Insert Picture dialog box, 281–282
Insert Table dialog box, 160
Insert⇨Annotation command, 212–213
Insert⇨Break command, 143
Insert⇨Field command, 194
Insert⇨File command, 245
Insert⇨Footnote command, 156
Insert⇨Frame command, 285
Insert⇨Object command, 290, 294–295
Insert⇨Page Numbers command, 150
Insert⇨Picture command, 281, 301
Insert⇨Symbol command, 120–121
inserting, fields, 355
Insertion pointer, 12
installation, applets, 291–293
inverse printing, 315–317
Italic tool, 113
Italics (Ctrl+I) keyboard shortcut, 113
Italics command, 113

• J •

Justify (Ctrl+J) keyboard shortcut, 127
Justify tool, 127

• K •

kerning, 124
key combinations, 33–34
keyboard shortcuts

Beginning of Current Page (Ctrl+Alt+PgUp), 45
Beginning of Document (Ctrl+Home), 46
Beginning of Paragraph (Ctrl+Up Arrow), 45
Bold (Ctrl+B), 112
Bookmark (Ctrl+Shift+F5), 49
Bottom of Current Screen (Ctrl+PgDn), 44
Center (Ctrl+E), 126
context-sensitive help (Shift+F1), 40
Copy (Ctrl+C), 38–39, 72
Ctrl+Arrow (directional) keys, 43
Ctrl+Esc, 10
Cut (Ctrl+X), 38–39, 73
Delete Word (Ctrl+Backspace), 54
Delete Word (Ctrl+Delete), 54
documents, Ctrl+Arrow keyboard shortcuts, 43
End of Document (Ctrl+End), 45–46
Exit (Alt+F4), 242
Flush Right (Ctrl+R), 127
Fonts (Ctrl+Shift+F), 118
Go Back (Shift+F5), 46, 49, 338
Go To (Ctrl+G), 47
Hanging Indent (Ctrl+T), 134
Hard Page Break (Ctrl+Enter), 141–142
Indent (Ctrl+M), 132
Italics (Ctrl+I), 113
Justify (Ctrl+J), 127
Left Align (Ctrl+L), 126
Mark Entire Document (Ctrl+5), 70
New (Ctrl+N), 29, 243
Next Page (Ctrl+Alt+PgDn), 45
Next Paragraph (Ctrl+Dn Arrow), 44
Next Window (Ctrl+Shift+F6), 236
Open (Ctrl+O), 20, 104, 243, 259
Paste (Ctrl+V), 38–39, 72–73
Previous Window (Ctrl+F6), 236
Print (Ctrl+P), 33–34, 80, 99
Print (Ctrl+Shift+F12), 33–34, 80
Repeat (Ctrl+Y), 40
Repeat Find (Shift+F4), 40
Repeat Go To (Shift+F4), 40
Replace (Ctrl+H), 64
Reset Character (Ctrl+spacebar), 117–118
Save (Ctrl+S), 27, 242
Select All (Ctrl+A), 71
Subscript (Ctrl+=), 117
Superscript (Ctrl+Shift+=), 117

• Q •

• R •

• *U* •

• *V* •

7/29/

Windows® 3.11 For Dummies,® 3rd Edition
by Andy Rathbone

ISBN: 1-56884-370-4
$16.95 USA/
$22.95 Canada

Mutual Funds For Dummies™
by Eric Tyson

ISBN: 1-56884-226-0
$16.99 USA/
$22.99 Canada

DOS For Dummies,® 2nd Edition
by Dan Gookin

ISBN: 1-878058-75-4
$16.95 USA/
$22.95 Canada

The Internet For Dummies,® 2nd Edition
by John Levine & Carol Baroudi

ISBN: 1-56884-222-8
$19.99 USA/
$26.99 Canada

Personal Finance For Dummies™
by Eric Tyson

ISBN: 1-56884-150-7
$16.95 USA/
$22.95 Canada

PCs For Dummies,® 3rd Edition
by Dan Gookin & Andy Rathbone

ISBN: 1-56884-904-4
$16.99 USA/
$22.99 Canada

Macs® For Dummies,® 3rd Edition
by David Pogue

ISBN: 1-56884-239-2
$19.99 USA/
$26.99 Canada

The SAT® I For Dummies™
by Suzee Vlk

ISBN: 1-56884-213-9
$14.99 USA/
$20.99 Canada

Here's a complete listing of IDG Books' ...For Dummies® titles

Title	Author	ISBN	Price
DATABASE			
Access 2 For Dummies®	by Scott Palmer	ISBN: 1-56884-090-X	$19.95 USA/$26.95 Canada
Access Programming For Dummies®	by Rob Krumm	ISBN: 1-56884-091-8	$19.95 USA/$26.95 Canada
Approach 3 For Windows® For Dummies®	by Doug Lowe	ISBN: 1-56884-233-3	$19.99 USA/$26.99 Canada
dBASE For DOS For Dummies®	by Scott Palmer & Michael Stabler	ISBN: 1-56884-188-4	$19.95 USA/$26.95 Canada
dBASE For Windows® For Dummies®	by Scott Palmer	ISBN: 1-56884-179-5	$19.95 USA/$26.95 Canada
dBASE 5 For Windows® Programming For Dummies®	by Ted Coombs & Jason Coombs	ISBN: 1-56884-215-5	$19.99 USA/$26.99 Canada
FoxPro 2.6 For Windows® For Dummies®	by John Kaufeld	ISBN: 1-56884-187-6	$19.95 USA/$26.95 Canada
Paradox 5 For Windows® For Dummies®	by John Kaufeld	ISBN: 1-56884-185-X	$19.95 USA/$26.95 Canada
DESKTOP PUBLISHING/ILLUSTRATION/GRAPHICS			
CorelDRAW! 5 For Dummies®	by Deke McClelland	ISBN: 1-56884-157-4	$19.95 USA/$26.95 Canada
CorelDRAW! For Dummies®	by Deke McClelland	ISBN: 1-56884-042-X	$19.95 USA/$26.95 Canada
Desktop Publishing & Design For Dummies®	by Roger C. Parker	ISBN: 1-56884-234-1	$19.99 USA/$26.99 Canada
Harvard Graphics 2 For Windows® For Dummies®	by Roger C. Parker	ISBN: 1-56884-092-6	$19.95 USA/$26.95 Canada
PageMaker 5 For Macs® For Dummies®	by Galen Gruman & Deke McClelland	ISBN: 1-56884-178-7	$19.95 USA/$26.95 Canada
PageMaker 5 For Windows® For Dummies®	by Deke McClelland & Galen Gruman	ISBN: 1-56884-160-4	$19.95 USA/$26.95 Canada
Photoshop 3 For Macs® For Dummies®	by Deke McClelland	ISBN: 1-56884-208-2	$19.99 USA/$26.99 Canada
QuarkXPress 3.3 For Dummies®	by Galen Gruman & Barbara Assadi	ISBN: 1-56884-217-1	$19.99 USA/$26.99 Canada
FINANCE/PERSONAL FINANCE/TEST TAKING REFERENCE			
Everyday Math For Dummies™	by Charles Seiter	ISBN: 1-56884-248-1	$14.99 USA/$22.99 Canada
Personal Finance For Dummies™ For Canadians	by Eric Tyson & Tony Martin	ISBN: 1-56884-378-X	$18.99 USA/$24.99 Canada
QuickBooks 3 For Dummies®	by Stephen L. Nelson	ISBN: 1-56884-227-9	$19.99 USA/$26.99 Canada
Quicken 8 For DOS For Dummies,® 2nd Edition	by Stephen L. Nelson	ISBN: 1-56884-210-4	$19.95 USA/$26.95 Canada
Quicken 5 For Macs® For Dummies®	by Stephen L. Nelson	ISBN: 1-56884-211-2	$19.95 USA/$26.95 Canada
Quicken 4 For Windows® For Dummies,® 2nd Edition	by Stephen L. Nelson	ISBN: 1-56884-209-0	$19.95 USA/$26.95 Canada
Taxes For Dummies,™ 1995 Edition	by Eric Tyson & David J. Silverman	ISBN: 1-56884-220-1	$14.99 USA/$20.99 Canada
The GMAT® For Dummies™	by Suzee Vlk, Series Editor	ISBN: 1-56884-376-3	$14.99 USA/$20.99 Canada
The GRE® For Dummies™	by Suzee Vlk, Series Editor	ISBN: 1-56884-375-5	$14.99 USA/$20.99 Canada
Time Management For Dummies™	by Jeffrey J. Mayer	ISBN: 1-56884-360-7	$16.99 USA/$22.99 Canada
TurboTax For Windows® For Dummies®	by Gail A. Helsel, CPA	ISBN: 1-56884-228-7	$19.99 USA/$26.99 Canada
GROUPWARE/INTEGRATED			
ClarisWorks For Macs® For Dummies®	by Frank Higgins	ISBN: 1-56884-363-1	$19.99 USA/$26.99 Canada
Lotus Notes For Dummies®	by Pat Freeland & Stephen Londergan	ISBN: 1-56884-212-0	$19.95 USA/$26.95 Canada
Microsoft® Office 4 For Windows® For Dummies®	by Roger C. Parker	ISBN: 1-56884-183-3	$19.95 USA/$26.95 Canada
Microsoft® Works 3 For Windows® For Dummies®	by David C. Kay	ISBN: 1-56884-214-7	$19.99 USA/$26.99 Canada
SmartSuite 3 For Dummies®	by Jan Weingarten & John Weingarten	ISBN: 1-56884-367-4	$19.99 USA/$26.99 Canada
INTERNET/COMMUNICATIONS/NETWORKING			
America Online® For Dummies,® 2nd Edition	by John Kaufeld	ISBN: 1-56884-933-8	$19.99 USA/$26.99 Canada
CompuServe For Dummies,® 2nd Edition	by Wallace Wang	ISBN: 1-56884-937-0	$19.99 USA/$26.99 Canada
Modems For Dummies,® 2nd Edition	by Tina Rathbone	ISBN: 1-56884-223-6	$19.99 USA/$26.99 Canada
MORE Internet For Dummies®	by John R. Levine & Margaret Levine Young	ISBN: 1-56884-164-7	$19.95 USA/$26.95 Canada
MORE Modems & On-line Services For Dummies®	by Tina Rathbone	ISBN: 1-56884-365-8	$19.99 USA/$26.99 Canada
Mosaic For Dummies,® Windows Edition	by David Angell & Brent Heslop	ISBN: 1-56884-242-2	$19.99 USA/$26.99 Canada
NetWare For Dummies,® 2nd Edition	by Ed Tittel, Deni Connor & Earl Follis	ISBN: 1-56884-369-0	$19.99 USA/$26.99 Canada
Networking For Dummies®	by Doug Lowe	ISBN: 1-56884-079-9	$19.95 USA/$26.95 Canada
PROCOMM PLUS 2 For Windows® For Dummies®	by Wallace Wang	ISBN: 1-56884-219-8	$19.99 USA/$26.99 Canada
TCP/IP For Dummies®	by Marshall Wilensky & Candace Leiden	ISBN: 1-56884-241-4	$19.99 USA/$26.99 Canada

For scholastic requests & educational orders please call Educational Sales at 1. 800. 434. 2086

FOR MORE INFO OR TO ORDER, PLEASE CALL ▶ 800. 762. 2974

For volume discounts & special orders please call Corporate Sales, at 415. 655. 3000

Title	Author	ISBN	Price
The Internet For Macs® For Dummies® 2nd Edition	by Charles Seiter	ISBN: 1-56884-371-2	$19.99 USA/$26.99 Canada
The Internet For Macs® For Dummies® Starter Kit	by Charles Seiter	ISBN: 1-56884-244-9	$29.99 USA/$39.99 Canada
The Internet For Macs® For Dummies® Starter Kit Bestseller Edition	by Charles Seiter	ISBN: 1-56884-245-7	$39.99 USA/$54.99 Canada
The Internet For Windows® For Dummies® Starter Kit	by John R. Levine & Margaret Levine Young	ISBN: 1-56884-237-6	$34.99 USA/$44.99 Canada
The Internet For Windows® For Dummies® Starter Kit, Bestseller Edition	by John R. Levine & Margaret Levine Young	ISBN: 1-56884-246-5	$39.99 USA/$54.99 Canada

MACINTOSH

Title	Author	ISBN	Price
Mac® Programming For Dummies®	by Dan Parks Sydow	ISBN: 1-56884-173-6	$19.95 USA/$26.95 Canada
Macintosh® System 7.5 For Dummies®	by Bob LeVitus	ISBN: 1-56884-197-3	$19.95 USA/$26.95 Canada
MORE Macs® For Dummies®	by David Pogue	ISBN: 1-56884-087-X	$19.95 USA/$26.95 Canada
PageMaker 5 For Macs® For Dummies®	by Galen Gruman & Deke McClelland	ISBN: 1-56884-178-7	$19.95 USA/$26.95 Canada
QuarkXPress 3.3 For Dummies®	by Galen Gruman & Barbara Assadi	ISBN: 1-56884-217-1	$19.99 USA/$26.99 Canada
Upgrading and Fixing Macs® For Dummies®	by Kearney Rietmann & Frank Higgins	ISBN: 1-56884-189-2	$19.95 USA/$26.95 Canada

MULTIMEDIA

Title	Author	ISBN	Price
Multimedia & CD-ROMs For Dummies® 2nd Edition	by Andy Rathbone	ISBN: 1-56884-907-9	$19.99 USA/$26.99 Canada
Multimedia & CD-ROMs For Dummies® Interactive Multimedia Value Pack, 2nd Edition	by Andy Rathbone	ISBN: 1-56884-909-5	$29.99 USA/$39.99 Canada

OPERATING SYSTEMS:

DOS

Title	Author	ISBN	Price
MORE DOS For Dummies®	by Dan Gookin	ISBN: 1-56884-046-2	$19.95 USA/$26.95 Canada
OS/2® Warp For Dummies® 2nd Edition	by Andy Rathbone	ISBN: 1-56884-205-8	$19.99 USA/$26.99 Canada

UNIX

Title	Author	ISBN	Price
MORE UNIX® For Dummies®	by John R. Levine & Margaret Levine Young	ISBN: 1-56884-361-5	$19.99 USA/$26.99 Canada
UNIX® For Dummies®	by John R. Levine & Margaret Levine Young	ISBN: 1-878058-58-4	$19.95 USA/$26.95 Canada

WINDOWS

Title	Author	ISBN	Price
MORE Windows® For Dummies® 2nd Edition	by Andy Rathbone	ISBN: 1-56884-048-9	$19.95 USA/$26.95 Canada
Windows® 95 For Dummies®	by Andy Rathbone	ISBN: 1-56884-240-6	$19.99 USA/$26.99 Canada

PCS/HARDWARE

Title	Author	ISBN	Price
Illustrated Computer Dictionary For Dummies® 2nd Edition	by Dan Gookin & Wallace Wang	ISBN: 1-56884-218-X	$12.95 USA/$16.95 Canada
Upgrading and Fixing PCs For Dummies® 2nd Edition	by Andy Rathbone	ISBN: 1-56884-903-6	$19.99 USA/$26.99 Canada

PRESENTATION/AUTOCAD

Title	Author	ISBN	Price
AutoCAD For Dummies®	by Bud Smith	ISBN: 1-56884-191-4	$19.95 USA/$26.95 Canada
PowerPoint 4 For Windows® For Dummies®	by Doug Lowe	ISBN: 1-56884-161-2	$16.99 USA/$22.99 Canada

PROGRAMMING

Title	Author	ISBN	Price
Borland C++ For Dummies®	by Michael Hyman	ISBN: 1-56884-162-0	$19.95 USA/$26.95 Canada
C For Dummies® Volume 1	by Dan Gookin	ISBN: 1-878058-78-9	$19.95 USA/$26.95 Canada
C++ For Dummies®	by Stephen R. Davis	ISBN: 1-56884-163-9	$19.95 USA/$26.95 Canada
Delphi Programming For Dummies®	by Neil Rubenking	ISBN: 1-56884-200-7	$19.99 USA/$26.99 Canada
Mac® Programming For Dummies®	by Dan Parks Sydow	ISBN: 1-56884-173-6	$19.95 USA/$26.95 Canada
PowerBuilder 4 Programming For Dummies®	by Ted Coombs & Jason Coombs	ISBN: 1-56884-325-9	$19.99 USA/$26.99 Canada
QBasic Programming For Dummies®	by Douglas Hergert	ISBN: 1-56884-093-4	$19.95 USA/$26.95 Canada
Visual Basic 3 For Dummies®	by Wallace Wang	ISBN: 1-56884-076-4	$19.95 USA/$26.95 Canada
Visual Basic "X" For Dummies®	by Wallace Wang	ISBN: 1-56884-230-9	$19.99 USA/$26.99 Canada
Visual C++ 2 For Dummies®	by Michael Hyman & Bob Arnson	ISBN: 1-56884-328-3	$19.99 USA/$26.99 Canada
Windows® 95 Programming For Dummies®	by S. Randy Davis	ISBN: 1-56884-327-5	$19.99 USA/$26.99 Canada

SPREADSHEET

Title	Author	ISBN	Price
1-2-3 For Dummies®	by Greg Harvey	ISBN: 1-878058-60-6	$16.95 USA/$22.95 Canada
1-2-3 For Windows® 5 For Dummies® 2nd Edition	by John Walkenbach	ISBN: 1-56884-216-3	$16.95 USA/$22.95 Canada
Excel 5 For Macs® For Dummies®	by Greg Harvey	ISBN: 1-56884-186-8	$19.95 USA/$26.95 Canada
Excel For Dummies® 2nd Edition	by Greg Harvey	ISBN: 1-56884-050-0	$16.95 USA/$22.95 Canada
MORE 1-2-3 For DOS For Dummies®	by John Weingarten	ISBN: 1-56884-224-4	$19.99 USA/$26.99 Canada
MORE Excel 5 For Windows® For Dummies®	by Greg Harvey	ISBN: 1-56884-207-4	$19.95 USA/$26.95 Canada
Quattro Pro 6 For Windows® For Dummies®	by John Walkenbach	ISBN: 1-56884-174-4	$19.95 USA/$26.95 Canada
Quattro Pro For DOS For Dummies®	by John Walkenbach	ISBN: 1-56884-023-3	$16.95 USA/$22.95 Canada

UTILITIES

Title	Author	ISBN	Price
Norton Utilities 8 For Dummies®	by Beth Slick	ISBN: 1-56884-166-3	$19.95 USA/$26.95 Canada

VCRS/CAMCORDERS

Title	Author	ISBN	Price
VCRs & Camcorders For Dummies™	by Gordon McComb & Andy Rathbone	ISBN: 1-56884-229-5	$14.99 USA/$20.99 Canada

WORD PROCESSING

Title	Author	ISBN	Price
Ami Pro For Dummies®	by Jim Meade	ISBN: 1-56884-049-7	$19.95 USA/$26.95 Canada
MORE Word For Windows® 6 For Dummies®	by Doug Lowe	ISBN: 1-56884-165-5	$19.95 USA/$26.95 Canada
MORE WordPerfect® 6 For Windows® For Dummies®	by Margaret Levine Young & David C. Kay	ISBN: 1-56884-206-6	$19.95 USA/$26.95 Canada
MORE WordPerfect® 6 For DOS For Dummies®	by Wallace Wang, edited by Dan Gookin	ISBN: 1-56884-047-0	$19.95 USA/$26.95 Canada
Word 6 For Macs® For Dummies®	by Dan Gookin	ISBN: 1-56884-190-6	$19.95 USA/$26.95 Canada
Word For Windows® 6 For Dummies®	by Dan Gookin	ISBN: 1-56884-075-0	$16.95 USA/$22.95 Canada
Word For Windows® For Dummies®	by Dan Gookin & Ray Werner	ISBN: 1-878058-86-X	$16.95 USA/$22.95 Canada
WordPerfect® 6 For DOS For Dummies®	by Dan Gookin	ISBN: 1-878058-77-0	$16.95 USA/$22.95 Canada
WordPerfect® 6.1 For Windows® For Dummies® 2nd Edition	by Margaret Levine Young & David Kay	ISBN: 1-56884-243-0	$16.95 USA/$22.95 Canada
WordPerfect® For Dummies®		ISBN: 1-878058-52-5	$16.95 USA/$22.95 Canada

Order Center: **(800) 762-2974** *(8 a.m.–6 p.m., EST, weekdays)*

Quantity	ISBN	Title	Price	Total

Shipping & Handling Charges

	Description	First book	Each additional book	Total
Domestic	Normal	$4.50	$1.50	$
	Two Day Air	$8.50	$2.50	$
	Overnight	$18.00	$3.00	$
International	Surface	$8.00	$8.00	$
	Airmail	$16.00	$16.00	$
	DHL Air	$17.00	$17.00	$

*For large quantities call for shipping & handling charges.
**Prices are subject to change without notice.

Ship to:

Name _____

Company _____

Address _____

City/State/Zip_____

Daytime Phone _____

Payment: ☐ Check to IDG Books Worldwide (US Funds Only)

☐ VISA ☐ MasterCard ☐ American Express

Card # _____ Expires _____

Signature _____

Subtotal _____

CA residents add
applicable sales tax _____

IN, MA, and MD
residents add
5% sales tax _____

IL residents add
6.25% sales tax_____

RI residents add
7% sales tax_____

TX residents add
8.25% sales tax_____

Shipping_____

Total _____

Please send this order form to:

IDG Books Worldwide, Inc.
Attn: Order Entry Dept.
7260 Shadeland Station, Suite 100
Indianapolis, IN 46256

Allow up to 3 weeks for delivery.
Thank you!